The Vitor'
 to
KENT

INDEX TO 1:50 000 MAPS OF GREAT BRITAIN

Reproduced from the Ordnance Survey map with the permission of the
Controller of Her Majesty's Stationery Office, Crown copyright reserved.

Shading indicates maps used in this guide.

THE
VISITOR'S GUIDE TO
KENT

KEV REYNOLDS

MPC

HUNTER
PUBLISHING INC

Published by:
Moorland Publishing Co Ltd,
Moor Farm Road,
Airfield Estate,
Ashbourne,
Derbyshire DE6 1HD
England

British Library Cataloguing in
Publication Data:
Reynolds, Kev
   The visitor's guide to Kent.
   - 2nd ed.
   1. Kent. - Visitor's guides
   I. Title
   914.22'304858

ISBN 0 86190 383 8 (paperback)
ISBN 0 86190 382 X (hardback)

Published in the USA by:
Hunter Publishing Inc,
300 Raritan Center Parkway,
CN 94, Edison, NJ 08818
ISBN 1 55650 263 X (USA)

Colour and black & white
origination by:
Scantrans, Singapore

Printed in the UK by:
Richard Clay Ltd, Bungay, Suffolk

Cover photograph: *Scotney Castle,
Lamberhurst* (International Photo-
bank).

Illustrations have been supplied as
follows: MPC Picture Collection:
pp 194 (top), 207 (both), 210, 218
(large).

All other illustrations are from the
author.

CONTENTS

Key to Symbols Used in Text Margin and on Maps

 Recommended walk

 Parkland

 Archaeological site

 Nature reserve/Animal interest

 Birdlife

 Garden

 Golf facilities

 Picnic Sites

 Church/Ecclesiastical site

 Building of interest

 Castle/Fortification

 Museum/Art gallery

 Beautiful view/Scenery, Natural phenomenon

 Other place of interest

 Sailing

 Interesting railway

 Industrial archaeology

Key to Maps

 Main road

 Motorway

Railway

River

Town/City

 Town/Village

 Lake/Reservoir

 Canals

 County Boundary

 Railway

INTRODUCTION

'Kent, sir — everyone knows Kent — apples, cherries, hops and women.' So said Jingle on behalf of Dickens, one of the county's best-loved adopted sons. It is an opinion shared by many who know it by reputation or by journeys made to and from the bustling channel ports.

Kent is, of course, the garden of England and has orchards heavy with fruit in summer, rows of currants on the sides of sheltering hills, hop gardens strung taut and amassed with bines, rhododendrons colouring the verges of country lanes and the blazing shrubberies of cropped parkland, stately avenues of trees, neat lawns and dog roses and honeysuckle in the hedgerows. This is but one picture among many, however.

It is a complex county. Since local government reorganisation, it is the largest non-metropolitan county in England, and lying as it does at the south-eastern corner of England, has a long and difficult coastline to manage and maintain. The boundaries that divide Kent from Sussex and Surrey are distinctly rural but, in the north-west, London is an encroaching neighbour whose influence is felt rather more strongly than might be wished in this predominantly agricultural county. It is a county undergoing constant change and under pressure. Villages and towns within easy rail link of the capital have grown dramatically in post-war years to give commuters a taste of country living at weekends, and with mechanisation in agriculture the drift away from traditional farm work has meant considerable changes to village life and labour. There has been an increase in industry and commerce, and many towns have expanded to accommodate factories and office blocks, altering the landscape. Many a skyline has changed from a tree-scape to a vista of smoke-belching factories, and ugly pylons have been erected across the county. In recent years tens of thousands of acres have been flooded with the concrete of broad-laned motorways to cope with an explosion of motorised traffic, in the process releasing numerous small villages and towns from what was becoming an intolerable burden of vibration and noise.

Such pressures are not, of course, solely felt in Kent, but without doubt this corner of England has increasing problems to face. One of the more serious of these problems is the development of the Channel Tunnel, the construction of which is one of the most controversial of any project ever to be foisted on the county. Between Folkestone and Dover a section of Heritage Coast has been sacrificed. Ashford is expanding and will have an international railway station and an inland clearance depot for customs checks on freight, while at the northern end of the county major upsets have been caused by plans for a new rail link to be built from London to the Cheriton terminal. Feeder roads are also being upgraded to meet the projected demands for an increase in Channel-bound traffic. Although the tunnel is not scheduled to be opened until 1993 and the full extent of its impact is unlikely to be known before then, it is the manner by which the Tunnel Bill was handled in Parliament, and the subsequent bulldozing of large areas of much-loved landscape, that have caused great anxiety to the people of Kent. It is not sentimentality to prefer wheatfields and woodlands to motorways and man-made landscapes of concrete and brick, but an eye to the future and the quality of life for other generations.

Scenically Kent is a county of contrasts, and in those contrasts lies much of its charm. There are the hills; the North Downs that arc across Kent as a long ridge of chalk offering splendid panoramas over the valleys stretched below. There are the glorious heights of the Greensand Ridge with their canopy of beechwoods and sudden, breath-taking vistas. Sadly, some of these beechwoods were devastated in the early hours of 16 October 1987, when hurricane-force winds ripped across south-east England. Kent was among the worst hit of any county, with thousands of acres of woodland destroyed, not only along the Greensand Ridge, but in the low-lying Weald and on High Weald ridges too. Beechwoods were not alone in their dev-astation, for many orchards were also levelled by the scything winds, and some of Kent's finest parklands were similarly hit. The scars remain, but the work of clearance and tree planting has been taking place ever since, and in time these much-loved landscapes will be restored to a semblance of their former glory.

There are the noted viewpoints of the High Weald around Goudhurst where vast panoramas can be seen, patterned with hops and churches and meadows and the lowlands, too, like Romney, Walland and Denge marshes, and the Hoo Peninsula where cold winds blow without check in winter with sea mists rolling and hiding their secrets day after day. There are tight valleys with streams in their clefts and broad open levels such as Thanet and Sheppey and the Low Weald. There are the gaunt and majestic cliffs that guard Dover, and wide sandy bays such as that at Pegwell, near Ramsgate. Each has its own charm, personality and identity.

Over the centuries man has moulded these landscapes and made them gentle, homely, workable; a living countryside that welcomes rather than challenges. Here there are no moorlands or mountains, but chequered fields laid out with ancient hedges and lines of oak, ash and beech. In the woodlands pheasants are reared and in the great parks deer roam as they did in the days of Henry VIII and Elizabeth I.

Spread throughout the county there are forty country parks, or public open spaces, ranging from the 2-acre picnic site at Pillory Corner near Bewl Bridge Reservoir, to the 1,400 acres of Kings Wood, Challock, where visitors who wander the footpaths quietly stand a chance of seeing deer stepping lightly among the trees — and more than 2,000 acres of Bedgebury Forest, with the superb Bedgebury Pinetum adjacent to it. Trosley Country Park is located on the very lip of the North Downs, with spectacular views over the deep patchwork of the Weald. Teston Bridge Picnic Site occupies 24 acres of watermeadow on the banks of the Medway, and at Pegwell Bay, another site is all coastal grassland with big broad panoramas and a delight of birdlife.

One of the first in the line of *homo sapiens,* a sub-species of human being that lived perhaps 200,000 years ago, dwelt on the banks of what is now the Thames. At Swanscombe, near Gravesend, three fragments of skull have been found to give a brief clue to the existence of such a man alongside the flints with which he worked, and relics of animals of the time. Swanscombe Man is the first recorded Kentish man.

At Oldbury Hill between Seal and Ightham, Old Stone Age dwellers sought the protection of a series of rock shelters that give the earliest evidence of primitive man's simple home in the county, but more impressive by far are the stone monuments along the downs to either side of the Medway Gap. The Coldrum Stones at Trottiscliffe below the Pilgrims' Way and North Downs Way look across the Medway plain to the continuation of the downs where Kits Coty House stands in its open meadow above Aylesford. Here these ancient pillars have stood for some 4,000 years marking Neolithic burial chambers, the oldest constructions in Kent. They resemble more the monuments of the Low Countries than those like Stonehenge in Wiltshire.

Even before Julius Caesar proclaimed Kent to be the most civilised part of Britain in about 55BC, a Greek sailing the Channel 2,300 years ago, in the first written record mentioning Britain, referred to Kent with the name by which it is known today. The cliffs of Dover were the same then as they are now, but elsewhere the coast had different features and other channels. The Romans found Kent to be culturally far ahead of most of Europe and on a level with occupied Gaul. They found it occupied by Belgic tribes who had brought under control the native Celts. But under the influence of Rome, Kent emerged to become a centre of commerce and administration, and in consequence prospered with roads, ports, villas, towns and forts built at strategic points.

After the departure of the Roman legions in the fifth century, Kent became the focus of numerous warring bands, her coast being raided and invaded in turn by Jutes, Saxons and Vikings. Hengist and Horsa came ashore at Pegwell Bay and battled their way through the countryside; the first battle in the centuries of power struggles that were to follow. St Augustine arrived at Pegwell Bay in AD597 with his forty monks, bound on a mission from Rome to bring Christianity to these pagan shores, and as the arrival of Hengist and Horsa had signalled an era of violence, so that of Augustine signalled an era of religious growth.

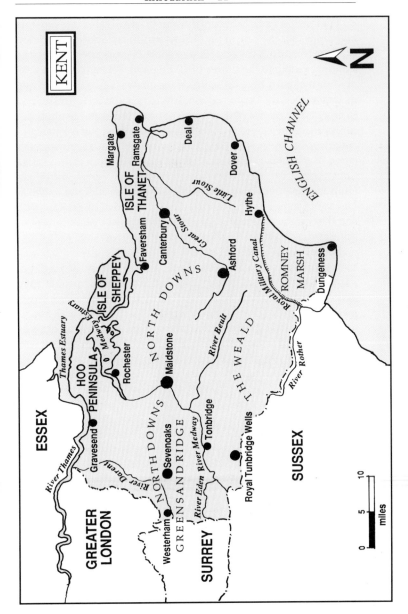

For much of its early history the county was divided into separate kingdoms, but the rule of the Saxons was to last for six centuries, until the Norman invasion of Sussex some 24 years after Edward the Confessor came to the throne of all England. William and his conquerors bypassed Kent in the first wave of invasion, but recognising its importance, they soon began to strengthen Roman fortresses and to erect many castles of their own. Thus can be seen the imposing fortifications of Dover and Rochester and numerous remnants of lesser castles scattered about the county. William also inspired a surge of religious rebuilding in Kent with the Saxon cathedrals of Canterbury and Rochester and making that great statesman Lanfranc his Archbishop of Canterbury. Under him the Archbishopric of Canterbury gained supremacy over that of York in 1072, and the document recording this transfer, signed by Lanfranc himself, survives to this day in the cathedral archives.

So begins the written history of Kent; a county which was frequently to assume a leading role in the history of England. Through the centuries many rich, famous and noble people have built their grand houses here, lavishing upon them the finest craftsmanship, surrounding them with grounds landscaped with imagination and genius. To these houses have come a succession of kings and courtiers, poets and princes. By the fourteenth century Kent was the richest county in the land, while pilgrimages to the shrine of Thomas á Becket in Canterbury gave inspiration to Chaucer and elevated the importance of its magnificent cathedral in the minds of all Englishmen. Today pilgrims continue to make their way there.

Chaucer was not alone in drawing a wider awareness of Kent through his writing, and over the centuries many of Britain's finest authors have either lived here or drawn inspiration from the landscapes, buildings or people. England's first printer, William Caxton, was born in the Weald; Christopher Marlowe, whom some see as Shakespeare's greatest rival, was born in Canterbury in 1564; Sir Philip Sidney's romantic verse sprang from the indisputable romance of Penshurst. Jane Austen has Kentish connections and once said that 'Kent is the only place for happiness' (she wrote *Pride and Prejudice* at Godmersham, where her brother lived) while Dickens, of course, comes alive almost everywhere in Rochester and Broadstairs — Somerset Maugham was at Whitstable and Thackeray at Tunbridge Wells. Vita Sackville-West and Virginia Woolf both wrote about Knole, in Sevenoaks; Joseph Conrad sniffed the sea at Gravesend, W.H. Davies wrote his *Autobiography of a Supertramp* in Edward Thomas's cottage in Sevenoaks Weald, while Richard Church's lyricism has brought out the very essence of the county in books and essays written from his various homes deep in the Kentish countryside.

Kent also had those who demanded reform. Wat Tyler led the Peasants' Revolt of 1381, inspired by John Ball, 'the mad priest of Kent', and in 1450 Ashford's Jack Cade rose against the misgovernment of Henry VI, defeated royal forces at Sevenoaks, occupied London and, having extracted promises of reform and pardon, dispersed his followers only to be hunted down and executed by the king.

During the Middle Ages the Cinque Ports of Sandwich, Hythe, Dover, Romney and Hastings brought renewed prosperity to the county through their maritime enterprises. The Wealden cloth trade flourished and its importance is indicated in the architecture of places like Tenterden and Cranbrook where, it is said, Elizabeth I walked through the town on a mile of local broadcloth.

In the eighteenth century the iron industry, which had for so long played an integral part in the county's financial success (particularly in the Weald), died out. The hammers lay silent, the ponds which drove them silted up and grew over. The Industrial Revolution took place elsewhere, while Kent looked to the safety of her shores in fear of Napoleon. Martello Towers were erected along the south coast and the Royal Military Canal dug along the fringe of Romney Marsh between Hythe and Rye. Fortunately neither the towers nor the canal were ever tested in combat for by the time the building work had been completed Napoleon was fighting elsewhere.

Throughout English history, Kent has often stood at the front line of attack. To Kent came Romans, Saxons and Vikings. William the Conqueror thought again about landing on her shore, as did Napoleon almost 800 years later, and in 1940 the pilots of Biggin Hill and Malling repelled another prelude to a planned invasion. Reprisal bombing followed, but by some miracle the best of Kent's past was spared the worst of Hitler's destructive powers — Canterbury Cathedral still stood in the settling dust of a city's ruin and Dover Castle remained above the port's shell-wrecked town while the architectural gems of Kent's countryside continue to grace the villages and byways.

That architectural heritage is extremely rich and varied. The Roman Pharoes lighthouse, dwarfed by the vast fortress of Dover Castle, is the oldest building still standing in England. At Lullingstone the beauty of Roman mosaic floors can now be seen, some 1,600 years after they were laid, demonstrating the wealth of that civilisation.

The legacy of the Roman legions was added to by the Saxons and Normans. The little church of St Martin's in Canterbury is England's oldest religious building in use for Christian worship. It was there when St Augustine came. It was in use when the Normans arrived and when Hitler attempted to level the city around it, and it is here to this day. Canterbury Cathedral owes its glory to the faith and genius of many ages, each marked by the greatest heights of craftsmanship of that era. Rochester too is etched with marvellous works from numerous eras, different in style and tone to those of Canterbury.

The county also has fine landscapes: the rolling downs, plunging cliffs, the great expanse of the Weald with its hop gardens, its orchards and its new vineyards. They are very different landscapes to those which the Romans knew. In Roman times the Weald was a vast forest with few tracks and fewer clearings; Romney's marshes had ships sailing where sheep now graze and Thanet was a true island separated from mainland Kent by the broad waterway of the Wantsum Channel. Under the Romans, however, Romney Marsh began to be reclaimed from the sea, although for several more centuries ships would continue to sail to the edge of Appledore and Smallhythe, now some miles inland. As for the Wantsum Channel, it was used by shipping as a short cut between the Thames estuary and the English Channel right into the Middle Ages before it silted up and dried out. Today it is a rich farmland and motorists bound for Thanet's resorts drive over it. Elsewhere along the Kentish coast, cliffs have eroded under the constant pounding of the tides, and into the waves have gone the walls of a Roman fort as well as a number of houses and acres of pasture.

The north Kent marshes are noted for their birdlife. Along the mudflats of the Swale there is a gathering of vast numbers of seabirds and waders. In a patch of woodland near High Halstow is England's largest heronry; there is the country's oldest heronry at Chilham, and down by the shingle spit of Dungeness great flocks of migrating birds make their twice-yearly landfall. At various points along the coast butterflies drift across from the Continent. There are flowers along the downs that draw botanists as well as butterflies, and a number of nature reserves have been established in recent years to protect the county's plantlife and wildlife.

Kent has numerous footpaths, as well as a number of long distance routes. The Saxon Shore Way follows the old coastline from Gravesend to Rye. The North Downs Way and the older Pilgrims' Way share parallel lines on their arc through the county, and the London Countryway crosses northern Kent on its circuit of the capital. There is also the Weald Way which heads south from Gravesend on a beeline for the coast, and the Greensand Way, which enters the county from Surrey at Crockham Hill and follows the ridge of hills on a south-easterly curve to Ham Street, where it joins the Saxon Shore Way.

Kent's coast has long been popular with holidaymakers. There are many fine beaches of clean sand, and the popular resorts have rides, ice cream parlours and deckchairs. Kent can offer something for everyone.

Not all of Kent's churches are like Canterbury, nor all her villages like Chilham or Chiddingstone or Smarden. Not all her castles have the romance of Leeds nor the power of Dover and not all her towns are as attractive as Tenterden or Cranbrook, nor all her houses as stately as Knole. But wherever one travels in this complex county there is something of interest to discover. There are castles and quiet churches to marvel at and the legacy of the past is there in yeoman houses, Tudor cottages, ancient priories, and Jacobean mansions. In village streets there are timber framed houses, while weather-boarding and tile-hung dwellings are characteristic of the area. It is a county of oast-houses, windmills and watermills; fishermen's huts, seaviews and mudflats acry with birds, but above all it is the garden of England.

1
DARENT AND THE THAMES

At first glance north Kent has little to attract the visitor. With London's sprawl edging beyond the downs, its suburban demands spilling into once-peaceful valleys and motorways sprouting over woodland, meadow and orchard alike, the map contains more grey areas than the country lover would care to see. Yet this is largely a blinkered view, for upon close scrutiny it is possible to find corners of quite remarkable beauty, the more surprising because of their close proximity to the capital.

In this comparatively small corner, framed by the downs, by London's political boundary, the busy Thames and the low marshes of the Hoo Peninsula, there are landscapes of great variety. There are the ruins of a Roman villa, the remains of ancient castles, elegant mansions set in gardens of splendour and buildings and scenes plucked straight from Dickens. Streams meander through a countryside as peaceful as one could wish, yet lying within an hour of the heart of London. There are wonderful village churches, tiny isolated hamlets, and a hilltop wood that contains Britain's largest heronry. Thus, a journey through this part of Kent is well worth the effort, especially if it is made without preconceived notions. That journey can best be started in the little town of Westerham, a mile or so from the birth of the River Darent.

Westerham has Surrey's border on its shoulder. It stands astride the A25, happily freed from the worst of its traffic since the opening of the motorway. To the north rise the downs, to the south the woodlands of the Greensand Ridge from which the Darent rises. The countryside surrounds the town and imposes its sense of unhurried pleasure. Here on the green, backed by a row of lovely old buildings that lead to the fine church, stands a statue to Westerham's hero, General James Wolfe, holding his sword aloft. Nearby there is a bronze statue of the town's more recent hero, Winston Churchill; the work of sculptor Oscar Nemon.

Wolfe was born at The Vicarage in 1727, but spent his childhood at the red-brick, multi-gabled house formerly known as 'Spiers', but renamed 'Quebec House' after his famous victory in Canada. Built in the seventeenth century, **Quebec House** stands at the eastern end of town and now belongs to the National Trust. In the old stable block at the rear the Trust has created a fine exhibition about the Battle of Quebec, and in the house itself four rooms allow the visitor to study items of personal interest to the Wolfe family.

At the western end of town stands another house with Wolfe connections. **Squerryes Court** was often visited by the young Wolfe, and it was in these grounds, at the age of 14, that he received his first commission. The house, a well-proportioned red-brick manor built in the William and Mary style in 1681, passed into the ownership of John Warde in 1731. It, and the extensive estate, have been in Warde hands ever since. Squerryes Court contains various items of Wolfe memorabilia, and in addition a collection of Old Masters; works by Rubens, Van Dyck and Van Goyens among them. The gardens are formal and extensive and contain a pretty lake as a foreground while it is in the picturesque valley of Squerryes Park that the Darent rises, and through it run one or two paths of considerable charm.

A walk (2 miles, 1 hour) from the High Street turns into Lodge Lane, which is opposite the B2024 Croydon Road junction. Walk past some delightful cottages to find a footpath bearing off to the right. This leads into Mill Lane where an old corn mill once stood. Turn left and follow the lane as far as an attractive lodge with a five-bar gate and a stile. The path through the gateway leads along the Darent upstream (Lake Walk), while the stile connects with a steep climbing path going almost due south. Take either path, for they meet again after half a mile, and both have much to commend them. (If you take the uphill path, bear left along a track about 400yd beyond the cricket pitch.) After the paths meet, the way continues through the meadows of Squerryes Park with the woodlands of Crockham Hill Common ahead, and those on either side of the park banked with rhodo-

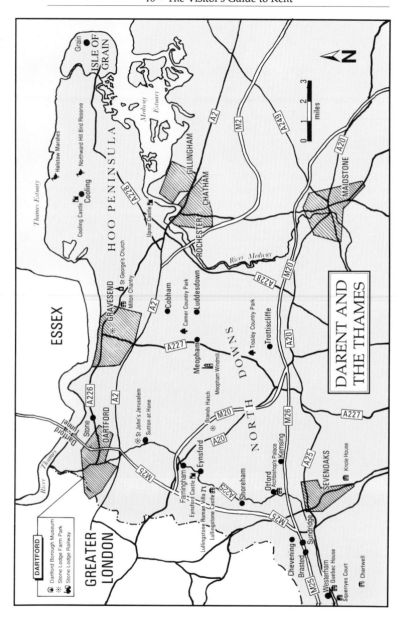

DARENT AND
THE THAMES

The statue of James Wolfe, Westerham

dendrons. The infant Darent runs through the meadows, here little more than a brook. It rises in the grounds of Crockham House which can just be seen tucked behind shrubs at the head of the valley, on the left. Return to Westerham by the alternative path.

By extending the above walk ($2^1/_2$ miles, $1^1/_4$ hours) some magnificent views can be obtained from the southern edge of Crockham Hill Common, or it is possible to include a visit to Chartwell. From the head of the valley cross out of Squerryes Park by way of a stile and bear right, then immediately take the narrow path left which climbs very steeply uphill into the woods of the common. At the junction with a main crossing track turn right, then first left to reach an isolated house. The path goes to the left of the house, then heads south once more to present the walker with a beautiful vista over the Weald. Go left downhill to meet the Westerham-Edenbridge road, cross it and climb steps leading to Mariners Hill. Across this more paths lead through beechwoods and over a further section of the common before plunging down to Chartwell.

The little one-time market town of Westerham has a long history and roots that go back to the Iron Age, while even earlier than that along the crest of the downs to the north, nomadic Neolithic tribes moved to and fro some 6,000 years ago. Much later there was a defended Saxon village here on the banks of the Darent, and during these times the Neolithic trail along the North Downs was virtually replaced by a trackway along the lower slopes of the downs — the route later adopted as the Pilgrims' Way. Today, of course, both the North Downs Way (tracing the crest of the downs) and the Pilgrims' Way below it are popular throughout the year with long distance walkers.

Apart from Wolfe and Churchill, Westerham claims a link with William Pitt who, at the age of 24, became Prime Minister in 1783. Originally he lived in Keston, between Biggin Hill and Bromley, but while his house was being repaired he came to live for a while in a small but attractive house in Westerham High Street. Today this house is a popular restaurant known as Pitt's Cottage.

Elsewhere in the town there once lived Sir Francis Younghusband, the former army officer who became variously political officer, political agent and British commissioner to Tibet from 1902-4. Younghusband was also a great explorer, something of a mystic, President of the Royal Geographical Society in 1919, and is remembered in mountaineering circles for his involvement in the early attempts to climb Mount Everest.

Eastwards out of Westerham the A25 and the Darent stream take

Places to Visit
In and Around Westerham

Chartwell (NT)
2 miles south of Westerham
The former home of Sir Winston
Churchill for 40 years, now
opened to the public. House and
gardens, studio containing many
of Churchill's paintings.

Quebec House (NT)
Westerham
A seventeenth-century gabled
house in which General James
Wolfe spent his early life. Now in
the hands of the National Trust,
with Wolfe memorabilia on show
in the house, and in old stable
block an exhibition detailing the
Battle of Quebec.

Squerryes Court
Westerham
Privately owned, but open to the
public, Squerryes is a William
and Mary manor house built in
1681. House contains a collection of Old Masters, especially
Dutch, plus items relating to
Wolfe who spent childhood days
here. Formal gardens, woodland
walks.

the traveller to **Brasted**, whose attractive little green is backed by a row of lovely Tudor cottages. In 1788, the rector of the time wrote that his parishioners were 'a very quiet, good sort of people, rather less polished and perhaps less corrupted than might be expected so near the capital.' The church lies down a side road, across the Darent, a survivor of a World War II flying bomb. However, this was de-stroyed by an arsonist late in 1989. Southwards another narrow road plunges among the wooded hills of the Greensand where paths and lanes explore a wonderland of colour and natural grace.

At Brasted Place, Prince Louis (who was to become Napoleon III and Emperor of France in 1852), spent a restless period in one of only two Kent houses designed by Robert Adam and now used as a training college. Here he planned his return to France and drilled a band of fifty-six supporters in the parkland that surrounds the mansion, before sailing for Boulogne in the summer of 1842.

Sundridge sits at a crossroads with the Darent, still no more than a brook running by. As with Westerham and Brasted, this village is hemmed in by the hills and an exploration to north or south would repay the time taken by such diversions. To the south a lane leads to Ide Hill's fine viewpoint. To the north another delves into a working countryside with the downs standing ahead, and even the motorway is forgotten in the peace of this green corner. Here lies **Chevening**, a village that is little more than a small collection of splendid cottages set against the high wall that surrounds the big house, Chevening Place. This was once the home of the Stanhopes, but is now the official country residence of the Foreign Secretary. It is a fine house dating from the time of Charles I and set in glorious parkland at the foot of the downs below Knockholt. The North Downs Way is surreptitiously guided round the park at a discreet distance from the mansion, then brought down to the few cottages that are practically all there is of the village. Across the road from the one-street hamlet stands the church. The village itself has an air of peaceful seclusion.

Not far from Sundridge the downs are cleft by the Darent where it sweeps northward. In this basin there is now a knot of motorways and trunk roads. To one side is **Otford**, with its duck pond, willows and backing cottages forming a welcome scene. Nearby are the remains of one of the palaces owned by the Archbishops of Canterbury in which Becket once lived.

There were palaces for the archbishops all over Kent of course, but Otford's was one of the grandest. In Becket's day it was a mansion of more modest proportions, and it was Archbishop Warham who enlarged it on the grand scale early in the sixteenth century. Henry VIII stayed here on his way to the Field of the Cloth of Gold, and soon after this took the palace from Archbishop Cranmer. However he never stayed long in it as he complained it made him 'rheumaticky', preferring instead Knole at nearby Sevenoaks. But it was not long before the lead was stripped from the roof to make ammunition. As a consequence the building very quickly fell into a state of disrepair and became little more than a ruin. Today there is just a section of tower and pieces of wall to be seen standing to the south of the church.

But the history of Otford goes back 2,000 years, for here settled Romans — there are Roman remains all along the Darent's valley. It was also here that Offa, King of *Mercia*, fought a momentous battle with the men of Kent in AD774; another battle, this time with the Danes, brought Otford into focus in 1016. But the latest battle of Otford, that which is fought against the remorseless tide of development, has seen the virtual swamping of a once-peaceful village into

Village pond, Otford

a road-girt suburb.

Be that as it may, Otford is still a charming place with plenty to interest the visitor. The church, dedicated to St Bartholomew, is certainly worth a visit. It stands back for breathing space, a homely building within, grey and intimating age without. It has very much the feel of a country church, and as you emerge from it to wander across to the village duck pond, that rural feeling remains. The duck pond itself is a rarity, for it is said to be the only area of water in England designated a listed building and even has its own official keeper to take care of the wildlife. (The pond is mentioned in an eleventh-century document, so it has been a feature of the village for a very long time.) Along the High Street are several interesting buildings, among them the Old Forge which is now a restaurant, while opposite stands The Bull Inn containing an oak settle apparently used by Becket when he stayed at Otford Palace.

North of Otford the Darent imposes an air of pastoral tranquillity on a valley that holds so many quiet pleasures. As it cuts through the downs, with the heights of Otford Mount to the right and Polhill to the left forming the gateway to the valley, the stream comes into its own. A narrow lane, entered from the outskirts of Otford between the village and the motorway, suddenly plunges into a landscape of farms, oast-houses, orchards and hop gardens. In places it is a sunken lane, in others it is level with the fields to give an expansive view of a valley just saved from being flooded with concrete. The valley which was loved and painted by Samuel Palmer who lived for a time in Shoreham.

There is a footpath (2 miles, $^3/_4$ hour) leading through the valley linking Otford and Shoreham. It follows the stream at the start, but after a while the Darent bears left while the path continues straight ahead, and passes through a golf course to reach Station Road, Shoreham. Turn left here into the village.

Shoreham is a delightful, straggling village with a fair selection of pubs, fine houses, and a church at the end of an avenue of stately yews. It has great names from history and a cross cut in the chalk of the hill overlooking the village in memory of those who died in two wars. The Darent gives Shoreham its identity and its colour. It runs beside the road leading from the church and sweeps beneath a little bridge at the roots of wading trees on its journey below the village proper. It draws the visitor with its detail, painting bright pictures for the camera. Beside it there are footpaths, across it a little hump-backed bridge, where there is a rugged memorial set in stone. On the village side of the bridge the King's Arms has a sentry-like 'ostler's box' where the inn's own ostler would be stationed until called upon to look after a customer's horse. Today a dummy ostler occupies the box.

Not far from the bridge is The Water House in which Samuel Palmer lived for 7 years. 'Everything connected with the little village in those happy times,' he wrote, 'seemed wrapped about with a sentiment of cosy quiet antiquity, full of assocation that carried you far back into the pastoral life of Merry England years ago.' Palmer was influenced by the great poet and artist William Blake who visited him here, and together the two might perhaps have strolled among the pollarded willows that line the stream and drew from them inspiration for their various works. But even before Palmer and Blake, the village had been visited regularly over a period of 40 years by John Wesley. In this village, in its church and in its vicarage, the evangelist delivered his sermons. For two generations his friend

Vincent Perronet was vicar here, and Wesley would make an annual visit to preach his individual style of worship, travelling with Perronet's son with whom he shared a missionary zeal.

Today, although it attracts many weekend visitors, the village somehow manages to retain its appeal. The Darent continues to wind its course among the meadows where footpaths lead to Lullingstone and Eynsford. Along it heron stand silent watch for an unsuspecting meal, and snipe paddle through the mud. On occasion deer may be seen, too. The path ($2^1/_2$ miles, $1^1/_4$ hours) which leaves the village on the left bank of the stream comes to a road before following the stream towards Eynsford, and a sudden sheen of tree-lined water indicates that Lullingstone Castle is near, seen as a mansion on the far bank of the lake.

Lullingstone Castle is more mansion than castle, although the gatehouse has pretensions. The house itself is Tudor behind a Queen Anne façade, with great oaks adorning the lawns and the lake spread out to one side. On the other side, squat upon the lawn, is the little flint church of St Botolph which is virtually a mausoleum for the owners of the castle; first the Peche family, then the Harts, the Dykes and the Hart-Dyke families. On one tomb lies Sir George Hart holding his wife's hand; a touching monument to a devoted couple.

There are two ways to approach Lullingstone Castle; from the A225 shortly after the junction with the narrow road from Shoreham, or from the north, along a delightful lane that begins in the crowded village street of Eynsford. **Eynsford** is one of those Kentish villages with many surprises. To the motorist travelling along the A225 it is an obstacle course of parked cars, a few beamed buildings to note briefly, and a church with a wood shingled spire standing above the road. However, halfway through the village a side road dips to the left, where a picture-postcard scene of hump-backed bridge and water-splash ford renews acquaintance with the Darent. This smiling, nostalgic corner leads along a quiet lane for a mile or so among green pastures and beside the stream. A majestic red-brick viaduct over the Darent carries the Swanley to Sevenoaks railway line, but all else is as nature intended. The lane leads to a car park, toilets and an ugly-roofed building erected by the Department of the Environment to protect one of Kent's great finds: **Lullingstone Roman Villa.**

Here is history brought vividly to life, for the villa's glorious mosaic floors have been carefully preserved, and the layout of individual rooms is easily recognised from the gallery overlooking the site. Glass cases contain small items found during excavations, which began in 1949, and the casts of a pair of ancestral portrait busts give a clue to the apparent wealth of the owner. The original busts, worked in Greek marble, are now in the British Museum.

Even before the Romans came, Iron Age farmers lived in the valley nearby, but during the Roman occupation a small villa was erected here around AD280, built of flint and mortar, with a thatched roof. About 100 years later this modest villa cum farmhouse was converted into a more imposing dwelling in keeping with the standards expected of an important official. There were baths, underfloor heating, finely decorated walls, servants' quarters and a new kitchen block. But then, for some reason, the villa was abandoned for almost a century until about AD480 when it was once more occupied as a rather grand farmhouse. The new occupants made a number of alterations and built a sizable granary on the banks of the Darent.

It was in the middle of the fourth century that the two splendid mosaic floors were laid; one in the dining room, the other in the reception room. The first shows Jupiter, here turned into a bull, carrying off Europa on his back while cupids look on. The other depicts Bellerophon mounted upon the winged horse Pegasus and spearing a frantic Chimaera within a border of dolphins. But perhaps the most surprising feature of this particular Roman villa is the existence of a Christian chapel. It dates back to about AD370 when a room was converted as a place of worship. The walls were re-plastered and decorated with representative figures in the attitude of prayer, six of them with arms outstretched; sacred monograms adorned other walls. Towards the end of the century the villa was once more abandoned and early in the fifth century, following a fire, almost the whole building collapsed and the ruins were steadily covered by soil washed from the hills. There it remained unknown to all for more than 1,000 years.

Half a mile farther along the lane is Lullingstone Castle with its trim surroundings of manicured lawns, mature trees and the gleaming lake. But while Lullingstone is a castle in name only, back in Eynsford are to be found remains of a true Norman castle standing in its dry moat above the Darent, 200yd from the main road.

The ford at Eynsford

Eynsford Castle has occupied this site for about 900 years and replaces an earlier one that was recorded in the *Domesday Book* of 1086. At that time it was held by Ralph, son of Unspac, who took the name of the village as his surname. It was his son, the first William de Eynsford, who built the curtain wall that the visitor sees today, and William's successors — there were six more with the same name — added various refinements in the following years. But in 1312 it was ransacked by Nicholas de Criol, one of the descendants of the fifth William, and the castle was never again used as a residence, although in the eighteenth century it was used to kennel the hunting dogs of the Hart-Dykes of Lullingstone.

The remains of Eynsford Castle consist of a good portion of the curtain wall, built of flint and some 30ft high, adorned here and there with adventurous plants. Within the grounds are assorted low and craggy ruins that tell of flights of steps and long-forgotten rooms, some of which had reused Roman tiles in their fabric. Once the Darent flowed around the castle and filled the moat. Now it flows peacefully below the white walls that have known more turbulent times.

The Darent reaches Farningham to be crossed by both the M20 and A20. These two major highways have jointly saved the village from being shaken to pieces by nose-to-tail traffic, for it used to stand astride the London road when travellers moved at a more sedate pace than today. As a result, **Farningham** lies snug and surprisingly peaceful down by the river. As Edward Hasted put it: '...in the midst of a valley of fertile meadows when the hills rise both towards the east and west. As you approach it from the hills on either side, it forms the most beautiful and picturesque landscape imaginable.' The Lion Hotel is a Georgian coaching inn whose lawns slope to the Darent near the brick bridge which dates from 1773 and has a fossil tree beside it. By The Lion, and beside the river, a notice board draws the attention of visitors to the Darent Valley Path, a walk which follows the river all the way to Dartford on the Thames. But best of all is the white weatherboarded mill across the road with its handsome mill house and fine cottage seen end-on along a lawn that borders the river. Above the Darent the main street rises between neat shops and typically Kentish houses, while back on the other side stands the much-restored thirteenth-century church whose main item of interest is an eight-sided font carved with the sacraments.

The village guards the best stretch of the Darent's valley, for northward one senses an overpowering encroachment of concrete on what once was a distinctly rural scene. Yet having said that, just north of the village and bordered on two sides by the M20 and M25 motorways which separate it from Swanley's urban fringe, Farning- ham Woods give 175 acres of mixed woodland, with access via paths and rides. Sevenoaks District Council manages the woodland as a nature reserve. By taking the A20 the motorist comes to Brands Hatch, one of the country's premier motor racing circuits for over 60 years and where the British Grand Prix used to be held.

On the Darent is the site of another Roman villa and soon after, in the village of **Sutton at Hone** on the very edge of town, is a manor house set within a charming garden in which peace and solitude seem all the more special for the contrasting noise and bustle just beyond. St John's Jerusalem was once a commandery of the Knights Hospitallers, and remnants of the original twelfth-century house have been incorporated into the present manor which was substantially improved by Hasted, the great Kent historian. It is said that work on the house bankrupted him and, indeed, he spent 5 years in prison for debt. Today the house is in the hands of the National Trust, who open the chapel and garden to the public. Through the garden flows the Darent, and all around the house the stream forms a moat.

Despite the notorious bottleneck of the Dartford Tunnel which takes the M25 beneath the Thames, and the forthcoming bridge over the river which should relieve some of these hold-ups; despite its unlovely marriage of urban and industrial development, **Dartford** has managed to retain a hold on sanity with a car-free High Street and several places of interest to make it worth seeking out. It has a long history and in fact it is one of Kent's oldest settlements. Among its claims to fame it has the distinction of being the place where Wat Tyler, who led the peasants' rebellion against the imposition of a poll tax in 1381, stopped with his followers during their march on London. A half-timbered pub on the corner of Bullace Lane commemorates his name, but it is doubtful whether Tyler actually lived here, as has been claimed. (He is said to have been born in Maidstone.)

A nunnery was founded in Dartford by Edward III and Anne of Cleves died here, but long before all of these, the Romans chose the site just south of the Thames marshes as a convenient place for Watling Street's crossing of the River Darent — the name is derived from its Saxon equivalent, 'Darentford'. Dartford Borough Museum recalls much of that history, and includes among its exhibits a unique glass bowl, the so-called 'Darenth Bowl' discovered in 1978. This priceless Saxon relic, decorated with a religious symbol and inscription, dates from the fifth century and suggests that an early form of Christian worship took place here.

A little to the east of the town, and reached from the A226, **Stone Lodge Farm Park** is both a Rare Breeds Survival Centre and a traditional working farm in a distinctly urban area. The farm, which

Flint and brick bridge over the Darent, Farningham

has its own museum, picnic sites and wagon rides, is open to the public from April to September, during which period ploughing with shire horses, milking, shearing and haymaking can be seen, as well as the farm's collection of more than 200 animals and rare birds.

Nearby, and overlooking the Thames, **Stone Lodge Railway** is a recent addition to the steadily expanding list of steam railways to be restored or developed by a preservation society. When completed it will run from a railway heritage centre to a new station at Stone Lodge Farm round a site that is earmarked for development as one of the largest leisure-oriented centres in the south-east of England. On the other hand, to the south-west of Dartford, **Joyden's Wood** is a surprisingly tranquil expanse of mixed woodland recently bought by The Woodland Trust, that acts as a much-needed green lung for this otherwise brick-and-concrete congested corner of Kent.

Leaving the Darent and heading towards Gravesend, the landscape becomes less and less attractive. It once had appeal — a raw, unsophisticated appeal, to be true — yet now only those with business to attend, or with a set aim, travel these roads.

Pocahontas statue in St George's churchyard, Gravesend

✳   **Gravesend** has an indefinable atmosphere and is a haunting
place, when all but deserted. It is a grey town on a grey river; a
delightful place for those who care for atmosphere, with its smell of
the river bearing more than a hint of the sea just around the bend. For
here passes the heavy traffic of the Thames, and just across the water
is Tilbury with its ferry plying daily between Essex and Kent. Here
the Thames pilots guide shipping from all over the world to the port.
Down by the river, the town planners have set aside walkways with
grassy strips and flower borders where you can picnic and watch the
life of the Thames. In mid-June there is the spectacle of old Thames
sailing barges in competition, their rust-coloured sails and black timbers forming a magnificent sight. Gravesend has its own regatta, and
for 3 months in summer there are many events taking place. It is fitting that Joseph Conrad, that great writer of sea stories, should have
woven parts of the town into some of his tales, including the Three
Daws pub.

       Above the river new buildings jostle with a few sad remnants of
seafaring days. Black weatherboarded structures have a Victorian
sense of melodrama, lining a climbing street that appears to have
come straight from Dickens. Not far from here, and a short walk from
the ferry entrance but standing back on the hill, is the parish church
of St George, topped with an off-white pinnacle. It occupies the site
of a former church, burned down in a great fire that destroyed much
of the old town in 1727. The church is often visited by American
tourists, for in the churchyard there is a delightful statue of the Indian
princess, Pocahontas, who was buried in the old church in 1617.
According to popular history, Pocahontas, the daughter of an important Red Indian chief, fell in love with Captain John Smith, whom she
saved from execution at the hands of her father. They were parted,
for Smith was sent from Virginia, and she later heard that he was
dead. Eventually Pocahontas married another settler, James Rolfe,
who was Recorder of the colony of Virginia. He brought her to
England where she was presented at the court of James I. But the
damp English climate made her ill and arrangements were made to
send her back to Virginia. However as she sailed down the Thames
her condition worsened and she was taken ashore at Gravesend.
There she died and was laid to rest. Other stories tell that she died of
a broken heart after finding John Smith was still alive, but fact and

Places of Interest In and Around the Darent Valley

Brands Hatch Motor Racing Circuit
Off A20 between Farningham and Wrotham
Various major motor sports events held throughout the year. Home of the Brands Hatch racing school.

Eynsford Castle (EH)
Eynsford
Remains of flint-walled Norman castle dating back to about 1100.

Lullingstone Castle
Eynsford, 1 mile south of village, off A225
An historic family home set in park-like grounds with small church nearby. About $^1/_2$ mile from Roman villa.

Lullingstone Park
Eynsford, on hill above Roman villa, reached from road to Well Hill off A225, 1 mile south of village
Nature trail, woodlands and typical chalkland flora in an idyllic setting.

Lullingstone Roman Villa (EH)
Eynsford, reached by narrow road from Eynsford, off A225
Excavated remains of a Roman nobleman's villa, containing some of the finest mosaic floor work yet discovered in Britain. Also early evidence of Christian chapel.

St John's Jerusalem (NT)
Sutton at Hone, on A225, 3 miles south of Dartford
Garden moated by the Darent. The house stands on the site of twelfth-century Knights Hospitallers commandery. Only the garden and old chapel incorporating original walls are open.

Stone Lodge Farm Park
Stone, east of Dartford, just off A226
Both a traditional working farm and a Rare Breeds Survival Centre. Farming processes to be seen; large collection of animals and birds, farming museum, wagon rides and indoor and outdoor picnic sites.

Stone Lodge Railway
East of Dartford, near junction 1a on M25
Standard gauge steam and diesel railway built by a local preservation group, the North Downs Steam Railway Co Ltd. Contains a collection of carriages and wagons, and is being developed as a demonstration line running from a railway heritage centre to Stone Lodge Farm.

fiction have become blurred with time.

Two centuries after Pocahontas died here, General Gordon

commanded the Royal Engineers in the rebuilding of the Thames fortifications. Gordon, who is best remembered for his activities in Khartoum, spent 5 years in Gravesend and while here he took a great interest in the life of the town; his name lives on in local schools, a promenade and there is a statue of him here.

Long before Gordon came to Gravesend, and even before Pocahontas was brought ashore here, Milton Chantry stood as the chapel of a leper hospital. Today, this medieval building (founded by the Earl of Pembroke in 1322) is run by English Heritage as an arts centre, with local history and craft exhibitions often held there.

While Gravesend is very much a town of the river, it also marks the starting place of two long distance footpaths; the Saxon Shore Way and the Weald Way.

The first, the **Saxon Shore Way**, follows Kent's coastline for 140 miles (9 days walking) between Gravesend on the Thames and Rye on the edge of Romney Marsh, just across the border in East Sussex. It is an interesting concept of the Kent Rights of Way Council to link a number of historic sites, including four forts built by the Romans as defences against Saxon raiding parties, and to explore the rich and varied coastal scenery that ranges from low-lying estuarine mud flats to the dramatic cliffs around Dover; from sandy bays to reclaimed marshland. The journey will delight the bird watcher, for there are many opportunities to observe the birdlife of the sea shore as well as woodland varieties, and there are nature reserves not far from the route on several sections.

Unlike the shoreline walk, the **Weald Way** is very much an inland countryside route. It leaves Gravesend heading towards the North Downs, passing through several little villages and surprising panoramas. It crosses the Medway and enters the Weald which it traverses both in Kent and in Sussex; it rises over Ashdown Forest and greets the sea from the crest of the South Downs. Thus in 80 miles (5 days) the Weald Way links the Thames with the English Channel; a lovely walk that is full of variety, rich in its scenery and in its architecture.

East of Gravesend lies the **Hoo Peninsula** edged with marshlands whose border trees stand hunched against the winds that sweep from the sea and the river. To the north is the Thames estuary, to the south and east that of the Medway. Inland, Hoo is clustered

Cooling Castle on the Hoo Peninsula

with orchards and fields of cabbages. A hilly spine runs across bearing patches of woodland, sheep graze the meadows and there are many gulls. It is a strange patch of country, dismissed by many writers on Kent as being unworthy of attention. Indeed, the visitor in search of the picturesque will be disappointed in this area, and those in need of organised entertainment would be better sent elsewhere. Hoo does have an appeal in its drabness, however, especially for those with more than a passing interest in Dickens. Here is the countryside which provided the opening landscape of *Great Expectations*; here in these lanes wandered the young Pip; in one of its churchyards lie buried Pip's brothers and sisters. The atmosphere of brooding which Dickens painted makes for a certain mystery, and that very same atmosphere may well be experienced anew. 'The dark flat wilderness beyond the churchyard', he wrote 'intersected with dykes and mounds and gates, with scattered cattle feeding on it, was the marshes...the low leaden line beyond, was the river...the distant savage lair from which the wind was rushing, was the sea.'

In contrast to so much of Kent, this countryside has an other-

Places of Interest on the Hoo Peninsula

Cooling Castle
2 miles west of High Halstow
Remains of fourteenth-century castle with fine drum towers at gateway. Privately owned and not open to the public, but may be seen from road.

Cooling Church
A small ragstone church in whose graveyard are the stone mounds taken by Dickens as the graves of Pip's brothers and sisters in *Great Expectations*.

Halstow Marshes
Bird watching all along the marshes and water meadows at the northern end of Hoo. Ducks, waders, white-fronted geese in winter. Footpath access only.

Northward Hill Bird Reserve
1 mile north of High Halstow
RSPB and NCC Reserve, Britain's largest heronry. Access by permit only.

Upnor Castle
2 miles north of Rochester on the left bank of the Medway
Remains of castle built in 1559, later used as gunpowder and munitions store.

worldliness about it; its villages seem to belong to no other part of the county, they have a sense of isolation about them.

Cooling, a bare hamlet, has two points of especial interest, one also connected with Dickens. In Cooling's churchyard, among the graves, there is a melancholy collection of thirteen lozenge-like stones depicting a sad family's infant mortality. When Dickens put Pip in this churchyard to be met in the fog by the escaped convict Magwitch, he gave only five such graves, but there can be little doubt that this corner was his inspiration. Half a mile away stand the remains of Cooling Castle, one-time home of Sir John Oldcastle, on whom Shakespeare modelled his Falstaff.

Cooling Castle is privately owned and not open to the public, but much of interest may be seen from the road which passes by; the impressive twin drum towers at the entrance gate, a good amount of walling, the moat. From within the boundary walls the visitor catches sight of something incongruous in this bleak country: palm trees growing. There are lawns and flowers which have a tended, well-loved look about them.

The Saxon Shore Way comes through Cooling, for at one time the tide would have flowed to its edge. This explains the castle's existence, for in 1379 French ships raided the Upper Thames estuary and 2 years later John de Cobham was granted a licence to fortify his manor house, as much out of a sense of national duty as of personal safety. In a grand gesture of self-congratulation he fixed to one of the gateway towers an inscription in copper, like a charter and seal, declaring that he was 'mad in help of the country'.

The Shore Way continues out of Cooling, and 2 miles beyond, just north of the hilltop village of High Halstow, it skirts **Northward Hill**, Britain's largest heronry and a reserve of the RSPB. Not only is this patch of mixed woodland on the edge of **Halstow Marshes** an important site for herons, there are also long-eared owls roosting in winter, and many nightingales and woodpeckers breed there. The marshes themselves, all around the Hoo Peninsula, provide a rich habitat for numerous ducks and waders, with geese coming through in winter, and along the water meadows and mudflats ornithologists will find plenty of interest. The sea wall at Allhallows, between the caravan park and the foreshore, is easily accessible and offers a fine observation point, while from it footpaths run in either direction, skirting the various marshes.

The road links High Halstow with **Grain**, a village whose view of the broad estuary does not compensate for the abominable forest of shining storage tanks and slimline chimneys of the oil refinery that overshadow it, nor for the power station nearby. It is understandable for anyone to shy away from its landscape and head back towards a Kent of old beamed houses and woods, of hills and valleys and vast panoramas, epitomised by the sweeping arc of the North Downs.

2
THE NORTH DOWNS

The escarpment of the North Downs forms the very backbone of Kent. Entering from Surrey above Westerham, this long chalk ridge sweeps in a gentle arc across the whole county before breaking off dramatically at the white cliffs of Dover.

The downs give an element of drama to the scenery of Kent. To one side they slope off gradually, to the other they plunge steeply to the valleys, making an effective barrier to London's suburban sprawl and forming a natural boundary to the Weald.

For centuries the downs have been used as a route to and from the Continent; in prehistoric times settlements were linked by trackways that were adopted by later occupants, yet today they seem strangely empty. Within the folds of the downs are surprising vales, with hamlets and villages tucked into them, linked one with another by narrow lanes that wriggle around fields and woodlands, deep-rutted in antiquity. No major roads run their length, they keep their distance to north or south, crossing only rarely. In consequence this is excellent cycling or walking country. The North Downs Way leads for 124 miles between Farnham in Surrey and Dover, and the Pilgrims' Way links Winchester with Canterbury by 120 miles of footpath, track or minor road. There are numerous other pathways too, traversing the sides of the downs, crossing them, leading from village to village, from wood to farm to ancient site. Whether by foot, bicycle or car, the traveller along the downs will find an absorbing countryside with plenty of variety. In their villages and hamlets, adorned with fine churches or lovely cottages, there are rewards for those who will make the diversions required to find them; and of

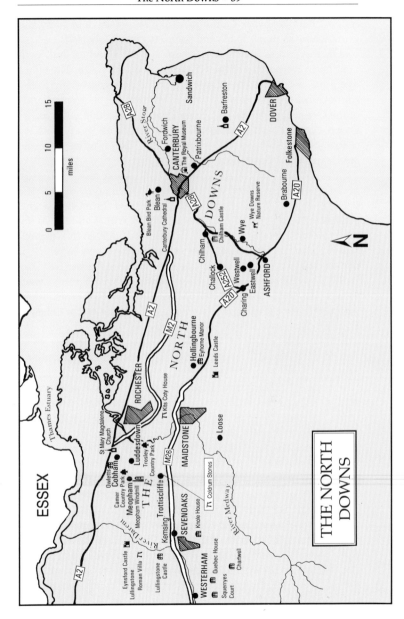

THE NORTH
DOWNS

course, there is always Canterbury, natural objective of every pil-grim, where so many roads and pathways inevitably lead.

On the downs above Westerham is Kent's highest hill, with London to the north and lush countryside to the south. The views along this section of the ridge are grand indeed, especially to the south across the valley of the young Darent to the thick woodlands of the Greensand, and all along the brow of the ridge as far as the Darent Gap north of Sevenoaks there is a contrast of city and country so that the long-distance walker finds himself balanced between one landscape of concrete and another of foliage.

The boundary of Greater London claws its way towards the top of the downs. **Biggin Hill** is up here, a name synonymous with the Battle of Britain. The airport here is today used for more peaceful activities, but few who lived through World War II will forget the contribution made by the young airmen who manned this airfield.
 Not far from Biggin Hill at **Downe** stands the house in which, a century ago, there lived one of the most brilliant figures from the world of natural sciences: Charles Darwin. It was here in Down House that Darwin wrestled with his conscience for years before submitting for publication his remarkable work, *On The Origin of Species*, which sparked off bitter controversy. During the 40 years that he lived here, he truly stamped his character on the place. Now owned by the Royal College of Surgeons, the rather gaunt, rambling house has been turned into a Darwin museum.

On the lip of the downs cluster woodlands stocked with pheas-ants, and during an autumn walk the birds rise startled from the scrub. There are foxes and squirrels in great number, and deer may on occasion be sighted along their edges. But at Polhill, where the River Darent breaks through, there is a tangle of busy roads and a railway line taking traffic from London to the south, while on the eastern side of the valley the downs resume their interrupted course, rising again to offer beautiful views along their crest. Below, tucked against their southern slopes, **Kemsing** is an expanding village marooned between the ancient trackway of the Pilgrims' Way and the modern express route of the M26. The heart of the village has some pleasant corners, an attractive covered well with a war memo-rial nearby, one or two fine houses in its street and a glorious church rich in the work of craftsmen of another age. Behind its surrounding wall is the former vicarage, now a Youth Hostel, overlooking the broad valley beyond the village.

Tucked as it is against the downs, with Youth Hostel and bed and breakfast accommodation available, Kemsing makes a fine base for weekend walking tours. A steep pull up onto Green Hill, where the trees and scrub tangle with wild clematis (traveller's joy, or old man's beard), long vistas show a delightful stretch of country. Of the many tempting walks from here, one that is particularly recommended takes in an easy 3-mile circuit ($1^1/_2$ hours), passing near the imposing Hildenborough Hall and onto Whiteleaf Down, before cutting 'inland' among woods and open meadowlands to a lost-world flint-walled pub, The Rising Sun. It has no village to service, just a farm or two and a scattering of cottages caught among the folding downs. It is hard to believe that another world of towns and motorways is merely 'just across the hill'. From The Rising Sun another path leads back, crosses the North Downs Way and drops steeply down the scarp slope to Kemsing once more.

The Pilgrims' Way, running along the slope of the downs, skirts the northern edge of the estate of St Clere, a stately mansion built in the reign of Charles I for Sir John Sedley, the 'hottest Parliamentarian in the county'. Beyond it, past meadows and orchards, is **Wrotham**, very close to a knot of highways that show little respect for the rural delights of the hills. The heart of the village itself (pronounced Rootum) is, visually at least, a classic example of a small English community. There is a neat little village square, two inns, a sturdy thirteenth-century church, a red-brick manor (originally Elizabethan), a war memorial and remnants of an archbishop's palace, all of which make a pleasing contrast to the M20 motorway which scuttles its traffic to the north. The church was dedicated to St George even before he became adopted as England's patron saint. It is a large, cool building with an atmosphere all its own, and behind it there once stood one of those palaces used by the peripatetic Archbishops of Canterbury. This was pulled down in 1349, and the stone from it carted to Maidstone in order to build Archbishop Islip's palace on the banks of the Medway.

Wrotham was a staging post on the London road, and history tells us that it was here that Henry VIII learned that the execution of Anne Boleyn had been carried out in 1536. More than 200 years later, during the Napoleonic Wars, Lieutenant Colonel Shadwell was shot by a deserter in the village. Set in a wall opposite the gates to Wrotham Place a stone commemorates the murder in simple terms. On Wrotham Hill, one of the loveliest viewpoints along this ridge, is the intrusion of an ugly BBC aerial.

There are woodlands again along the tops, and among them a new village called **Vigo** has sprung up. Trosley Country Park is to the south, an extensive area of woodland and downland, with nature trails and superb panoramic views over the Weald. These views are less troubled by trees than they used to be, for the hurricane of 1987 wrought considerable havoc here. But walks are once again made accessible. There is an information centre where various leaflets may be obtained, including guides to the nature trails and several walks. One walk leads off the scarp and descends the southern slope to reach the charming village of **Trottiscliffe**. This village offers typical downland views of sweeping meadows and a neat agriculture, with the hills fading blue towards the east and across the Medway Gap. The artist Graham Sutherland once lived here, in a weatherboarded house near the village centre. But charming though it undoubtedly is, both in itself and in its setting, Trottiscliffe's visitors come mainly to visit the Coldrum Stones.

First it is worth a visit to the church, isolated from the rest of the village and occupying a patch of ground among farm buildings and flat meadows with the downs rising behind as a wall. Its flint-studded tower is seen from far away. It is a simple Norman church, which nonetheless contains a magnificent pulpit with a carved canopy, originally made for Westminster Abbey where it stood until 1820. In scale it is quite out of keeping here, but it is a remarkable piece of work and a piece of London's history transported to the quiet countryside. Also displayed here are Neolithic bones and other relics from the Coldrum Stones.

The **Coldrum Stones**, the remains of a complex burial chamber, are reached from Trottiscliffe's church by way of a narrow road, track and footpath, and are found on a low terrace above the valley with broad views around. Here these weighty stones were raised about 2000BC to form columns, and though many have long since collapsed in a rough circle measuring 160ft in circumference, four of the original twenty-four columns remain standing. They are very heavy,

A trail through Trosley Country Park

some almost 12ft by 10ft, manhandled from who knows where, for they are not of any local stone. The burial chamber, or barrow, would have consisted of this circle of upright sarsen stones covered by a huge mound of earth with only the entrance kept clear. Even without the covering mound, and with a majority of stones missing, it is still an impressive site. In it were found skeletons and other remains of twenty-two people, as well as the bones of assorted animals. In 1910 the site was excavated and given to the National Trust in 1926 in honour of Benjamin Harrison, the archaeologist. Although it is perhaps not so obviously impressive as Kits Coty it is nevertheless a site of enormous interest. From it one looks across the patchwork of meadows and woodlands to the curve of the downs upon whose slopes Kits Coty rests.

One of the Trosley Country Park walks includes in its 6-mile (3-hour) loop Trottiscliffe village, church and Coldrum Stones. It is a fine walk with plenty of scenic variety. Begin at the car park information centre, taking to a woodland track before descending the scarp of the downs, crossing the Pilgrims' Way and several fields as far as the village. From the village head east towards the church and Coldrum Stones, continuing over more fields and along woods to the outskirts of Ryarsh village before turning north and making a way back to the downs. Climb steeply onto the North Downs Way whose waymarkings lead back to the country park.

The visitor travelling by road should continue eastwards beyond the entrance to Trosley Country Park along the crest of the downs for a couple of miles or so. The lane winds staccato fashion between broad fields and leafy woods. Then suddenly light floods in from the right and there is a superb view off to the south. The downs here have been broken by the Medway, but you can see across its meandering course to a resumption of the escarpment, now veering south-eastwards in a determined arc.

A narrow lane cuts back to the left by this viewpoint, and in about 500yd leads to one of the highest points in Kent, **Holly Hill**. There is a car park here on the edge of the 32 acres of Holly Hill Wood, some glorious views to north and east, and enticing footpaths that plunge into the woods and off to remote and secluded villages. The North Downs Way long distance path comes this way, and the Wealdway and London Countryway also pass nearby. It is an area well worth exploring.

Away from the dramatic lip of the escarpment there are some rather lovely valleys that are worth exploring at leisure. They are threaded by narrow lanes, often leading from one lonely farm to another, or to tiny villages. One such is **Dode**, a village deserted at the time of the Black Death. Today there is just a stretch of pleasant valley, a minute disused church barricaded against vandalism by a high surrounding fence, a farm, and woodlands at the head of the valley. Its lane snakes away northwards and leads to the marvellous hamlet of **Luddesdown**. It has a church with Roman tiles in its tower walls, while nearby Luddesdown Court is one of England's oldest inhabited houses which was once owned by Bishop Odo. Both the small barn-like church of Dode and tiny Luddesdown can be easily reached by footpath from Holly Hill. From the hamlet of Great Buckland you wander north through sloping fields in a gentle moulded vale known as the Bowling Alley, which leads directly to Luddesdown, bringing you onto a lane near both Luddesdown Court and church. A return to the car park at Holly Hill by way of Horseholders Wood would make a very pleasant 5-mile (2-hour) circular walk.

West of Luddesdown, on the crown of the downs astride the busy A227, is the straggling village of **Meopham** said to be the longest in Kent. At its heart is a very fine green, where cricket is played, and which looks across to a well-preserved windmill. Meopham's impressive church stands to the north, and Camer Country Park is on the right of the B2009 which branches from the main road towards Cobham. It offers 46 acres of parkland and woods.

Around Meopham there is gentle rolling downland, not so dramatic perhaps, as may be found in some areas of the North Downs, but sufficiently so to repay an afternoon's unhurried exploration. Occasionally one comes across a time-worn hall house, or perhaps a hidden village tucked around its central pond.

Ridley and Stansted, both tiny hamlets, are among the loveliest. **Ridley** is minute and consists of little more than a turreted church among flint walls, a farm, a cottage or two and an unusual thatched well-head dating from 1810. By comparison **Stansted** is a teeming metropolis, for it boasts a pub and a playing field in addition to its church, farm and cottages set in a tilt of meadows. The narrow hedge-lined lanes are a cyclist's delight, while the walker has many

A footpath through the Bowling Alley vale to Luddesdown

Great Buckland Farm, near Luddesdown

Stansted Church

Stansted

Thatched well-head, Ridley

more discoveries to make in this downland of intimate valleys and hilltops. There are woodlands and orchards, too. Charles Dickens used to travel extensively in this area, and some of his best-known characters acted out their adventures here. At **Cobham** The Old Leather Bottle inn was immortalised in *Pickwick Papers*, and today it incorporates the author's portrait in its sign. The Old Leather Bottle is a sizeable old coaching inn whose half-timbering is the result of much rebuilding after damage by fire in 1880; it stands at the western end of the High Street opposite St Mary Magdalene Church, one of the riches of the downs. In this church, with its wide chancel, is a veritable picture gallery of brasses, noted beyond the county boundary for the remarkable detail and beauty of their workmanship. They lie rank upon rank just below the altar, memorials to the Cobham and Brooke families, while elsewhere, scattered in various parts of the church, are other brasses to Masters of Cobham College.

Cobham College is hidden from the High Street by the church, but it is a lovely piece of architecture, set to the south of the churchyard with the downs as a background. Set around a courtyard of neat lawns, the mellow houses of the college have been here for 500 years or more. Sir John de Cobham founded the college in 1362 to say masses for his ancestors, and the buildings were later erected to house the master and priests, but in 1598 they were altered to provide almshouses for the poor of the parish. Beyond them broad landscapes hold several footpaths worth taking; to Luddesdown, Sole Street, or farther still traversing the downs to Trottiscliffe.

To the north-west of the village stands **Owletts**, a modest-sized seventeenth-century red-brick house with a notable staircase and especially fine plasterwork above it. In 1917 it became the home of the architect, Sir Herbert Baker, who made certain alterations and additions, designed a formal garden and then passed it all to the National Trust.

At the other end of the village, set in its great park, is **Cobham Hall**, 'an ancient hall displaying the quaint and picturesque architecture of Elizabeth's time'. So said Dickens, who used to walk regularly from his home at Gads Hill to Cobham Park. It is one of Kent's most lavish mansions, a red-brick sixteenth-century house from which project extensive wings; it has domed towers and lofty chimneys and inside, a vast picture gallery 130ft long. Nowadays it serves as a girl's school, but it is open to the public during some parts of the school holidays.

Dickens' Gads Hill lies not far from Cobham on the edge of Higham village, where he spent his last years writing in a little Swiss chalet which has since been removed to Rochester's Dickens Centre. 'I have many happy recollections connected with Kent, and am scarcely less interested in it than if I had been a Kentish man bred and born and had resided in the county all my life,' he wrote. And presumably Mr Pickwick merely voiced the great Victorian novelist's own feelings when he proclaimed Cobham to be '...one of the prettiest and most desirable places of residence.' Perhaps it was a sharing of such sentiments that inspired the authorities to declare practically the whole village a conservation area.

Cobham is the last of the downs west of the Medway. To the north the country slides to the levels of Hoo, while to the east the rural landscape is too soon exchanged for the cluster of buildings that make up Strood. Here the Medway has carved a deep channel through the chalk hills. The surprisingly delicate looking Medway

The Old Leather Bottle, Cobham

Cobham College and church

Kits Coty House

Bridge carries the M2 high above the river, but both cyclist and walker are also catered for, and the mile-long crossing gives some spectacular views, especially downstream to Rochester Castle looming above the river.

Beyond the Medway the downs change direction and arc in a rough south-easterly line. Along their edge some wonderful panoramas are revealed over the low Medway plain and into the Weald. At times it is necessary to blinker one's view in order to ignore the industry clustered along the river, or the pylons that cross the landscape. But late afternoon when the sun is sinking there is a wonderful view.

Above Burham the downs achieve considerable height toward Bluebell Hill. To the north, Chatham's suburbs spread across once-green meadows, sliced now by the motorway and the Rochester to Maidstone road. But overlooking the Medway Gap the chalk downland offers sanctuary; there are splendid panoramic views, footpaths lead to the north, south, east and west; there are finches and warblers among the scrub and kestrels are often to be seen hovering overhead.

There is a 13-acre picnic site on Bluebell Hill with the North Downs Way leading along its northern edge, and a little farther on, where the way bears south, is the most spectacular of Kent's archaeological sites.

Kits Coty House, like the Coldrum Stones at Trottiscliffe, the Countless Stones or Little Kits Coty half a mile below, is the remains of a Neolithic burial chamber; but here the capstone is still resting where it was placed some 4,000 years ago. There are three bulky upright stones, almost 8ft tall, on which the 10-ton capstone has been laid. This is one of the oldest monuments in England and occupies a site above the valley gazing out across the Medway Gap.

The North Downs Way and Pilgrims' Way follow parallel lines above Maidstone, and on the top of the downs beside the Sittingbourne road (A249) the spacious grounds of the Kent County Agricultural Showground teem with activity for a short period every summer. Up here it is necessary to leave the main roads to explore the heart of downland Kent, where farms lie scattered in hollows; cottages are sited by woods; villages lie dotted along the trackways that mark their slopes. East of the county town, a short distance from magnificent Leeds Castle, the Weald comes to the ankles of the downs, to provide a notable contrast of valley and ridge. The very best of the downs is to be found along these edges which catch this contrast, and along the lower slopes some of the loveliest of its villages are found. Unfortunately it has recently been announced that the route of a new high-speed Channel Tunnel rail link will pass this way, and there are fears that this will greatly reduce the charm and peace of the area. At present the narrow lane of the Pilgrims' Way which traces the foot of the downs gives an opportunity to sample a 'lost world' of isolated farms, tiny villages and broad landscapes. Once the high-speed trains come hurtling through, that world will be lost forever.

Hollingbourne is one such village which sits among the foothills. If approached from the downs one plunges in a steep descent on a narrow road sunken into the chalk with a bower of trees hanging over. This is the route taken by Cobbett in 1823: 'When I got to the edge of the hill and before I got off my horse to lead him down this more than a mile of hill, I sat and surveyed the prospect before me, and to the right and to the left. This is what the people of Kent call the

Places to Visit Around Meopham

Camer Country Park
North of Meopham, off B2009
46 acres of parkland with some
fine trees.

St Mary Magdalene Church
3 miles north-east of Meopham
Dates from the thirteenth century
and contains one of the finest
collections of brasses in Britain.
Behind the church, Cobham
College almshouses may be
viewed at times given on notice
board in churchyard.

Cobham Hall
3$^1/_2$ miles north-east of Meopham
An impressive sixteenth-century
mansion set in a vast area of
parkland. Now a girls' school, it
is open to the public during
Easter and summer holidays.

Coldrum Stones (NT)
5 miles south of Meopham, 1
mile east of Trottiscliffe
Remains of a Neolithic long
barrow some 4,000 years old.

Four upright stones of the central
chamber are still in place, but
others lie scattered in a rough
circle. An impressive site. Car
park nearby.

Meopham Windmill
Well preserved smock mill, built
1801, standing by the main A227
road and open to the public on
Sunday afternoons in July and
August, and summer Bank
Holidays.

Owletts (NT)
Cobham, 2$^1/_2$ miles north-east of
Meopham on B2009
A seventeenth-century red-brick
house with fine staircase and
plasterwork, set in pleasant
gardens.

Trosley Country Park
4 miles south of Meopham off
A227
160 acres of downland and
woodland, with nature trails and
circular walks. Information centre
with guides for sale.

Garden of Eden.' It is a very lovely view, but the approach from the
Weald is no less dramatic, for it comes off the busy A20 by way of a
lane that suddenly dips into the past. Eyhorne Street is the lower half
of this two-part village, and it consists of a marvellous street of old
cottages representing various periods. Some are timber-framed,
some weather-boarded, some of old brick. A stream flows past the
doors of one or two houses and a tannery on its course to the River
Len. It rises in a spring in a pond near the church that forms the focus
of Upper Hollingbourne; the two parts of the village being separated
by the railway and meadows with footpath access.

All Saints Church has a lovely approach, beautiful views across the fields to a group of farmbuildings, the manor and the downs behind. Inside there is much of interest. It owes much of its ornateness to the Culpeper family who occupy some of the more lavish corners of Kentish churches, but its particular treasure is a richly decorated altar cloth — not in everyday use — which was worked by four Culpeper daughters while their father was in exile with Charles II.

There is a definite aura of peace about Hollingbourne, in its lanes and its footpaths and in its street. It is a corner of Kent which shares the sweep of the downs with the tranquillity of the lower meadows. Eyhorne Manor is but one of its glories; it is a fifteenth-century manor restored with loving care in a splendid garden of herbs and flowers. Near the church is Hollingbourne Manor, with its Tudor chimneys, a fine example of an Elizabethan manor house, but unfortunately it is not open to the public.

A green track keeps to the foot of the hills to link Hollingbourne with Harrietsham, another village split not only by the railway but also by two roads, and from there one climbs the downs among beeches to join a criss-cross of lanes, all of which offer pleasant diversions to the visitor.

After walking along the topmost lanes, or one of the many well-signposted paths, it is worth coming down once more to have a look at **Charing**. It is on the junction of two main routes; Maidstone to Ashford and the cross-country road that leads to Canterbury, yet fortunately it has been bypassed by most of the traffic. Charing has seen the comings and goings of Canterbury pilgrims for centuries, lying as it does close to the ancient route. Those who now turn off the main road to walk along its climbing street will be rewarded by its fine timbered or weatherboarded houses, Georgian frontages, the lovely church tower of Kentish rag-stone with superb battlements, and remains of the Archbishop's Palace, home once to Cranmer and where Henry VIII stayed on his way to meet the Emperor Charles V at the Field of the Cloth of Gold. There were 4,000 or so people accompanying the king on his journey, and many of these would have been entertained in the huge banqueting hall, now a flint-walled barn belonging to Palace Farm, seen through an archway on the approach to the church.

Charing Church

The A252 misses the best of Charing, climbs on to the back of the downs and runs among woods to **Challock**, a village that was originally built around its church, but after the plague moved to its present site, a mile or so away. Challock Forest dominates the countryside south of the road, but approaching Chilham the folding hills lose some of their height and the woodlands fall back. The Canterbury road skirts below and to the north of Chilham, but the fame of this village is sufficient to send thousands up to its square.

 Chilham is a victim of its own splendour. It is a small village built on a steep hill with a marvellous square, with a church at one end, a Jacobean mansion hidden behind high walls at the other, and Tudor and Jacobean houses lining both sides. From each corner, lanes lead away with their own charming houses. Little wonder that on fine summer days, and at weekends, Chilham is crowded with visitors. As one of Kent's prettiest villages it must on occasion be extremely trying to live in.

It was near here that the Romans are said to have fought their last great battle in England, burying their dead in a Neolithic long barrow 2,000 years old. The site is today known rather picturesquely as Julliberrie Downs; according to some authorities, in honour of Julius Laberius who was killed in 54BC. Roman finds have also been made near the castle, and there are suggestions that the ruined Norman keep could have Roman foundations. Certainly Chilham's hilltop perch is an obvious defensive site. There are traces of Saxon defences here, and Henry II built an octagonal castle to replace an earlier construction commissioned by Odo, Bishop of Bayeux. Only the keep and inner bailey of Henry's castle remain today, but Sir Dudley Digges had the Jacobean 'castle' built for him on the site, and this was completed in 1616. It is an extraordinary building, occupying five sides of a hexagon around a courtyard, and believed to have been designed by Inigo Jones. Apart from the special medieval banquets held in the Gothic hall, the castle is closed to the public, but the grounds are extremely popular with visitors. They were originally laid out by John Tradescant, but now bear the stamp of Capability Brown. He designed the terraced lawns and the lake, the noble trees and the marvellous shrubs. There is some fine topiary, an ancient heronry, said to date back to the thirteenth century (which would make it the oldest in England), and from the ground there are distant views of Canterbury Cathedral. On Sundays in summer jousting tournaments are held in these grounds, and there are falconry displays and other medieval-style entertainments.

At the other end of the village square there is the lovely flint church of St Mary's, 600 years old, an airy, spacious place of worship in which to sit in quiet prayer away from the crowds. Pilgrims would have passed through Chilham, and no doubt many would have paused in this church too, to refresh their spirits before continuing on the final stage of their journey to Canterbury. Beyond the village there are orchards on the hillsides, and in the bowl of the valley lagoons of the Great Stour spread out with the railway line running alongside. Within a few miles the downs have opened and ahead is Canterbury, trapped within a commercial development that at times threatens to overwhelm it.

Canterbury has an indisputable majesty. Its glory is known to all who know anything of the history of England. Its great cathedral stands proudly as one of Britain's architectural triumphs, and is recognised immediately on sight, which may be from the top of the downs or across the jostling crowds by day, or floodlit from the Dover road by night; a tribute to the faith that inspired it and to the craftsmen who created it.

Within the Roman city walls there is the history of many centuries and races of men, and many remains. During World War II, enemy bombers destroyed nearly a third of Canterbury's centre, but miraculously little of great value disappeared, and in the devastation certain Roman discoveries were made. Unhappily, the post war development of the city leaves something to be desired, and recent building programmes have threatened almost to smother the very things that make Canterbury unique. Multi-storey car parks loom over winding streets to block the view of the cathedral, and plate glass and red-brick commercialism form an unworthy complement to the leaning Tudor buildings and dramatic arches that represent old Canterbury.

Apart from the distant view of its lovely towers and spires, the first notable feature for the visitor is the half circle of city wall with its grassy slopes, and here and there its inner trees and gardens. The Romans built it, but the Normans improved the structure and provided six gates and some twenty-one watchtowers. The old

Chilham — the classic view

burial mound known as Dane John has been enlarged, and from it there is a splendid view of the wall stretching onwards, the gardens below, and the cathedral caught across the intervening trees. There was an Iron Age camp beside the River Stour, and Belgic tribes settled the site around 300BC. The Romans set up an important administrative centre, known as *Durovernum*, from which they had roads stretching out to Richborough, Reculver and Lympne. Watling Street crossed the Stour here and it is not difficult to appreciate the importance of the site to an army of occupation. In their city the Romans built fine villas, baths and an amphitheatre; their roads and houses were several feet lower than today. In Butchery Lane, south of the cathedral, the Roman Pavement forms an underground

Canterbury Cathedral

museum where the remains of a town house, mosaic pavement and under-floor heating room may be seen, in addition to numerous other pieces of Roman Canterbury.

Although it was the Romans who introduced Christianity to Kent, it virtually died out with their withdrawal, and it was St Augustine who, sent by Pope Gregory in AD597 to convert our Saxon ancestors, re-established the Christian religion here. At this time Ethelbert was king of Kent with Bertha as his queen and Canterbury as the capital of their kingdom. Queen Bertha was French and already a Christian, and Ethelbert gave her a Roman building in which to practice her religion while he had his own pagan temple elsewhere in the city. Bertha's chapel became St Martin's Church and this, with Roman material seen in its walls, stands today as the oldest church in England still in use. It was here that Augustine converted Ethelbert and, celebrating Whitsunday, baptised him into the faith. Ethelbert's former temple was given for dedication to Christian purposes, and Augustine also established a monastery which became the burial place for a succession of kings and queens of Kent. Today, St Augustine's Abbey lies in ruins.

When Augustine proclaimed Canterbury as the centre of the Roman church in Britain, there was already a place of worship on the site of today's cathedral. It was rebuilt several times following Danish raids and fires, but the foundations of the building seen today were laid by the first Norman archbishop, Lanfranc, in 1070. His work remains in parts of the crypt and the ground plan of the nave. It was added to over several centuries by countless masters. Before Becket, it was a small yet glorious place. Following his murder in 1170 and Henry II's barefooted pilgrimage 2 years later, the cathedral received the gifts of thousands of pilgrims who visited Becket's shrine over the next 300 years. The city became immensely prosperous but Becket's shrine was desecrated and the cathedral plundered in the fever of dissolution. Again it was restored to glory, again it suffered destruction at the hands of the Puritans in the Civil War when much of the beautiful stained glass and a number of statues were smashed. Yet the cathedral church of Christ, the seat of the Primate of All England, the ultimate symbol of English Christianity has received the skills of master craftsmen to create the wonderful edifice that is, arguably, the finest cathedral in Britain.

Canterbury Cathedral is light and airy; pillars soar to a forest of arches that support a ceiling full of majesty. Steps lead up and up from one level to another, worn by the millions of feet of pilgrims down the centuries, leading past monument after monument, moving among works of art in wood and iron and stone, past screens and under windows that demand a detailed scrutiny that time never properly allows. The windows are particularly beautiful; ancient and not so ancient, they are inspired representations of biblical themes, the history of martyrs, pages of scripture and history written in coloured glass.

The choir has iron gates and an exquisite screen etched in stone. Around it are chapels many hundreds of years old; there are other chapels farther on, and countless figures, tombs and shrines to many of the great and famous in English history. But the shrine that made Canterbury one of medieval Europe's greatest centres of pilgrimage is today a simple affair. Just a few words on the Murder Stone where Thomas á Becket was slain by four knights 800 years ago.

Thomas Becket. Archbishop. Saint. Martyr. Died here Tuesday 29th December 1170.

Only the knee-worn pavement that surrounded the original shrine signifies its previous importance, but Erasmus indicated its former magnificence when he wrote in 1512 that Becket's shrine was so magnificent that 'gold was the meanest thing to be seen.' On Henry VIII's orders, Thomas Cromwell destroyed it in 1538. If the cathedral was Canterbury's sole attraction it would still be enough to warrant time in the city.

As well as the Roman ruins there is the interesting **West Gate** on the banks of the Stour, last of the fortified gatehouses, rebuilt in 1380. For many years it was used as a prison, but it now houses a museum and in the guard chamber there is a collection of arms and armour. There are the remains of the castle that the Normans built within the city walls, Poor Priests' Hospital, a fourteenth-century hospice restored now as a museum of Canterbury, and Greyfriars Friary which dates from 1276 and was the first such Franciscan friary to be established in England. There are other interesting churches such as St Mildred's in Castle Street, or St Peter's in St Peter's Street, or St Dunstan's not far from the West Gate, in which there is a vault containing the head of Sir Thomas More. When Henry VIII executed him, his head was tossed into the lap of Margaret Roper, his daughter, and for the remainder of her unhappy life she preserved it in spices and kept it in her house, not far from where it now lies.

In the heart of the city there are narrow streets crowded with splendid old buildings which have seen countless pilgrims through the ages. Heavy gabled houses hang over the streets and the river. Shadows fall from timbered frontages, mellow stone catches the changing moods of light as one street leads to another, and all the time there is the cathedral. It is never far away and whether it is seen in all its splendour through the magnificent Christ Church Gate or in a brief glimpse, it is beautiful. Within its precinct stands the long-established King's School, one of the oldest still in existence. Among the school's old boys are Shakespeare's contemporary, Christopher Marlowe, and W. Somerset Maugham.

South of Canterbury the downs fold away towards the English Channel. Along their eastern edges runs the extremely busy Dover road, the A2. To the north-east, roughly following the course of the River Stour, runs the A28 towards the low-lying Isle of Thanet. As it leaves Canterbury, and almost before you realise the city has gone, the road brings you to Sturry, whose heart was destroyed by two of Hitler's bombs in 1941. The main road curves to the left, but as it does so another, more narrow road breaks off to the right, hiccups over a tight, hump-backed medieval bridge, and enters **Fordwich**, an ancient 'limb' of the Cinque Ports.

Now here is a village worth dallying in. There are two good pubs on the tree-lined banks of the Stour that serve meals. There are several attractive cottages, a delightful church containing box pews, a Norman font and a stone once thought to have been part of the tomb of St Augustine. And there is England's smallest town hall; a red-brick, herring-bone building with black timbers and a fine roof, set behind iron railings on what at one time was an important riverside quay. (It was here that the Caen stone used for building Canterbury Cathedral was unloaded.) The town hall is open to visitors. It holds a few exhibits of local historical interest, including a ducking stool.

While the A28 continues out of Sturry and away from the downs, a more narrow road twists away from Fordwich to meet the Canterbury to Sandwich road with John Aspinall's Howletts Zoo Park (between Littlebourne and Bekesbourne) drawing numerous visi-

The River Stour at Fordwich

tors with its collection of exotic animals set in 55 acres of mature parkland.

There are other minor roads, though, that explore the hills and valleys without haste; for instance, that which goes through the now-quiet village of **Bridge**. Until 1976 this was the main London-Dover road, a horror story of congestion and a catalogue of accidents that made life almost intolerable for the residents of Bridge who campaigned for a bypass for 14 years and made national headlines by repeatedly blocking the village street with their massed sit-down protests. In one action, 1,000 people joined the protest and held up traffic for an hour, and the tail-back was of such proportions that the government was forced to take action. Work began on the bypass during the following year, and when the new road was finally opened, the villagers' victory was celebrated far and wide. Just south of the village it is possible to walk in green pastureland, lovely vales, or woodlands crowning the hills. There are footpaths through Bourne Park that lead to the hamlet of Bishopsbourne where Joseph Conrad spent the last 5 years of his life, and from there through

Charlton Park to Kingston where a railway once ran linking Canterbury with Folkestone. It is all lovely soft country, but a short diversion to **Patrixbourne**, a little north of Bridge, gives a glimpse of one of the most attractive villages in the area which is worth a visit if only for the magnificent Norman doorway of its church. Doorways seem to be a speciality of this corner of the county, for a few miles farther south-east of Patrixbourne, reached by a complex of lanes off the A2 is **Barfreston**. This tiny village has a gloriously decorated Norman church whose south doorway of the nave is one of the treasures of England, a joy to behold, a marvel of craftsmanship. Barfreston (or Barfrestone as some signs have it) is a secluded little hamlet caught in a fold of the downs. Henry Moore lived in a cottage above the church for a while during the 1930s, during which time the surrounding countryside was being scarred and scoured for coal. There were coalfields at nearby Snowdown and Tilmerstone — both

Barfreston,
south doorway

Places to Visit
In and Around Canterbury

Blean Bird Park
Blean, 3 miles north-west of
Canterbury
A collection of exotic tropical birds
offers an unusual outing. There is
also a childrens' corner.

Canterbury Cathedral
One of the finest church buildings
in Britain and seat of the Primate
of All England. Wonderful nave,
choir, crypt and various tombs,
monuments and shrines. Its
windows are magnificent.
Guided tours twice daily.

Chilham Castle Gardens
5 miles south-west of Canterbury,
off A252
The grounds of a Jacobean
mansion built on the site of a
Norman castle, with terraced
lawns, lake, fine shrubs and trees
and ancient heronry. In the
grounds jousting and other
medieval entertainments are held
on Sundays in summer. Medieval
banquets may be booked in
advance in the Gothic hall.

Howletts Zoo Park
3 miles south-east of Canterbury,
between Bekesbourne and
Littlebourne
Numerous exotic animals in a
lovely parkland owned by John
Aspinall.

Norman Castle
Canterbury
Built in the eleventh-century within
the city walls, it was later used as
a county jail. Ruins only.

Roman Pavement
Canterbury
Archaeological finds and Roman
remains of a town house, mosaic
pavement and hypocaust room in

an underground museum in
Butchery Lane. Considered by
many to be the most outstanding
Roman site in Canterbury.
Combined tickets available for this
and West Gate.

Royal Museum and Art Gallery
The main museum in Canterbury,
houses a number of the city's
archaeological finds. The art
gallery adjoins the museum which
is in the High Street.

St Augustine's Abbey
Canterbury
Foundations of the abbey church
set up by St Augustine in AD597,
now in ruins.

Wealden Forest Park
5 miles north-east of Canterbury,
on Herne Bay road, A291
An extensive area of woodland
with a wide range of attractions
including nature trail, adventure
playground and wildlife park
containing British animals and
birds. There is also a covered
garden and butterfly centre with
British and tropical butterflies.
Other facilities are planned to
broaden the scope even further.

The Weavers
Canterbury
Now a shop in St Peter's Street, it
was originally built in 1485. Beside
it runs the Stour on which boat
trips are arranged from The
Weavers.

West Gate Museum
Canterbury
Rebuilt in 1380 by Archbishop
Sudbury, this is the last of the
city's fortified gatehouses.
Now contains museum of arms
and armour in the guard chamber.

of which are now closed, and although Kent drew migrations of miners from South Wales during the Depression, the only remaining colliery in Kent today is at Betteshanger, near Deal, although the National Coal Board has proposed its intention that this too, should cease operations.

The North Downs Way explores the countryside and the tiny villages that lie to the east of the A2, while to the west there are sufficient minor vales, hamlets and woodlands where several days could be spent unravelling some of their secrets with footpaths for the rambler, and lanes to entice the cyclist and the leisurely driver.

On the southern slopes, resuming once more fom Charing, the downs are every bit as attractive as on their northern counterpart, and keeping away from the main roads that lead to Ashford and

Hythe some pleasant corners can be found. **Westwell** is an ancient place with a history of 1,000 years. It is not a large village but it will delight the botanist in spring, will repay the lover of old churches, and in addition it contains a disused watermill now converted into a private dwelling but set beside the road for all to see.

The alternative routing of the North Downs Way, which avoids Canterbury, comes this way and shortly after passing through Westwell enters the grounds of **Eastwell** Park with its 40 acres of lake, popular with herons and anglers alike. It used to be the major feature of the park, whose manor house is now a hotel, and was considered by Daniel Defoe as the finest he had ever seen. On the northern bank, partly shrouded in trees, stand the remains of a white, flint-walled church that partly collapsed in a storm in 1951, having been considerably weakened during World War II. It is being slowly repaired by the Friends of Friendless Churches, but in spite of its precarious state (or maybe because of it) the white church set in a landscape of so much greenery proclaims a message of peace and tranquillity. In an unnamed tomb here, the body of Richard Plantagenet — son of Richard III — is reputedly buried. Legend has it that he escaped from the Battle of Bosworth Field and came to the Eastwell estate where he worked out his days anonymously as a carpenter. The church and lake are discovered along a narrow, hedge-lined no-through-road that cuts away from the lane linking Westwell with the Ashford to Faversham road. Where lane meets road stands the large and lavishly decorated neo-Jacobean gate-

The gatehouse, Eastwell Park

house, an eye-catching structure when first seen from the south by travellers journeying from Ashford. Here, though, a vast sweep of downland and valley draws one's attention to the east.

This is an attractive land of wide views and a sense of space. Take a side lane once more, this time branching off from Boughton Lees, and follow through a cleft of hedgerow to another tiny hamlet almost submerged in a brash of field and meadow; **Boughton Aluph** — church, manor and a few cottages on a lane that goes nowhere. The downs spread around. The North Downs Way comes right past the church, so the long-distance walker absorbs the full flavour of this surprisingly 'empty' region of Kent before marching on to **Wye**, which sits on the right bank of the Great Stour, framed to the east by the impressive wall of the North Downs again, here marked by a crown cut out of the chalk to commemorate the coronation of Edward VII in 1901. This little town has many lovely houses, a church, and a college founded by John Kempe who, born here in 1380, became Archbishop of Canterbury. His college for priests was dissolved in 1545 and the buildings became a grammar school, but today it is used as an agricultural college for the University of London. At the western end, a small stone building with mullioned windows represents the oldest part, and was once a portion of Archbishop Kempe's College. There is a certain harmony about the college buildings that the passage of centuries has done nothing to diminish.

A number of footpaths serve Wye and its position at the foot of Crundale and Wye Downs makes it an attractive base for a few days' leisurely walking. Above the town are some of the best remaining areas of chalk downland in Kent. There are orchid banks and dry valleys, woodlands and delightful views. Armed with a map, there is much to explore. One 10-mile (4-hour) loop provides a good introduction. It leaves Wye churchyard and heads roughly eastwards to the nose of the downs. A series of paths and lanes lead up to the hamlet of Hassell Street, and from there northwards along the scarp among trees and open downland to reach Crundale Church, isolated from its village by half a mile of lane or path. The footpath loses height, either by heading directly back to Wye and thereby saving $1^1/_2$ miles, or preferably diverting towards the village and then cutting back through woods on a rise before going down across fields and through more stretches of woodland into the town once more.

South-eastwards the downs stretch in an imposing wall. Along Wye Downs there is a nature reserve managed by the Nature Conservancy Council where the chalk downland is rich in flowers and butterflies. From the slopes there are views south towards Romney Marsh and the sea. There is a nature trail and a convenient car park on the Hastingleigh road about 2 miles from Wye, and by combining footpaths and lanes there is plenty of scope for some lovely walks.

The hamlet of **Brabourne** lies along the slope of the downs among orchards and a mesh of lanes, with footpaths leading to the broad valley that forms a step above Romney Marsh. Brabourne (not to be confused with Brabourne Lees a couple of miles away) with its inn at one end of the street and its church at the other, with the downs above and the valley below, is a delightful place. The aged flint-walled church squats quietly; around it are the few dignified houses and neat farms which form the entire community. It has not the quaintness to make it a pretty village like Chilham or Chiddingstone, but it is representative of those hamlets of old that were tied to the land.

The road climbs out of Brabourne and runs along the downs near. Stowting to give some lovely views from Farthing Common. Here the Roman road of Stone Street which linked Canterbury, or *Durover-num*, with *Portus Lemanis*, or Lympne, ends its straight run across the downs and curves suddenly to the east before descending to the edge of the marshes. Other roads cut off into the downs here away from the North Downs Way and the Saxon Shore Way, and enter the very pleasant **Elham Valley** which flows north-east from the overgrown village of Lyminge. In this valley flows the infant Nail Bourne stream and its pastures provide some lovely walks. One footpath (5 miles, 2 hours) follows the right bank of the stream between Lyminge and Breach to the south of Barham, taking in the pleasant village of Elham on the way. **Elham** escapes the crowds, like Brabourne, by being not quite pretty enough, by not having a showpiece. But those with a feeling for such places will not be disappointed, either by its location or by its unobtrusive architecture. It is one of the unsung discoveries of the downs.

Between Elham's valley and the coast there are few villages on

*Hastingleigh, on the
downs above Wye*

the downs; there are more isolated farms. The land is criss-crossed
with footpaths and lanes which should be travelled through without
haste. From the crown of Castle Hill above Folkestone one can gaze
down upon the Cheriton terminal of the Channel Tunnel, and west
along the valley through which travellers pour by road and rail,
bound for France.

 EAST KENT COUNTRY TOUR (50 miles, 2-3 hours)
This is one of three signposted tours in Kent developed specifically
with the visiting motorist in mind. The route, which is outlined in an
anti-clockwise direction, leads to some of the most interesting places
in the area — historic buildings, gardens, viewpoints or other attractions — the majority of which are described in some detail elsewhere
in this guidebook. Signs to watch out for have a white tree and
direction arrow on a brown background; some are also marked 'East

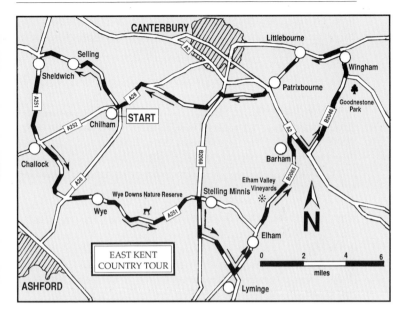

Kent Country Tour'. As a circular route, the tour could be joined at any point, but is described here from the lovely village of Chilham, south-west of Canterbury above the junction of the A252 and A28.

From **Chilham** (one of the finest villages in Kent, complete with Jacobean 'castle') the tour heads north-westwards on a minor road through orchards and past **Perry Wood** (150 acres of woodland; many footpaths) to **Selling** (The White Lion is a 400-year-old coaching inn). Through Selling continue to the A251 where you turn left into **Sheldwich** (the parish church is of Norman origin) and travel through open meadowlands to the crossroads at **Challock**. The original village was badly hit by the plague in the fourteenth century but survivors built a new village at a safe distance from it. Challock Church stands a mile or so away to the south, and is dedicated to St Cosmus and St Damian.

Continuing along the A251 the route goes through King's Wood, then along the perimeter of **Eastwell Park** (neo-Jacobean gatehouse, lake and ruined church accessible by a short detour.) At **Boughton Lees** break away left along a minor road through charming countryside, across A28 and into the small market town of **Wye** at the foot of the North Downs (watermill and mill house on the Great Stour, 400-year-old timber-framed house, Wye College, memorial crown carved in the downland chalk).

Signs direct the tour now onto the downs and beside **Wye Downs Nature Reserve** — one of Kent's finest chalk downlands for flowers and butterflies with magnificent views and the Devil's Kneading-trough which is a dry valley thought to have been shaped some 10,000 years ago). The narrow road follows the edge of the downs, then breaks away north-eastwards and comes to the B2068, the former Roman highway of **Stone Street**, not far from **Stelling Minnis** (weatherboarded smock windmill, built 1866).

South now along Stone Street for $1^1/_2$ miles, then head left on a minor road through **West Wood** (440 acres of woodland, picnic area, public toilets and waymarked footpaths) on into the Elham Valley to the village of **Elham** (many fine buildings). Continue through the valley (good views) and pass **Elham Valley Vineyards** (open to the public, except Mondays, between June and September), and cross the A2 outside Barham to join the B2046 heading northward.

Along this road you will pass signs for **Goodnestone Park** (Jane Austen connections; walled garden open on set days from April to September) and come to **Wingham** (village with fine houses of all periods from Tudor to present day, on either side of wide High Street). Turn left to head through countryside of orchards and hop gardens to reach **Littlebourne** (mill astride the Nail Bourne river and interesting group of oast-houses) where the route turns left again towards **Howletts Zoo Park** (large collection of exotic animals, including a breeding colony of gorillas). Orchards are a major feature of the drive to **Patrixbourne** with its several lovely half-timbered and thatched houses and twelfth-century church with beautifully carved stone doorway.

Over the A2 again, the tour veers westward among more orchards, hop gardens and oast-houses, along the edge of **Chartham Downs** (fine views) to Shalmsford Street where the A28 leads back to **Chilham** once more.

3
THE MEDWAY

T he valley of the Medway, and the towns and villages that have grown up along its banks and on the hills that overlook it, make a tour along its course a journey full of interest. It runs right across the county, for it rises among the hills of Sussex beyond the south-western boundary and flows out to the sea among marshes and little islands of its estuary, squeezed between Sheppey and Grain. On its route it draws other streams, which drain Greensand hills and the chalk downs. In its waters canoes and dinghies and narrow boats share the currents with swan, moorhen and duck. Medieval bridges span its width; splendid pieces of ancient architecture which add another touch of serenity to an already serene stretch of water. Manicured lawns come down to its edge. Village houses can be found on its banks, and from the towpath that follows its course for many miles, some of the loveliest of all Kent's acres are shown in all their glory.

The Medway combines history with scenic splendour. It contrasts the tranquillity of rural innocence with, downstream, the vigour of industrial power. The old distinction between Kentish Men and Men of Kent was a product of the river's division of the county into west and east. To the west lived Kentish Men; east, Men of Kent.

The Medway has not always been a lovely river, for like so many major waterways it suffered deplorably from pollution. Now, however, the Kent River Board has restored the river; it is stocked with fish, and flowers, birds, voles and insects again find it a congenial habitat.

For a few short miles west of Groombridge, the infant Medway forms the Kent-Sussex border. It flows below Ashurst, where footpaths lead into a wonderland of high Wealden hills overlooking Sussex and the rising blue ridge of Ashdown Forest; a landscape full of summer romance when the meadows are cut and spread with drying hay, with gentle streams and isolated farms breaking the chequerboard of greenery with their white-tipped oasts. This is a landscape that draws some of the best features of both Kent and Sussex; it can only be guessed from the road. The rail passenger travelling through from Edenbridge to Eridge and Uckfield has a better chance of understanding this countryside. But best of all is the wanderer of footpaths who absorbs the full splendour of this almost secret corner where the Medway is but a small feature of a much greater whole.

The river breaks away from Sussex (marked by a meagre stream called Kent Water) where green hills rise out of the low-lying meadows down the slope from **Fordcombe**, a small village sitting on a minor crossroads with a village green and a cricket pitch giving it a distinctly spacious quality. On the left bank rises **Hobbs Hill** with its farm and oasts gazing south from a prominent position. This is all good walking country — the Wealdway heads through Fordcombe — with footpaths leading over Hobbs Hill to Chiddingstone Hoath and Penshurst, or alongside Kent Water to Cowden. Since this chapter deals primarily with the Medway, there is a fine walk ($3^1/_2$ miles, $1^1/_2$ hours) to be had beside the river all the way from the watermeadows below Fordcombe as far as Penshurst, going through low-lying pastures nobbled here and there with solid-looking wartime pillboxes, past an occasional half-timbered manor house and along the edge of hop gardens until you come at last to a pleasing introductory view of the cottages, church and hump-backed bridge of Penshurst itself, where the Medway is swelled by the River Eden in the Eden Valley. Since the boundaries of each chapter necessarily overlap here and there, Penshurst is dealt with more thoroughly in Chapter 5, Eden Valley and The Greensand Ridge.

More than a century ago, there were plans to make the Medway navigable to barges upstream as far as Penshurst, but work was never finished, and the plan was abandoned a little beyond Tonbridge. A green track known as the Straight Mile, downstream and some distance from the village, indicates where the scheme foun-

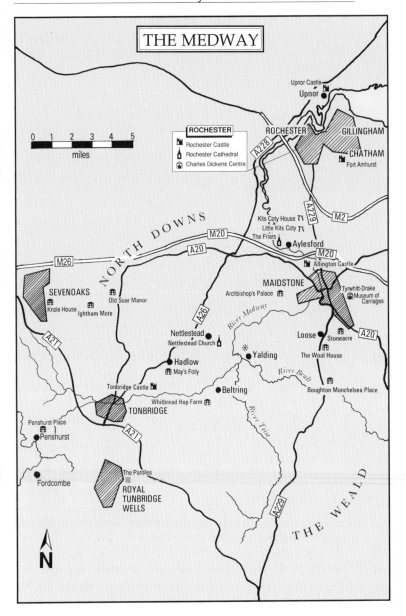

THE MEDWAY

0 1 2 3 4 5
miles

ROCHESTER
- Rochester Castle
- Rochester Cathedral
- Charles Dickens Centre

Upnor Castle
Upnor

ROCHESTER

GILLINGHAM

CHATHAM
Fort Amhurst

A228

A229

M2

NORTH DOWNS

Kits Coty House
Little Kits Coty
The Friars
Aylesford

M20

A20

M26

M20

Allington Castle

SEVENOAKS

Old Soar Manor

Knole House
Ightham Mote

MAIDSTONE

Archbishop's Palace

Tyrwhitt-Drake
Museum of
Carriages

A26

River Medway

Loose
Stoneacre

A20

Nettlestead
Nettlestead Church

Yalding

The Wool House

A21

Hadlow
May's Folly

River Beult

Tonbridge Castle

Beltring

Boughton Monchelsea Place

Whitbread Hop Farm

TONBRIDGE

Penshurst Place
Penshurst

A21

River Teise

Fordcombe

The Pantiles

ROYAL
TUNBRIDGE
WELLS

A229

THE WEALD

N

dered. A path leads along the Straight Mile, around the open stretch of Hayesden Water and by the railway; a tangle of river, road and rail with the encroaching sprawl of Tonbridge spreading from the east. It is in **Tonbridge** that the Medway navigation starts.

The remains of Tonbridge Castle, a stark Norman stronghold with huge round towers built on a mound overlooking the river, gives good views of the Medway and surrounding gardens and the sports ground nearby, created on 50 acres of greenery encircled by the river.

It is the castle's commanding position that gives a clue to the town's significance, for even during Iron Age times the site was recognised as being an important Medway crossing. The Weald was then an almost impenetrable forest, and there were few north-south trackways through it. One, however, came through here, and a stronghold was established to guard the crossing. It is thought that the name of Tonbridge comes from *dun burgh*, meaning 'hill fort'. The original castle, built by the Saxons on the site of the Iron Age hill fort, was strengthened soon after the Norman Conquest, but this was almost completely destroyed by fire in 1087. A replacement was built immediately; motte and bailey surviving to this day, although when the Norman keep that stood on the motte was razed, a large gatehouse with double drum towers was constructed in the thirteenth century. Horace Walpole considered the gateway to be 'perfect' when he visited in 1752. Today there is a very agreeable contrast to be seen between the stark curtain wall and drum towers, and the sweep of trim lawns brightened with flower borders; past and present, power and pleasantry, easily reached from the town's main street. In the main street stands Tonbridge School, founded in 1553 by Sir Andrew Judde as a free grammar school, but almost completely rebuilt in Victorian Gothic style in 1864. Seen from the road it appears to be the archetypal English school, with neat lawns, boaters and blazers; it also boasts a library dating back to 1760.

Across the Medway bridge which takes traffic through the town, Medway Wharf Road, on the left, leads to a lock. From here to Maidstone the walker is treated to a towpath walk of great beauty. It is a long walk, about 16 miles (7 hours) in all, but there are numerous possibilities for cutting short the journey at any one of the villages along the way. At first the path follows the right bank of the

Tonbridge School

river, but shortly after, when a road is reached, it crosses to the left bank. For many miles the river is crossed from one side to the other, usually at convenient locks. At no stage is the route difficult to follow, but it goes through such delightful countryside that a spring or summer's day ought to be devoted to its exploration by any keen rambler.

In his *Rural Rides*, William Cobbett covered much of Kent, not all of which drew his enthusiasm; but one particular corner was sufficient to inspire his praise. 'The ten miles between Maidstone and Tonbridge,' he wrote, 'I believe to be the very finest, as to fertility and diminutive beauty, in the whole world...There are, on rising grounds, not only hop gardens and beautiful woods, but immense orchards of apples, pears, plums, cherries and filberts, and these, in many cases, with gooseberries and currants and raspberries beneath.'

Heading out of Tonbridge along the Medway Valley, the first place of any size is **Hadlow**. As a village it has undisputed charm, a wide street with some pleasant buildings near the church, and a

The River Medway at Tonbridge

Tonbridge Castle

Gothic tower that dominates the surrounding countryside. It is this folly that catches the eye from so many corners of the Medway Valley. It is 170ft high and all that remains of Hadlow Castle, a large house built in the last year of the eighteenth century. The tower was an afterthought, the dream of a wealthy eccentric, Walter Barton May, an industrialist with enough money to indulge his fancy in an age noted for its eccentricities. There are two theories as to why the tower was built. One says that May wanted to be able to keep an eye on his wife after they had parted; the other, that he wished to be able to see the coast, far beyond his own land. Whatever the reason, the folly remains as an interesting feature of the landscape, a lofty pinnacle of imaginative design, all crenellations and spires. Cobbett again, is worth quoting, for in 1823 he saw Hadlow Castle as 'an immense house, stuck all over with a parcel of chimneys, or things like chimneys; little brick columns with a sort of cap on them at the top to catch the earwigs'.

May's Folly rises above the parish church of St Mary's in whose churchyard is a memorial to a group of hop pickers who were drowned in 1853. They were returning across the Medway from their day's labours when the two wagons in which they were being carried broke through the railings on Hartlake Bridge, and tipped into the river. All thirty-five men, women and children perished in the tragedy. The present Hartlake Bridge is a more sturdy, albeit rather bland, construction, unlike some of the splendid medieval stone bridges seen farther down-stream.

South of Hadlow, **Golden Green** sits among orchards and hop gardens, with oasts catching the eye here and there. The hamlet is not remarkable, a straggling place along the road to East Peckham where the B2015 takes the traveller over the river to **Beltring** and the largest hop farm in Kent. Beside the road a great cluster of conical oast-houses announces the Whitbread Hop Farm, which has become not simply a hop-drying centre, but a magnet for visitors with its museums, its country crafts exhibition, nature trail and its fishing. This is one of the few places in the county where a working farm may be visited during the busy hop harvest season, from September until mid-October. During this time the air is heavy with a musky fragrance as the hops are dried on special floors before being packed tightly into huge sacks, known as pockets.

Between Branbridges, where the road from East Peckham to Beltring crosses the river, downstream to the village of Yalding makes a very pleasant walk (3 miles, $1^1/_2$ hours). Go through the works entrance immediately south of the bridge and make for the river, where the path heads along the right bank. It goes under a railway bridge and then through a shaded region of trees and shrubs. It is a peaceful, leisurely stretch of river. An oast-house is eventually to be seen ahead on the opposite bank, a few moments later a lock gate with a weir and a superb fifteenth-century bridge. As a distant frame a wall of hop gardens and orchards stands some way ahead, but between it and the river lies the village of Yalding.

Yalding is probably the best of all the villages of the Upper Medway Valley, and therefore one of the busiest in summer. It stands a short distance away from the Medway's main course with one of Kent's longest bridges leading over the Beult to link two halves of the village. The better half, with the church and its onion dome off-centre on its tower, has a curving, climbing wide street with typical Kentish weatherboarded houses and some impressive oasts a few yards from the pavement. The church has some lovely features with a cobbled path at the top of the steps while the churchyard itself is a quiet, tidy place. Through the village the road climbs steeply to give wide views. There are orchards at the top of the hill and to the left the valley curves in a long sweep.

Over the river and on its western slopes is **Nettlestead**, whose church has occupied its site for more than 500 years. The tower is older. The stained glass inside the church was damaged by a catastrophic hailstorm on 19 August 1763, when 10in diameter hailstones smashed the windows and wrought havoc in neighbouring villages. Next door to the church stands Nettlestead Place, probably as old as the church in its foundations, with a thirteenth-century undercroft and a weathered stone gatehouse. The house is private, but some of its magic and mystery may be hijacked from the pathway that leads from the church to the river; a pathway of moss and crumbling stone. It is a beautiful and peaceful corner.

East of the Medway there are lanes worth following. They wind between orchards and fields, with views overlooking the river and westward to a line of hills, dark with woods on their crown. But for a continuing involvement with the Medway it is best to leave the

Places to Visit
In and Around Tonbridge

Hadlow

4 miles north-east of Tonbridge
An attractive village with extra-
ordinary tower known as May's
Folly.

Nettlestead Church

$7^1/_2$ miles north-east of Tonbridge
A lovely, small country church in
an idyllic setting, caught
between a cricket pitch and the
Medway. The main building is
fifteenth century, but with an
older tower. Wonderful windows.

Tonbridge Castle

Remains of a large Norman
castle, set in the midst of
attractive public gardens
overlooking the Medway. A small
museum is included in the
gatehouse. A nature trail has
been laid out through the
grounds.

Tonbridge Sports Ground

Near to the castle, an ideal place
for families. A paddling pool and
play area for young children;
putting green, crazy golf, tennis,
bowls and swimming pool in the
nearby castle grounds.

Whitbread Hop Farm

Beltring, 6 miles east of Tonbridge. A picturesque collection
of oast-houses in which the
visitor can see the hop industry in
action. Fine assortment of old agricultural implements, museum,
craft centre. Fishing, nature trail
and at times, the Whitbread shire
horses may be seen.

Yalding

8 miles east of Tonbridge
A delightful village of medieval
bridges, fine church, rivers, locks
and a weir. Good fishing, boating,
in lovely countryside.

lanes and wander the footpaths that allow a more intimate acquaintance. Follow the towpath (2 miles, 1 hour) which is reached from
Nettlestead Church by way of the ancient gateway and the tracks
across the railway. Down by the river the path leads to a row of
mobile homes with gardens around them below Wateringbury, a
village that suffered grievously in the same hailstorm which
smashed the glass of Nettlestead Church. Beyond, the river curves in
a broad bow through watermeadows, and the path leads to a lock
and a weir down which the currents race beside a heavily overgrown
wall of what appears to have once been a vast mill on the far bank.
This is Teston Bridge Picnic Site, an attractive spot with a car park
and toilets.

Oasts near Yalding

✳   **Teston Bridge** is another of those magnificent medieval crossings of the Medway, with five fine arches. Above the right bank is
West Farleigh, and the traveller taking the high road from Yalding
will have come along the hilltop to reach it. Between West and East

Farleigh, the large grounds of Court Lodge and an old church can be seen above the Medway.

East Farleigh is a little straggling village high over the river where Donald Maxwell, one of Kent's keenest advocates whose books conjure up the atmosphere of the county's odd corners, now lies buried in the churchyard. To the same churchyard, in earlier times, came William Wilberforce, the scourge of the slave traders, for his son Robert was vicar here and Wilberforce senior spent his old age at the seventeenth-century vicarage. A memorial cross in the churchyard recalls forty-three hop pickers who died of cholera in the village in 1849.

Down a steep hill beside the church the road comes to another of the Medway's great bridges. It was at this one, with ribbed arches, that Cromwell's men, under Fairfax, crossed in 1648 before taking Maidstone in a battle that saw 300 Royalists dead and another 1,300 taken prisoner. The bridge, 100yd long and some 500 years old, is a national monument, deservedly so. It looks lovely from all angles.

A short distance up-river there is a remarkable old wooden bridge at **Barming**, and a stroll along the river bank (1 mile, $^1/_2$ hour)

Teston Bridge

to see it makes good use of spare time. Go down to the towpath below East Farleigh bridge and follow the river along its bank for about a mile upstream. This narrow, simple crossing is slung in the midst of some pleasant country, with hop gardens climbing the steep hills to the south. The bridge takes traffic, though not a lot of it, but in 1914 apparently a traction engine being driven from Marden to Aylesford was directed to cross the Medway here without regard to its considerable weight. Predictably it failed to make the crossing, for the traction engine (complete with four-man crew) broke through the timbers and landed in the river, much to the amusement of the locals.

From East Farleigh it is but a short step into the county town of **Maidstone**. When Richard Church wrote his classic evocation of Kent shortly after World War II, he was scathing in his remarks about Maidstone. He ranted against the thoughtless siting of the bus station, about garages and car parks and the lack of local government care. In recent years the town has been transformed. It still has a traffic problem, but what town in the south-east has not? It has a new shopping precinct, but the past has been restored and brought into focus. Down by the river a thoughtful scheme has resulted in the creation of a waterside haven of peace where, on a bright summer's day it is pleasant to stroll or to sit and watch the boats go drifting by.

It is here that old Maidstone is so easily recalled, for clustered above its east bank are several historic buildings, among the oldest that Maidstone has. One, the former **Archbishop's Palace**, seems to rise almost directly from the water. It is a splendid piece of architecture, set above the river. Originally a manor house for the Archbishops of Canterbury, it was built over in the fourteenth century and added to by successive archbishops. However, it passed out of the hands of the church in 1537 when Cranmer exchanged it with Henry VIII, for other properties. The wealthy Astley family, into whose care the palace passed, added the east frontage during the seventeenth century. Nowadays it is owned by the local council who purchased it in celebration of Queen Victoria's jubilee and some of the rooms are rented out for receptions and private functions. There are dungeons beneath the palace on the side of the river where John Ball was imprisoned for preaching social revolution. It was from here that Wat Tyler, the leader of the Peasants' Revolt, caused his release, though Ball was soon recaptured and hanged.

Nearby stands the ragstone church of All Saints, where 1,500 people can be seated in the nave and aisles. It was begun in 1395 under Archbishop Courtney who rebuilt it from a former parish church. Now considered to be the grandest Perpendicular style church in all Kent, it had originally been planned as something grander. All Saints, however, is but one of several notable buildings of time-battered grey stone that form an interesting group on this Medway shore. There is the Master's House of the College of Priests, also founded by Courtney and now housing the Kent Music School, and at the entrance to the palace precincts there is the gatehouse which is even older than Courtney's creations. It is a small rectangular building and it may have been a mill for the Len, one of the Medway's tributaries, flows past, or it may have been simply a small house with an upper hall. Today it houses Maidstone's information centre.

On the other side of Mill Street, opposite the gatehouse, is one of the town's finest old places, the Archbishop's Stables. It is an impressive building which gives an impression of the past and has become the home of a unique collection of old forms of transport and accessories, the Tyrwhitt-Drake Museum of Carriages.

There are other corners of interest to be found in the town and the surrounding countryside. There is the green splendour of Mote Park with its lake butting on to the town; in the surrounding countryside are villages of charm and character. There are a great many houses, castles and estates that belong to another age.

Among the outlying villages is **Loose**. It has streams that in the past powered thirteen mills. It has millponds, lovely houses, a valley with a gentle walk and steep hills rising above it. In its churchyard there is the grave of a man who was chaplain of St Helena during Napoleon's exile there, and an ancient yew that has stood on the hillside for something like 1,000 years.

Loose is a village on the outskirts of town; it holds jealously to its own identity. During the sixteenth century the wool trade prospered here, and as a result, mills grew along the stream which gave its name to the village. When the south lost its wool trade to the industrial north these mills were converted for paper making. The village continued to prosper.

On the southern edge of Maidstone the Loose Road (A229) breaks away from the A274 at a roundabout marked by The Wheatsheaf public house. This makes a good starting point for a circular walk (4¹/₂ miles, 2 hours). Head south a short distance along Sutton Road to the left of The Wheatsheaf, and take the first turning on the right along a narrow lane. A path then leads between a cemetery on the left and a school on the right. Continue straight ahead, eventually finding a tarmac track leading to the junction with the Boughton Monchelsea road. Turn right here, then first left to find the path which goes to the road, then downhill into Loose village. At The Chequers take the footpath beside the stream along the village, then into the valley beyond. After a while it reaches a narrow lane going to Tovil, but just before this village is entered another path goes off to the right, and by cutting across South Park, The Wheatsheaf is gained once more.

Halfway between Maidstone and Aylesford the Medway makes a sweeping bend, and on its west bank rises **Allington Castle** with its towers and battlements. It has stood here for 700 years, seeing the best and the worst; it has housed kings, given rest to cardinals and courtiers, heard the songs of poets and has seen the withdrawal of

The former Archbishop's Palace, Maidstone

care and come close to ruin.

Long before the castle rose in local stone the site was important, for here the Romans crossed and before them the Britons created a moated village. The Romans built a villa by the Medway's ford, and in 1282 work began on the present building, then a fortified manor house with Norman links. By the sixteenth century it was almost in ruins, but then Sir Henry Wyatt brought it back to life by making substantial alterations and adding a Tudor house with a gallery stretching across the inner courtyard. His son Thomas, the poet who first loved Anne Boleyn, was born here, as was his son (also Thomas) who lost his head in the Kentish rebellion against Queen Mary in 1554. After this the castle began a slow and lengthy decline so that by the time Lord Conway bought it in 1905 it was little more than a shell. But Conway's wealth and great love of beautiful things were precisely what the castle required, and eventually it was restored to the glory it had known under the Wyatts. In 1951 Allington Castle was sold to the Carmelite Friars as a retreat and Christian centre.

Carmelite Friars have long been associated with this corner of

Places to Visit
In and Around Maidstone

Allington Castle
1 mile north-west of Maidstone
Moated, fortified castle dating back
to 1282 with Henry VIII connections. Now in the hands of
Carmelite Friars.

Archbishop's Palace and
Dungeons
Mill Street, Maidstone
Fourteenth-century palace on the
banks of the Medway. The
dungeons adjoining the palace
held John Ball at the time of the
Peasants' Revolt.
Open by appointment only.

Aylesford
4 miles north-west of Maidstone
Charming village set on the banks
of the Medway, one of the most
picturesque clusters of buildings in
Kent when seen from across the
river.

Bluebell Hill Picnic Site
5 miles north of Maidstone, on
A229
13 acres of lofty downland with
enormous views over the Medway
Valley. Popular footpath walks.

Boughton Monchelsea Place
4 miles south-east of Maidstone,
off B2163
Manor house built in 1567 of local
ragstone, set in landscaped
gardens with fine views. Displays
of costumes and old vehicles.

The Friars
Aylesford
Carmelite priory, built in 1242. The
Carmelites returned in 1949 to
restore the cloistered buildings.

Kits Coty House
and Little Kits Coty
4 miles north-west of Maidstone,
on the downs above Aylesford
Two Neolithic burial sites. Kits
Coty House is the larger and more
impressive, set in a high meadow
far above the valley.

Leeds Castle
4 miles east of Maidstone on A20
One of the loveliest castles in
Europe, set on two islands in a
large lake. Saxon origin, but
reconstructed in stone in 1119.
The 400-acre grounds landscaped
by Capability Brown.

Kent, for downstream at nearby **Aylesford** they built a priory in
1242, in which met the first Chapter of the Order in Europe. The
Friars, as the priory is known, changed hands several times following the dissolution, and among its owners was one of the Wyatts
from Allington. Later in the seventeenth century, Sir John Banks a
friend of Pepys, lived there, and when the diarist made a brief visit
in 1669 he recorded a favourable impression: '...he keeps the

Loose
2 miles south of Maidstone off
A229
Delightful village with cottages
rising in terraces above streams
that run through the streets.

**Maidstone Museum and Art
Gallery**
Chillington Manor, St Faith's Street
Housed in an Elizabethan building
with Tudor long gallery, a number
of fine exhibits, including Anglo-
Saxon jewellery, archaeology,
early Kentish industries and
twelfth-century Lambeth Bible.

Mote Park
Maidstone
450 acres of parkland east of the
town centre, with fishing and
sailing in the lake.

Stoneacre (NT)
Otham, 3 miles south-east of
Maidstone
A small half-timbered manor
house, dating mainly from the late
fifteenth century.

Museum of Kent Rural Life
Cobtree Manor Park, Sandling,
2 miles north of Maidstone
The history of Kent's countryside
on a 27-acre site by the Medway.
Displays in an oast-house, and
outdoor exhibits including hoppers'
huts, hop garden, orchard, apiary
etc.

**Tyrwhitt-Drake Museum of
Carriages**
Archbishop's Stables, Mill Street,
Maidstone
A magnificent collection of horse-
drawn carriages, vehicles and
accessories, contained in a
fourteenth-century stable block
that is in itself worth studying.

The Wool House
Loose, 2 miles south of
Maidstone, off A229
Fifteenth-century timbered house
formerly used for washing newly-
sheared wool.
National Trust owned, but open
only by written application.

grounds about it, and the walls and the house, very handsome.'
Some of the panelling that Pepys would have admired was destroyed by fire in 1930, but much remains, and it is only fitting that
after 400 years of exile from their first home, the friars returned to
Aylesford in 1949 to bring their original purpose to the historic
building, 'mighty finely placed by the river.'

Aylesford though, has other sites of interest. On the downs above

Aylesford almshouses

π the village is Kits Coty House, an awesome Neolithic tomb, 4,000 years old, on a belvedere overlooking the Medway Valley. Here came the Romans, and later the Danish invaders, Hengist and Horsa who, in AD455, 'fought against Wyrtgeorm the King at a place which is called Aegelsthrep, and his brother Horsa was slain, and Hengist after this obtained the Kingdom.' In 893 Alfred defeated the Danes here and drove them north.

The panorama of Aylesford's graceful medieval bridge spanning the river in five arches is one of the classic views of Kent. It has drawn the photographer and the artist so often that it has become hackneyed; yet no amount of photographs or paintings can detract from the perfection of such a scene.

But it is not only the fourteenth-century bridge, the crowded High Street, church and priory that draw one's admiration in Aylesford, for away from the river there stands a row of comfortable-looking almshouses overlooking a greensward. These almshouses, with their mullioned windows and little brook below, are almost Dickensian. They make a pleasing group beside the road which leads

Rochester High Street

to the downs, and Kits Coty House. Half a mile along this road, at the junction with another that heads to the right, a footpath (2 miles, 1 hour) cuts off diagonally to the right through orchards and fields to reach a lane. Go left along the lane for half a mile until it makes a zigzag turn. At the final sharp turn a track leads directly ahead. Along this can be seen the Countless Stones, or Little Kits Coty, a scattering of stone remains of a prehistoric long barrow. The track bears left to come to the road again at a junction. Cross this and take the path (North Downs Way) which heads steeply uphill until on the left are seen the Neolithic upright stones known as Kits Coty House.

North of Aylesford the Medway pushes itself through the broad gap in the North Downs, twisting and writhing in a series of ox-bows, but after all the miles of hop gardens, orchards and meadows it is now dominated by one industrial complex after another. The first of these are the papermills at New Hythe and Snodland (as Dickensian a name, surely, as any in Kent), on an ancient Medway crossing point on the Pilgrims' Way. It is then the cement factories at Halling and Cuxton that coat the air with dust and blot the sun, before you arrive at the graceful modern bridge that takes the M2 (and the North Downs Way) across the river with almost a bird's-eye view of Rochester.

At first glance **Rochester** is a dreary place of traffic and endless terraces, a point on a bend in the river immediately before it broadens into its estuary. That dreariness belies the power of its past, ignores the glories of its castle, its cathedral and its many corners of interest.

Even before the Romans came, Belgic tribes were here. However, Watling Street crosses the Medway here, and the Romans fortified their camp with a wall that encased a city of $23^1/_2$ acres. It must have been an impressive place then, with hills and woodlands to the west and the south-east, marshes to north and east and lookouts keeping watch on the estuary. Saxons succeeded the Romans, and they had to defend their hill against Viking raiders. They slung a wooden bridge across the river in place of the Roman one of timber and stone, and added their own work to the fortifications. Their stones are still here.

Rochester's first church was laid out in AD604, but the Vikings came and left it in ruins; King Alfred fought back, built a fleet of ships here and formed England's first navy. The Norman Bishop Gun-

Places to Visit In and Around Rochester

Charles Dickens Centre
Eastgate House, High Street, Rochester
Dickensian characters in wax, set in tableaux. An award winning exhibition in an elegant Elizabethan red-brick house built in 1590.

Chatham Dockyard
Dock Road, Chatham
A vast collection of historic buildings on an 80-acre site which served the Royal Navy for 400 years, and where *HMS Victory*, among others, was built. Craft museum, working ropery, sailmaking, covered slipways and much more.

Fort Amhurst
Dock Road, Chatham
An impressive Georgian fortress built in 1756 as part of the Royal Navy Dockyard's defensive system. Tunnels and lower batteries open to the public.

Guildhall Museum
High Street, Rochester
Local history exhibits from the Stone Age onward; arms and armour, Victorian dolls and toys.

Medway Heritage Centre
Dock Road, Chatham
Formerly St Mary's Church, the centre houses an exhibition giving the story of the Medway's history.

Northward Hill Bird Reserve
High Halstow, 5 miles north-east of Rochester
An RSPB reserve noted as the largest heronry in Britain. Nature trail from High Halstow.

Rochester Castle (EH)
Occupying a fine site above the river, the castle is one of England's greatest examples of a Norman fortress. Outer walls built in 1087, the keep dates from 1127.

Rochester Cathedral
First consecrated in AD604 the cathedral is second in age only to Canterbury. The present building contains work begun by Gundulph in 1080, but with additions from the twelfth and fourteenth centuries.

Royal Engineers Museum
Brompton Barracks, Gillingham
Contains the story of the regiment, whose proudest 'son' was General Gordon.

Temple Manor
Knight Road, Strood
Thirteenth-century Knights Templar hall house, with some seventeenth-century extensions.

Upnor Castle
2 miles north of Rochester on the left bank of the Medway
Built in 1559 to defend the ships of Chatham.

Watts Charity Almshouses
High Street, Rochester
An Elizabethan house, founded as a charity by Richard Watts 'for six poor travellers to stay one night', it features in Dickens's tale *The Seven Poor Travellers*.

Rochester Castle

dulph, William the Conqueror's great architect, built the cathedral and the castle side by side: one to defend the faith, the other to defend the city.

In the reign of Henry I, a massive keep was raised. This keep stands today as a symbol of the town; a defensive tower 120ft high, with walls 12ft thick, four floors, a unique well shaft and numerous openings. It stands at the top of a grassy mound within the old city walls, a magnificent sight with a panoramic view from its tower. Here, in 1215, rebel barons were besieged by King John for 7 weeks. Stones were hurled against the walls from huge machines in one of the greatest sieges of that time, but to no avail. A tunnel, however, was then burrowed beneath the tower and the pit props used to hold its ceiling were burned with the aid of fat from forty pigs. Only then did the tower surrender.

From the castle walls the cathedral is seen. Here Ethelbert the Saxon king, more than 1,300 years ago, established a base for Christianity, having relinquished Canterbury to St Augustine. The present cathedral was begun by Gundulph 400 years after Ethelbert, but much of his work has been hidden by later adaptations and additions.

Perhaps Rochester Cathedral would be more appreciated if it did not suffer from constant comparison with Canterbury. Each has its own individual beauty; they share a common purpose. Rochester's cathedral church is a place of great beauty. In the crypt, cool arches hold the secrets of centuries; the work of Norman masons remain unchallenged. These same Norman masons created a nave of magnificent proportions; 75ft wide and 100yd long where arch upon arch leads up to an oak roof.

The west door has a lovely archway with pillars and carved birds and animals. From it, the sloping moat of the castle can be seen, where Dickens wished to be buried. The graveyard there was closed to further burials and at Queen Victoria's request he was placed in Westminster Abbey; yet if the ghost of this best-loved of all Victorian novelists is to be found anywhere, it must surely be in the streets of Rochester.

To Dickens, Rochester was Dullborough and Cloisterham. In its streets today there are scenes described in *Great Expectations, Edwin Drood, The Uncommercial Traveller* and *Pickwick Papers*. In the High Street near Rochester Bridge the Royal Victoria and Bull Hotel is where the Pickwick Club assembled. To Pickwick it was The Bull Hotel, but in *Great Expectations* it appears as The Blue Boar. There is the Watts Charity, scene of the story *The Seven Poor Travellers* and nearby, also in the High Street, is the house in which Mr Jasper lived in *Edwin Drood*. Rochester came alive in Dicken's novels, and in Rochester today Dickens comes alive. A visit to the castle, for example, is to see immediately what Jingle meant when he said: 'Ah! fine place — glorious pile — frowning walls — tottering arches — dark nooks — crumbling staircases — old Cathedral too.'

The city makes the most of Dickens. There is a Charles Dickens Trail, and every year there is a Dickens Festival, a congregation of Dickensian characters converge on the town dressed in Victorian costume. There are torchlight processions, garden parties and street entertainments. At Eastgate House, which makes several appearances in his novels, there is now a Dickens Centre, one of Rochester's major tourist attractions. In its ground there stands the Swiss chalet from Gads Hill in which he worked during his last years. He had been writing there the day before he died, in June 1870.

Rochester runs into Chatham, and Chatham into Gillingham without any obvious boundary between them, but while Rochester has a light heart with a traffic-free High Street where musicians play and tourists drift from wine bar to delicatessen, and from one Dickensian scene to the next, **Chatham** is a working town of working people, although since the dockyard was abandoned by the Royal Navy in 1984 there has been a shift in its direction of labour.

Dickens' first taste of Kent was in Chatham, for as a child he was brought here to live at what is now 11 Ordnance Terrace when his father took work as a dockyard clerk. For 400 years the river was Chatham's focus, the dockyard being founded in 1547 as a repair yard for the navy but soon developing as a shipbuilding centre in its own right. Elizabeth I came here, as did Drake, Pepys, Nelson and Evelyn. The first ship to be built in Chatham was the *Sunne* in 1586, its best-known being *HMS Victory* in 1759. Chatham's shipwrights 150 years later, began to build submarines, and the last to be launched from here was the *Okanagan*, built for the Royal Canadian Navy in 1966.

Since its closure the former Royal Navy dockyard has been transformed into a dockyard museum, with rope making in the ropery, and sailmaker and rigger at work in the same loft where Nelson's flags were made; a collection of naval guns on display, the great covered slipways and the largest concentration of historic buildings to be found anywhere in Britain — all within a site of almost 80 acres.

Above the town, on a hill overlooking the docks, **Fort Amhurst** is a most unusual Georgian fortress with a vast labyrinth of tunnels, messrooms, powder magazines and storerooms, hewn from the chalk by French prisoners of war. On an upper floor the living conditions experienced by Wellington's soldiers have been recreated in a barrack room. On the ground floor a museum has been established, and during the summer re-enactments of scenes from the fort's history are played out for the benefit of visitors.

Beyond Rochester, the Medway flows past the remains of **Upnor Castle**, built in 1559 in order to protect Chatham Dockyard from attack. When attack came, the castle had been so neglected that it failed as a deterrent and the Dutch sailed up the river under Admiral de Ruyter on 10 June 1667, and destroyed or captured the ships of the Royal Navy at anchor there. The surprising village of **Upnor** itself, tiny though it is, is worth a visit. Reached by a side road breaking away from the A228 to the north-east of Strood, it is reminiscent at first glance of a Devonshire fishing village, although it was built primarily to service the ragstone and brick castle that is now in the care of English Heritage. Leaving your vehicle in a tree-shrouded car park on the edge of the village (there is no room to park in its three streets) a few paces will bring you to the High Street; a short sloping street lined by pleasant weatherboarded cottages and two pubs, it falls away to the shoreline of the Medway. Near the bottom of the street you enter the grounds of Upnor Castle. If you go a few paces beyond, you'll find yourself in the water which is a colourful stretch of river with a small marina on the last bend before the Medway's estuary opens out to the sea, but in the past it was full of pensioned-

*Upnor
Castle*

Upnor High Street

off ships holding miserable cargoes of prisoners.

Beyond Upnor the Medway flows into oozing marshes, tidal creeks with little islands, and its estuary, notable for its bird life. Waders and gulls are particularly in evidence. The journey from the hills of Sussex is complete; its mission, to drain the hills and meadows, the orchards and hop gardens of the garden of England is accomplished.

4
COASTAL KENT

Kent's coastline is ever-changing. Pounded by the restless waves, cliffs slowly crumble into the sea. There are also one-time islands whose tidal boundaries have been driven back to extend the frontiers of the mainland, and marshes that have been drained to put sheep where once were fish. It is a slow but insistent transformation.

Much of this coastline has been developed for tourism. Some has been given over to shipping while parts have become littered with caravan sites. There are still, however, stretches of magnificent solitude.

To the north, the Hoo Peninsula pokes out like a stubby thumb between the estuaries of the Thames and the Medway; marshlands overlooking the Thames, oil refineries and power stations bordering the Medway, and between the two an outpost of caravan and sail down at Allhallows-on-Sea overlooking Southend across the water. The 'on-Sea' part of Allhallows is a mile from the village, at the end of a no-through-road where the sun shines and the wind blows and a sea wall entices you to seek out the solitude of marshes away from caravan city. A strange place is Allhallows, having no equal anywhere else in Kent — not in Sheppey, nor Thanet, nor even on Romney Marsh.

Sheppey lies to the south, separated from Hoo by the Medway's estuary, an island cut from the mainland by the Swale, not a river but a tidal watercourse adorned with yachts and a crowded birdlife. The island itself is mostly flat and drab and without much to commend it. Yet thousands holiday there annually and find contentment on its beaches at Minster and Leysdown. At its farthest point **Sheerness** is growing as a commercial port with ferries bringing numerous visitors from the Netherlands and daily cargoes from the Continent and beyond. In years gone by there was a naval dockyard here, and it was to Sheerness that *HMS Victory* brought Nelson's body following his death at Trafalgar. In earlier times it was overrun by Vikings who based themselves on the island while they plundered mainland Kent. It was pillaged by the French and invaded by the Dutch, and smugglers dragged their illicit booty ashore where yachtsmen now gather for sport at weekends.

On the highest part of Sheppey stands **Minster**, once several miles from the sea, but now on the coast. On the highest point of the highest hill, is the finest building for many a mile; an ancient piece of England that overlooks a doleful collection of bungalows and shops and an expansive view of lowland Sheppey with its various watercourses. This is Minster's abbey church which occupies the hilltop with a simple gatehouse that dates back to the fifteenth century; yet when that was built, parts of the original abbey building were already 800 years old.

Minster Abbey, the church of St Mary and St Sexburga, is really two churches in one, joined by an archway cut in the south wall of the early Nun's Chapel. The nunnery was first established in AD670 by the widow of Ercombert, the Saxon king of Kent, but Sexburga's church was sacked by the Danes and it was not until the twelfth century that it was refounded as a priory of Benedictine nuns. After the dissolution in 1536 much of the abbey was destroyed, leaving the parish church to dominate. Now it is a place of pilgrimage. Inside an effigy of Robert de Shurland is accompanied by the head of his horse appearing from the waves to symbolise the story of his being saved by his mount from drowning. Another tomb, in the Nun's Chapel, has a figure thought possibly to be the Duke of Clarence who, under sentence of death for high treason, chose as his form of execution drowning in a butt of malmsey wine.

Minster Gatehouse Museum is concerned with Sheppey's history, and in it are photographs, fossils and exhibitions relating to the island's chequered past. Elsewhere there is a reminder of the isle's aviation history, for in the early years of the century many of the great names of flying, Moore-Brabazon, Sopwith, the Short brothers and Charles Rolls among them, operated from Eastchurch aerodrome,

Places of Interest On Sheppey

Church of St Thomas the Apostle
On the Isle of Harty, south-east corner of Sheppey
One of the most remote churches in Britain, it contains several magnificent items, including fourteenth-century carved chest and miniature organ.

Elmley Marshes
West of the Isle of Harty
RSPB reserve accessible only by footpath from Kings Hill Farm, and open only Wednesday, Saturday and Sunday.

Minster Abbey
Sheppey. A saxon church and a thirteenth-century church joined together to form the finest building on the island. It contains many interesting monuments and brasses. Minster Gatehouse Museum nearby.

Shell Ness National Nature Reserve. Isle of Harty
Popular among birdwatchers, this eastern-most corner of the island is only accessible by footpath, either from Harty Church or south from Leysdown on Sea.

whose buildings are now used as a prison, and on an attractive memorial wall opposite All Saints Church are carved replicas of early flying machines, biplanes and triplanes, and the names of the pioneers who flew them. Nothing else in this small, dreary place could possibly attract the visitor.

The **Isle of Harty** occupies the south-eastern corner of Sheppey and is reached by just one narrow road, off the B2231. It has two or three farms, a handful of houses, an inn and a church. It is a forgotten patch of country, a no man's land of marsh and meadow and fields of cabbages; of streams and ditches, mudflats and watermeadows. Signs lead to the Ferry Inn, now lonely without its ferry, perched on a grassy lip above the Swale, and looking across the water to Faversham with which it was once linked. Now to reach Faversham involves nearly 30 miles of driving; by ferry-boat it was little more than a mile. Down by the water there is a wonderful air of isolation.

Half a mile from the Ferry Inn, across the meadows by footpath, is Sheppey's second delightful building. The Church of St Thomas the Apostle is one of the most remote in Britain; it stands in a churchyard with a slightly sunken trail as a path to its door, with the water a short distance away at the rear, and a vista of Harty's levels sweeping northwards at the front. A farm track allows vehicular access. To one side there is a farm with a strange moat, to the other a small house. There are no distractions here, beyond those demanded by the seabirds. The church has no electricity, but it is lit by oil lamps or by the natural watery light that floods through the windows by day. It contains surprising treasures, like the tiny hand-powered organ, a table with five magnificently carved faces, a lovely rood screen and a delicate old chest, 600 years old and carved with a pair of jousting knights, thought to be German in origin. In the south wall, backlit by the sun, a window depicts a harvest scene to one side, sheep on the other and a pair of little harvest mice above.

Along this southern edge of Sheppey the marshes are known to birdwatching enthusiasts. At Elmley, west of Harty, there is a reserve managed by the RSPB, reached only by footpath from Kings Hill Farm; a little to the north-east of Harty's church lies Shell Ness National Nature Reserve controlled by the Nature Conservancy Council and accessible by path either from Leysdown or from the Church of St Thomas the Apostle. From here Shell Ness is only about 2 miles ($^3/_4$ hour) away and to reach it involves following the track which cuts off from the narrow lane 200yd north of the church, then bears left along the edge of the marshes. On the sea wall the walk may be extended northwards to reach Leysdown on Sea, but for bird-watching this is an unnecessary extension.

Between Elmley Island to the west and Shell Ness to the east there are stretches of reclaimed marsh and rough grasslands leading to the muddy foreshore of the Swale. Along here, an immense concentration of wildfowl can be seen, particularly in winter when approximately 20,000 waders may be found. There are dunlin, curlews, knot, oystercatchers, bar-tailed godwits and plovers in great crowds. There are Brent geese wintering too, and among those that breed here are redshank, gadwell and pochard. Mallard are here in abundance of course, as well as teal and wigeon, and when the tide rises and interferes with this feeding, they rise in huge flocks to fly across the water or to the marshes inland.

Across the Swale on mainland Kent are similar stretches of marshland which complement Sheppey's wonderful wildfowl habitats. Designated a Site of Special Scientific Interest, much of south

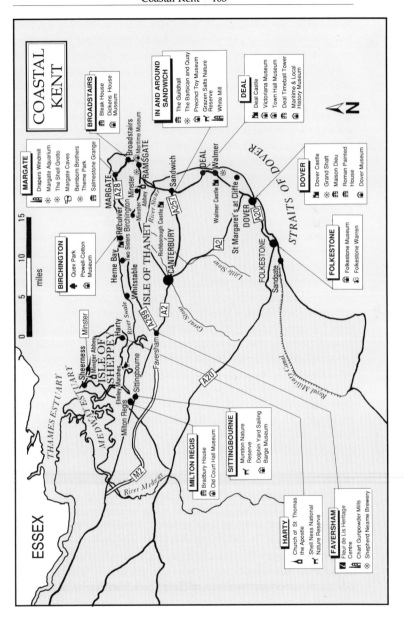

COASTAL KENT

MARGATE
- Drapers Windmill
- Margate Aquarium
- The Shell Grotto
- Margate Caves
- Bembom Brothers Theme Park
- Salmestone Grange

BROADSTAIRS
- Bleak House
- Dickens House Museum

BIRCHINGTON
- Quex Park
- Powell-Cotton Museum

IN AND AROUND SANDWICH
- The Guildhall
- The Barbican and Quay
- Precinct Toy Museum
- Grazen Salts Nature Reserve
- White Mill

DEAL
- Deal Castle
- Victoriana Museum
- Town Hall Museum
- Deal Timeball Tower
- Maritime & Local History Museum

DOVER
- Dover Castle
- Grand Shaft
- Maison Dieu
- Roman Painted House
- Dover Museum

FOLKESTONE
- Folkestone Museum
- Folkestone Warren

HARTY
- Church of St Thomas the Apostle
- Shell Ness National Nature Reserve

FAVERSHAM
- Fleur de Lis Heritage Centre
- Chart Gunpowder Mills
- Shepherd Neame Brewery

MILTON REGIS
- Bradbury House
- Old Court Hall Museum

SITTINGBOURNE
- Murston Nature Reserve
- Dolphin Yard Sailing Barge Museum

ESSEX

THAMES ESTUARY

MEDWAY ESTUARY

ISLE OF SHEPPEY

Sheerness

Minster Abbey

Minster

Harty

Elmley Marshes

Milton Regis

Sittingbourne

River Swale

Faversham

River Medway

M2

A299

A2

A20

Whitstable

Herne Bay

Reculver

Two Sisters

Birchington

MARGATE

Minster

Abbey

Richborough Castle

River Stour

CANTERBURY

Great Stour

Little Stour

Broadstairs

Maritime Museum

RAMSGATE

Sandwich

A257

DEAL

Walmer

Walmer Castle

St Margaret's at Cliffe

DOVER

A20

FOLKESTONE

Sandgate

Royal Military Canal

STRAITS OF DOVER

N

miles
0 5 10 15

Swale gives the ornithologist constant pleasure. There is a nature reserve outside Murston on Milton Creek, but farther to the east a much larger reserve, on the Nagden and Cleve Marshes, is a fine area for observing vast populations of breeding and migrant birds. The Saxon Shore Way goes along the sea wall and gives access to the area. Join the path at Nagden, $1^1/_2$ miles downstream from Faversham and reached by narrow road from Graveney. The path (5 miles, 2 hours) follows the creek wall as it curls out and around the Nagden Marshes to the edge of the Swale, with views across the water to Harty's church, then continues along the sea wall until it reaches the Graveney road. A full circuit may be made by following down the road for half a mile before joining another path on the right that cuts across to orchards on its return to the cottages at Nagden once more.

Sheppey is left by way of the practical but unlovely Kingsferry Bridge, and travelling inland a country of mixed industry, orchards and urban sprawl is found. The A2, formerly Watling Street and one of the most important Roman roads, misses the best of the old royal manor of **Milton Regis** on the outskirts of Sittingbourne. There is the renovated Elizabethan Bradbury House and Old Court Hall, now a museum, but perhaps the handsome fourteenth-century church with its massive tower is the best thing in this town. Between the church and Milton Creek runs the line of the Sittingbourne and Kemsley Light Railway, hauled by steam locomotives.

Sittingbourne was once an important staging post on the London to Dover road, but it has had much of its identity smothered by industry so that the modern traveller, fighting heavy traffic on the way through, takes with him an unfavourable impression. Apart from a few architectural curiosities, its twin attractions are the narrow gauge railway which runs on 2 miles of track between Mill Way and Kemsley Down, and a museum devoted to the sailing barge.

When Sittingbourne's industry developed during the latter half of the nineteenth century, hundreds of sailing barges were used as transport. Now a memory and a few well-preserved relics of what must surely have been one of the most peaceful of all forms of industrial transport are all that remain. Dolphin Yard Sailing Barge Museum is located along a rough track off Crown Quay Lane, set beside an extremely narrow stretch of Milton Creek. Here, barges lie at anchor, their sails furled, puffs of smoke coming from their chimneys, their black-tarred hulks decorated with colourful scrolls around the name plates. Beside the barges, the original boathouse contains photographs and memorabilia dealing with the history of these craft; it is still in use for barge maintenance. Dolphin Yard is the only survivor of eleven such yards that were used to build Thames sailing barges, and is a fascinating corner that attracts a growing number of visitors each summer.

Between the downs and the coast are orchards of cherries, their blossom enriching the whole area in spring. Between Sittingbourne and Faversham the flat country is broken here and there by small hills, and there are hop gardens mingled among the orchards. To the north the marshes are always evident, while to the south the neat fields and rows of fruit trees rise steadily towards the North Downs, with spruce villages linked by a tracery of narrow lanes and footpaths. **Rodmersham** is little more than a few Georgian farmhouses and a flint church; **Lynsted** is a bigger village that boasts a fine heart, while **Tonge** has a church and practically nothing else but a watermill, and **Teynham** with its orchards of fruit was once considered 'the most dainty piece of all our Shyre'.

On the edge of Faversham, **Ospringe** straddles the A2. There was a Roman settlement here centuries ago. Numerous coins and much pottery from that period have been discovered here, and on Judd's Hill there is an earthwork. In the main street, on the corner of Water Lane near the Faversham turn-off, there stands a lovely old building, all ancient beams and mellow walls; the Pilgrim's hostel known as Maison Dieu. It dates from the thirteenth century in part; its beamed ceilings are of the sixteenth century. It now contains a three-phase museum. One part deals with Roman objects, another with the house itself, and a third concerns itself with Faversham's past.

Turning down into **Faversham** is a revelation. Here is a town with many fine buildings; a town with pride in itself, a cared-for place that is a pleasure to visit. Its history is on display everywhere, but of course it also has modern shops and industries. Once it was an important and flourishing port, and gained the status of a 'limb' of the Cinque Port of Dover. It had a ship building industry on the creek leading to the Swale where fighting ships were made. It had a mill where gunpowder was made, and it had a lively trade in oysters. The

Stonebridge Pond, Faversham

❋ creek is still a busy part of Faversham, and nearby is Shepherd Neame Brewery.

On entering Faversham the visitor is advised first to go to the Fleur de Lis Heritage Centre in Preston Street where all the information that one might need to make the most out of a visit is on display. In a fifteenth-century former inn, the Heritage Centre has museum displays on three floors, as well as information leaflets and an excellent Kentish bookshop. Armed with leaflets and advice, the town may be explored at leisure. A marvellous collection of buildings line the streets, many of which are restricted to traffic, and there are as many as 400 fine buildings on a preservation list, maintained carefully and blending thoughtfully into modern society so that they are not simply quaint museum pieces, preserved and unfunctional.

With so many fine places it is difficult to pick out the highlights. Certainly the centre of town has a particular grace and charm. At the junction of three streets is the old covered Market Place, built originally in 1574; its pillars and arches support the rebuilt Guildhall, and standing behind it is a large Victorian pump painted a lurid red.

A Victorian pump near the old Market Place, Faversham

Nearby stands a fine Tudor house, and running away from this is Court Street which contains a number of good houses as well as the offices of the local brewer patterned with hops in the plaster. West Street also leads from the Market Place and has many lovely timbered buildings; it leads down to Stonebridge Pond which is crowded with ducks and geese and bullrushes. Standing on the hill behind it, and seen over a row of weather-boarded houses, is the delicate blend of Davington Priory and the Norman church of St Mary Magdalen; a scene quite exquisite in a town of exquisite scenes. A short walk from here are the oldest gunpowder mills in the world in which powder was manufactured for some of the greatest battles in English history. Partly restored by the Faversham Society, Chart Gunpowder Mills form an interesting item of industrial architecture and make a popular outing for the visitor.

Faversham is surrounded by gentle hills, with orchards and hop gardens down to the marshes bordering the eastern limits of the Swale. **Oare**, on one of the branches of Faversham Creek, has its yachts and a nature reserve. **Graveney**, on the edge of the marsh, boasts a fine church in which one of the masons of Canterbury Cathedral once practised his art. The horizon is bounded by the sea; caravans and simple chalets crowd the edges of the marsh, huddling below the protection of the sea wall which forms an obvious boundary along the front to Seasalter. Here, in 1971, a remarkably well-preserved Viking ship was discovered in the mud behind the sea wall. It is now in the Greenwich Maritime Museum.

Seasalter runs without a break into Whitstable, but still manages to retain a separate identity. Its beach is a mixture of sand, shingle and shells, while in the streams of the marshes there is good fishing for eel, roach or perch. Although the industry from which the town took its name dates back to prehistoric times, modern Seasalter has little of antiquity to give it appeal. **Whitstable**, however, wears age in some of its streets, and in spite of an intrusive industry in the heart of town around the harbour, it expresses a character that is busy without being boisterous, unpretentious yet still caters for the tastes of seaport enthusiasts. There is plenty of sailing here, with a yachting week drawing competitors from far and wide; as well as water skiing and sail-boarding and all the traditional activities associated with a coastal resort.

Places to Visit In and Around Sittingbourne and Faversham

Chart Gunpowder Mills
Westbrook Walk, Faversham
The oldest gunpowder mills in the world built in the eighteenth-century, but maintained by local Faversham Society.

Dolphin Yard Sailing Barge Museum
Crown Quay Lane, Sittingbourne
In a working boathouse beside Milton Creek various exhibits dealing with the history of Thames sailing barges are on display. The forge, sail loft and carpenters shop can be seen, and on the creek several operational barges are berthed.

Fleur de Lis Heritage Centre
13 Preston Street, Faversham
Information centre and displays of local history housed in former fifteenth-century inn.

Maison Dieu (EH)
Ospringe, Faversham, on A2 junction with Water Lane
Old pilgrims' hostel also used by royalty, now used as a museum with three displays; Roman, the Maison Dieu itself, and local Faversham history.

Murston Nature Reserve
2 miles north of Sittingbourne
Old flooded brickearth pits beside Milton Creek forming wetland habitat for a variety of birds. Approached along footpath from Murston (Saxon Shore Way).

Nagden Marshes
North-east of Faversham
Part of South Swale Nature Reserve, where countless wildfowl and sea birds may be observed. Accessible by Saxon Shore Way public footpath from Nagden.

Old Court Hall Museum
Milton Regis, 1 mile west of Sittingbourne
A museum of miscellaneous exhibits housed in renovated fifteenth-century buildings. Displays of finds made by the local archaeological society.

Shepherd Neame Brewery
17 Court Street, Faversham
Tours by appointment, with beer tasting, of this old Kentish family brewery.

Sittingbourne and Kemsley Light Railway
Milton Road, off B2005
A narrow gauge steam-hauled railway which runs for 2 miles as far as Kemsley Down. Originally built to convey paper between mills, it is now operated as a tourist attraction.

East of the harbour is a broad beach of rocks and shingle known as The Street. For a mile or so it stretches out to sea, and at high tide when it lies exposed the tidal pools display a rich and fascinating assortment of marine creatures. For centuries Whitstable was noted for its oyster beds, although it was only one of a number of Kentish towns producing this particular food — others included Faversham and Milton Regis — yet in recent years the industry fell into decline through over-fishing. Now the Whitstable oyster is making a come-back and an annual oyster festival is held in the town as an attempt to publicise the fact.

The world's first passenger railway line once ran between Whitstable and Canterbury. It opened on 3 May 1830, hauled by a steam locomotive named *Invicta*, and ran the $6^1/_4$ mile journey in 40 minutes. The line, alas, is no more, but *Invicta* remains as a museum piece and Whitstable has reason to remember with gratitude the entrepreneurs responsible for opening the town to a wider public. Two years after the railway began, the harbour was completed and in 1837 the first steamboat to travel from England to Australia sailed from it.

It is near the harbour that the best of Whitstable is to be found. To one side is its industrial face, on the other is tradition; the tradition of black tarred oyster sheds and fishermen's cottages, weather-boarded and tightly packed against the beach, separated by narrow alleyways. The streets nearby hold a flavour of the past with quaint shops and old inns. It is the 'Blackstable' of Somerset Maugham's *Of Human Bondage*; Maugham lived with his uncle at The Rectory for some time after his parents died, and the town features largely in this autobiographical novel.

Whitstable spreads itself along the coast eastwards to include **Tankerton** and **Swalecliffe**. The first has grassy slopes bordering the promenade, the second is a very old village protected by a projection at Long Rock that forms the eastern limits of Whitstable's bay. Beyond this, the full cluster of **Herne Bay** marks the first of north Kent's resorts. It is a town that grew out of a Victorian development; it has a typical Victorian seaside appearance adapted over the years to accommodate more modern tastes. In truth, its heyday is long gone and Herne Bay is becoming increasingly taken over by retired couples. But for those who desire a traditional seaside holiday it has numerous guest houses and hotels, a safe beach, all the traditional entertainments, and a stone clock tower on the promenade, erected in the year of Queen Victoria's coronation. It had another claim to fame in its pier, almost a mile in length, but this was virtually demolished in 1979. Rising from the waves like a man-made island, however, stands the seaward end of it, around which the pleasure boats make their tours.

Inland from the resort of Herne Bay, and separated from its growth by the A299, is the original village of **Herne**, a place that clings desparately to its own identity. Surrounded by agricultural land and woodlands not far off, the village is growing with modern estates, but at its heart there are some lovely old houses and a fourteenth-century flint-towered church in which the martyred Nicholas Ridley was once minister. It gazes down the High Street and across to the restored smock windmill rising among streets of new houses, with footpaths plunging out across meadows and off to the woods beyond.

On 20 acres of that woodland, midway between Herne Bay and Canterbury, the **Wealden Forest Park** contains one of the largest animal sanctuaries in southern England. Brambles English Wildlife is set in a typical English woodland where a nature trail leads visitors· to close-up views of fallow and sitka deer, owls and foxes. Farm animals are here for children to feed; there is an enclosed toad garden, a collection of Scottish wild cats and an adventure playground, making the park a popular venue for family outings.

Along the coast, the Saxon Shore Way has remained true to its line from Faversham to Herne Bay. It takes the promenade here through the crowds of holidaymakers, going eastwards to Beltringe cliffs with the towers of Reculver seen ahead. It is at **Reculver** that the Way deserts the modern coast, for in Saxon times the country beyond was separated from mainland Kent by the tides of the Wantsum Channel. The Shore Way retraces the steps of history, but it is certainly worth following the coastal path ($3^1/_2$ miles, $1^1/_2$ hours) as an outing in its own right from Herne Bay as far as Reculver's towers, up and over the cliffs with their wide panoramic views. There is a contrast between scenes ancient and modern, between Norman architecture and the regulated pattern of caravan parks, between the vast pitch of the sea and the variegated spread of a chequered land.

Reculver's towers

Rearing abruptly from the very edge of the encroaching sea, the pair of massive towers known as the Two Sisters are all that remain of an extraordinary church originally built 1,200 years ago on a site that has known the mark of Iron Age man, Roman, Saxon and Norman. The two towers were saved from destruction in 1809 by Trinity House in order to serve as an important landmark to shipping. On this site Iron Age man had a settlement. The Romans then came and recognising the strategic importance of the cliff top, built a fort to protect the mouth of the Wantsum Channel to the east. It guarded the town of *Regulvium*, their name for Reculver, which then stood $1\frac{1}{2}$ miles from the sea, but the sea has steadily eroded the cliffs and most of the fort has now crumbled beneath the waves. After the Romans left, King Egbert of Kent founded a church here in AD669, built within the walls of the fort and using materials that the Romans used. It survived the twin adversaries of a threatening sea and Danish raids, and in the twelfth century the Normans enlarged this Saxon place of worship, and dedicated their church to St Mary.

It would still be here today were it not for the obsessions of the mother of the last vicar, a Mr Nailor. Apparently she was convinced that the church was being used for puppet shows, and in her anger she persuaded her son to take it down. This act of vandalism in the early years of the last century was carried out, and only the great western towers and assorted fragments of walls remain of one of Kent's greatest and oldest churches.

East of Reculver is a flat land of low meadows and little streams, the silted bed of the **Wantsum Channel** that made Thanet an island. In Roman times the channel was more than a mile wide, an important stretch of waterway that for centuries gave shipping a short cut between the Thames and the Continent. Matching their fort at Reculver, the Romans protected the southern entrance to the channel with their fort and supply depot at Richborough, near Sandwich, where it entered the sea, but some time around the eighth century it began to silt up. It was a slow process, for throughout the Middle Ages shipping continued to use it, but by the end of Henry VIII's reign severe storms had rendered the channel unnavigable, and it was gradually reduced to its present size. Now as the traveller motors along the A299 there is little evidence to show that this was once an important shipping route.

There is something about **Thanet** which makes it different from other parts of the county. There is a feeling of change, and an island atmosphere in the landscapes and in some of the little villages. At **Sarre**, for example, several miles inland, many of the buildings seem to be facing a sea front. That sea is far off, of course, but when the Wantsum Channel lapped here Sarre had a ferry. Today Chislet Marshes, against which the village is set, fill the area once covered by the Wantsum — a region of dykes marking the lowland into a series of lozenges.

Linked with Sarre by footpath is the larger **St Nicholas at Wade** near a junction of roads. Larger than Sarre though it may be, it is still a small village whose name indicates that it originally stood beside a ford across the Wantsum when the channel had been reduced to a creek. It has some attractive features, not least of which are the Dutch gables on some of the older buildings. The church is especially fine and worth a visit. Alan Bignell's book of Kent villages tells how a workman in 1983 put his foot through a hole in the tiled floor and this led to the discovery of hundreds of human bones. They were

Minster Abbey, Thanet

reinterred in due course and the secret charnel house made safe once more.

The change in landscape that occurs as you go deeper into Thanet only serves to underline the difference between this one-time island and 'mainland' Kent. In his *Rural Rides*, Cobbett found Thanet different too, but he had little to praise about it: 'The labourers' houses, all along this land, beggarly in the extreme. The people dirty, poor-looking; ragged, but particularly dirty.' It was overrun by the Vikings and haunted by smugglers, but today one or two of its resorts are among the busiest in the south.

Birchington is the first town of any size, yet it has almost lost itself to nearby Margate. As a resort in its own right it has a long way to go to match its neighbour, but Minnis Bay has a beach with certain attractions. It is about 4 miles from Reculver and some of the land between the two, being below sea-level, is only saved from inundation by a high defensive wall. Its predecessor was breached during the notorious storm of 1953 when large tracts of land were flooded. East of Minnis Bay the chalk cliffs rise and serve as natural defences,

running around the coastline to Dover. From Birchington's main
centre there is little to indicate the proximity of the sea, but All Saints
Church has much of interest, and at its doorway is buried Dante
Gabriel Rossetti, the poet and artist who formed the Pre-Raphaelite
Brotherhood. His grave is marked with a memorial stone carved by
Madox Brown under whom he studied. Opposite the church a
narrow road runs south, along which can be found Quex Park. In it
are a mansion and Powell-Cotton Museum of natural history and
ethnography which, together with the gardens, are open to the
public.

Along the cliff road Westgate and Westbrook run one against
another, their green lawns and flower beds and little bays sharing a
calm prelude to the noisy vibrancy of Margate proper.

Margate is the quintessential seaside resort, a smaller Blackpool,
a Londoner's Bank Holiday venue; perhaps having a right to the
claim of birthplace of the seaside resort on account of the invention
here of the bathing machine in 1753. Around the same time its grand
villas sprang up to accommodate a wealthy clientele, and in Victorian times it had a sparkling reputation. The crowds then were small
compared with those of today, when Margate annually attracts
thousands of holidaymakers. It has everything the British seaside
holidaymaker apparently wants, except peace and solitude. Bembom Brothers Theme Park, which used to be known as Dreamland,
is the ultimate in amusement parks, just a stroll from the beach across
the broad promenade. Bembom has some 20 acres of giant fun fair,
blaring music, candy floss and the overpowering smell of hot dogs
and onions. Elsewhere the town has its famous shell grotto discovered in 1835, it has caves claimed to have been used as smugglers'
hideouts, a restored smock windmill and the remains of a medieval
priory at Salmestone Grange.

The past is little revered in Margate, however. The town is
unashamedly the brash tourist capital of Thanet, superficial and
brazen, and quite magnetic in its appeal to countless generations of
holidaymakers.

After Margate, Thanet's coast swings southwards around North
Foreland with a brief stretch of countryside before the first houses of
Broadstairs are reached. **Broadstairs** presents an air of gentility, of
respectability. A sandy bay is enclosed by a half-circle of cliffs with

the town built on them, steeply in layers with gardens in front and charming streets behind with interesting buildings in which is seen, yet again, the genius of Dickens. Dickens is in Broadstairs as he is in Rochester. He loved this town which he called 'Our Little Watering Place', and came here often between 1837-51. In one of Broadstairs' houses lived Miss Mary Strong, whom he called Miss Betsy Trotwood in *David Copperfield*; the house is now a Dickens museum. He wrote this novel in the study of a gaunt castellated house overlooking the harbour. The house was known as Fort House, but today it is universally called Bleak House. Although he did not write that book here, it was nevertheless the inspiration for it. In Broadstairs he finished *Nicholas Nickleby* and worked on *The Old Curiosity Shop*. His enthusiasm for the town comes through clearly in a passage he wrote: 'It is the brightest day you ever saw. The sun is sparkling on the water so that I can hardly bear to look at it. The tide is in and the fishing boats are dancing like mad. Upon the green-topped cliffs the corn is cut and piled in shocks, and thousands of butterflies are fluttering about, taking the bright little red flags at the mastheads for flowers.'

Broadstairs developed from a fishing village, and sea fishing remains one of its many attractions today. Its small harbour is picturesque, and the row of Victorian villas and hotels overlooking the beach set the tone; it is one of the best examples of a Victorian resort in Kent, and a direct contrast to its close neighbours, Margate and Ramsgate.

It is not easy to tell where Broadstairs finishes and Ramsgate begins, for endless housing complexes abut along this stretch of coastline. As Broadstairs grew from a fishing village, so did Ramsgate; but here the similarity ends. **Ramsgate** is very much a duplicate of Margate, another town offering fun-fair entertainment and amusement centres with flashing lights and loud music. The heart of Ramsgate is to be found down by its busy harbour, crammed with private yachts and fishing boats, while cross-channel ferries and container vessels ply an increasing commercial trade nearby. There is an international flavour about this harbour; even the yachts are moored in similar fashion to those on the French Riviera, and it was from here that the Dunkirk evacuation was orchestrated. Somehow Ramsgate has managed to retain its special atmosphere while

Broadstairs

keeping pace with modern tourist demands. It is a sort of halfway house between Margate and Broadstairs; leaning towards Margate with its vivacity, but with a little of the soul of Broadstairs.

At nearby **Pegwell Bay** there is an entirely different atmosphere. This is a broad sheltered bay where the Stour flows into the sea after following a long loop via Sandwich: a low curving bay of sand dunes and mudflats, stretching far out when the tide has gone, with many wading birds paddling among the shallows. It is a historic place, for here came the Saxons under Hengist and Horsa in AD449, landing at Ebbsfleet in fleets of longboats. Christianity came with the landing in AD597 of St Augustine with his missionary monks. This should now be a place of pilgrimage, marked perhaps with a Christian chapel, but there is only a Saxon-style cross in a field erected in 1884. However, the arrival of Hengist and Horsa at Pegwell Bay is commemorated with a replica of a Viking longship. The *Hugin* was ✳ brought across the North Sea by an adventurous crew of Danes in 1949 to celebrate the 1,500th anniversary of that momentous landing; it stands for all to see beside the road, its brightly coloured shields

Ramsgate harbour

and dragon's head making a fitting monument to history.

Inland the Minster marshes form a bland and watery landscape, made the more depressing by the construction of huge power station cooling towers. There are lavender fields here too, and following the lanes inland where one or two old timber-framed houses kindle a spark of interest, you come to the village of **Minster**, which is certainly worth visiting for its splendid abbey, which should not be confused with Minster Abbey on Sheppey.

This is a wonderful place of peace and prayer, inhabited by Benedictine nuns. It is an ancient piece of monastic England, founded in AD670 by Ermenburga of *Mercia*, later to be called Domna Eva, the first abbess. The first building occupied a site where now stands the parish church of St Mary, but by AD741 the community had grown to seventy nuns and as more accommodation was required, so a new convent was erected on the present site. This suffered at the hands of the Danes and it was not until 1027, after the monks of Canterbury had successfully petitioned King Canute to make the property theirs, that rebuilding began. Once more it was partly destroyed, this time on the express orders of William the Conqueror who demanded that all Thanet should be 'laid waste so that the Danish army might have no stronghold.'

The present Minster Abbey consists of a Saxon wing restored by monks after the 1085 devastation and the ruins of an adjacent Norman tower with a remarkable little crypt inside, offering cool sanctuary and contemplation. The Benedictine nuns in whose hands the abbey now rests returned in 1937 and opened it to the public. It is a fascinating place. St Mary's, the parish church of Minster, dates from 1150. It was restored in the Victorian 1860s and again just over 100 years later. Then, in the notorious hurricane of October 1987, the spire collapsed into the churchyard causing a considerable amount of damage.

If you drive away from Minster heading west you come to the Canterbury-Ramsgate road near Gore Street. The B2046 strikes away to the south, crosses the western edge of the Ash Levels at Plucks Gutter, and enters fruit-growing country. Three or four miles further on you come to **Wingham**, a handsome village on a broad street lined with chestnuts and lime trees and a rich assortment of houses representing the best architectural designs of various periods from Tudor to present day. Wingham's main street makes a dog's leg on the old Roman road that ran between Canterbury and Richborough. Follow it eastward, thus making the final break in the anti-clockwise diversion from Minster, and after passing through the neat, well-kept village of Ash (a long village that most rush straight through) you come to the ring road which bypasses Sandwich. This is the main road to and from Thanet.

The coast road that runs from Thanet to Dover crosses the Stour near the old Roman fort of **Richborough Castle**, once a place of great strategic importance occupying a small island in the Wantsum Channel. When the Romans landed here in AD43 they developed a port and supply depot and a small civilian settlement to administer it. Their buildings then were of timber and it was not until much later, in the second half of the third century, that they built the massive walls of the fort that survives, in part, to this day. From then until their final evacuation from Britain around AD410, the Romans used Richborough, or *Rutupiæ* as it was known, as one of their main ports of arrival and departure for the military.

Places to Visit In and Around Margate and Ramsgate

Bembon Brothers Theme Park
Margate
Numerous 'white-knuckle' rides on
Britain's tallest big wheel,
dodgems, ghost train, roller
coaster etc, all on a 20-acre site.

Bleak House
Broadstairs
Charles Dickens's holiday home
where he wrote *David Copperfield*.
Now a Dickens museum and
museum of maritime interest.
Rooms on show.

Crampton Tower Museum
Crampton Tower, opposite the
railway station, Broadstairs
Contains this Victorian railway
engineer's blueprints, drawings,
and some photographs. Also a fine
model railway. Of great interest to
rail enthusiasts.

Dickens House Museum
Broadstairs
One-time home of Mary Strong,
upon whom Dickens based Miss
Betsy Trotwood in *David Copper-*
field. Now a museum devoted to
the writer's association with
Broadstairs.

Drapers Windmill
Off College Road, Margate
Built about 1850, now restored and
in working order and open to the
public.

Hugin
Pegwell Bay, Ramsgate
A full-sized replica of the early
Saxon longship that brought
Hengist and Horsa to Britain. On
permanent view by A256.

Margate Aquarium
Palm Bay
Contains a large collection of
tropical fish.

Margate Caves
Lower Northdown Road
Large caverns cut in the chalk
more than 1,000 years ago.
Thought to have been used,
among others, by smugglers as a
hideout.

The road swings away from Richborough to make a detour around the outside of a town that should be on the list of all visitors to this corner of the county. **Sandwich** is one of the loveliest survivors of medieval England: all winding narrow streets, with fine old buildings, some of which stood here when the town was a port and busy with maritime trade. Now the sea lies almost 2 miles away and is separated from Sandwich by the river that gives colour to one of the town's most picturesque corners. The Barbican is an attractive

Maritime Museum
Ramsgate
Pier Yard, Royal Harbour
Four separate displays cover
differing aspects of maritime
history including relics of eight-
eenth-century wrecks on the
Goodwin Sands.

Minster Abbey
Minster, 4 miles west of Ramsgate,
off B2048
Wonderful ancient building. Now
housing Benedictine nuns.

The Model Village
Westcliff, Ramsgate
A reproduction in miniature of the
English countryside. Especially
popular with children.

Motor Museum
Westcliff Hall, Ramsgate
Displays of cars and motor cycles
from the Edwardian era to the
1950s.

North Foreland Lighthouse
Broadstairs
Lighthouse built in 1790 and open
to the public.

**Powell-Cotton Museum and
Quex Park**
Quex Park, Birchington, 1$^{1}/_{2}$ miles
west of Margate
A remarkable private natural
history collection and ethnography
display, plus collection of guns and
oriental porcelain and silver in
early nineteenth-century mansion.

RAF Manston Spitfire Pavilion
3 miles west of Ramsgate
Exhibits and memorabilia from
World War II; its highlight is a
Spitfire MK XVI. Also a Canberra
PR3 and Gloster Javelin flanking
the pavilion.

Salmestone Grange
Nash Road, Margate
Fourteenth-century priory building
that was owned by monks of St
Augustin's Abbey, Canterbury.
Chapel, crypt and kitchen are of
particular interest.

The Shell Grotto
Grotto Hill, off Northdown Road
An ancient shell temple with
winding passages decorated with
millions of seashells.

gatehouse built on the Quay in 1539, guarding the entrance from the ✳
Stour. Two hundred years after it was built, a bridge was slung
across the river here and tolls were levied on all who used it, until
1977. Under the protection of the timber arch a board displays the
charges as in 1905.

In the eleventh century Sandwich was a Cinque Port, but by the
end of the sixteenth century its harbour had silted up. However its
prosperity did not fail for Flemish clothmakers came to the town and

The Barbican, Sandwich

many of its finest buildings date from this period; in Strand Street, for example, where so many timbered houses vie for attention; the Dutch House in King Street and the timbered Guildhall. It has three churches, a building that was a grammar school in 1564, and a line of earth walling that was part of the ramparts of the town. A pleasant walk can be made along this wall, from river to river, then to complete the circuit along Strand Street and the Quay.

On the edge of town, wedged between the A257 and the River Stour, lies Gazen Salts Nature Reserve, accessible by footpath from St Mary's Church. Another nature reserve of some importance is found on Sandwich Bay, a coastal stretch that attracts a large number of migrant birds in spring and autumn, and butterflies from the Continent in summer. Access to Sandwich Bay is by footpath from the town, or by car on a toll road as far as Prince's Golf Club, followed by a short walk along the shore.

Between Sandwich and the sea is one of Britain's best known golf courses, Royal St George's, and farther down the coast towards Deal the Royal Cinque Ports Golf Links attracts its own band of enthusiasts. Inland, the traveller will find a pleasing rural scene in the countryside leading towards Canterbury. There are orchards producing some of Kent's finest apples; there are winding lanes and fine footpaths and villages such as Chillenden with its strange trestle post windmill, or Eastry, once capital of this kingdom.

Perhaps the first impression one gains of **Deal** is that of a little town which owes its allegiance more to the sea than to the seaside. It has made few concessions to the more garish requirements of many another modern seaside resort, and has courageously resisted a plan for modernisation which could have drastically altered its character. It remains a quiet place of old cottages, narrow streets and alleyways, of fishing boats drawn up on its shingle beach and a castle built by Henry VIII that stands to this day as a perfect example of a Tudor fort.

With neighbouring Walmer, its history is punctuated with great names. Julius Caesar landed here in 55BC. Thomas á Becket came here on his return from exile. Nelson worshipped at the church of St George the Martyr and both Pitt the Younger and Wellington spent time at Walmer Castle as Lord Wardens of the Cinque Ports. Wellington, in fact, died here in 1852.

When Caesar arrived in his initial invasion attempt (generally reckoned to have been between the present-day Deal and Walmer), it was certainly not his first choice as a landing and he was forced by weather and attack from the Britons to retreat.

The following year, with renewed determination Caesar was back, landing unopposed at the same beach in 800 ships. Subdued by the sight of so many ships coming to land, the Britons withdrew to their hillfort at Bigbury. The Roman invasion was under way. Marching inland Caesar fought his way to St Albans and destroyed the town, then withdrew once more to Gaul, leaving England untroubled for another 400 years. It was much later that Deal emerged from the obscure beach that had brought the Romans ashore.

Upper Deal was the original settlement, and down on the seafront there was little more than a collection of fishermen's cottages until the seventeenth century, but then a port was developed on account of the comparatively safe anchorage afforded to shipping taking the quiet water between the coast and the notorious Goodwin Sands. The Downs, as this waterway is known, would often shelter a number of sailing ships waiting for a favourable wind before heading into the Channel, so Deal was well suited for their provisioning. From earliest times fishing was an important ingredient in the town's economy, but it was the siting here of a naval station in the eighteenth century that increased both its importance and its prosperity.

It is a town worth spending time in, for there are many corners of old Deal to explore. Middle Street is a conservation area of period cottages and listed buildings; in South Street is the house of Elisabeth Carter, the 'blue-stocking' favourite of Dr Johnson who, apart from being a noted linguist and intellectual, was a great walker; there is the strange Timeball Tower built in 1795 at the dockyard entrance to signal the time to shipping in The Downs, and the mellow town hall with its small museum of local history.

Deal Castle is a splendid piece of fortification built in the shape of a Tudor rose; a central circular keep surrounded by six bastions, like petals, which in turn have an outer ring of six larger bastions. Round the whole there is a moat with a surrounding wall. It was built by Henry VIII as one of three spaced a mile apart — the others are at Walmer and Sandown — in a bout of frantic building for coastal defence during the time of his excommunication by the Pope when he, and England, were under direct threat of invasion from the Continent. Of the three, Sandown has almost entirely disappeared beneath the encroaching sea, but both Deal and Walmer Castles are in excellent condition, Deal being the larger and most complete.

Walmer Castle, just south of Deal, is surrounded by trees and linked to gardens laid out by the niece of William Pitt. It has been converted from a fort to the official residence of the Lord Warden of the Cinque Ports, and most of the wardens have left their own mark on its additions and adaptations. It is open to the public, as is that of Deal.

The coast road runs south as far as residential Kingsdown, then heads inland to join the busy A258 at Ringwould, but the Saxon Shore Way follows a cliff path, with fine views over the Goodwin Sands which have been the graveyard of many hundreds of ships over the centuries and, curiously, also the venue for some rather eccentric games of cricket. The first recorded game played on these shifting sands, some half a dozen miles off shore and only temporarily exposed by the tides, took place on 31 August 1813 between two

Places of Interest In and Around Sandwich and Deal

The Barbican and Quay
Sandwich
Gateway to the town from the river
and one of the most attractive
corners in Sandwich.

Deal Barracks History Museum
This has items connected with the
Royal Marines whose association
with the town goes back to 1664.

Deal Castle (EH)
Remarkably preserved fort,
designed like a Tudor rose and
built in the sixteenth century.

**Deal Maritime and Local History
Museum**
St George's Road
Relics of boats form a special
feature of this museum which
contains assorted exhibits relating
to the town's maritime history.

Deal Town Hall Museum
St George's Road
Georgian building containing items
of local and archaeological
interest. Open by appointment
only.

Gazen Salts Nature Reserve
North-west of Sandwich, between
A257 and River Stour
12 acres of lake, pond and
meadow offering a diversity of
habitats. Managed by the Kent
Trust for Nature Conservation.

The Guildhall
Sandwich
Delightful sixteenth-century
timbered building, with panelled
courtroom with folding jury box.
Items of local history relating to the
Cinque Ports on display.

Precinct Toy Museum
Harnet Street, Sandwich
Museum of childrens' toys dating
from 1870 to present day.

Richborough Castle (EH)
1 mile north of Sandwich
Remains of important Roman fort.
Domestic relics and coins on show
in the museum on site.

**Richborough Roman
Amphitheatre**
South of Richborough Castle
Open to view at all times.

Sandwich Bay Nature Reserve
2 miles north of Sandwich
Large coastal strip of shingle and
sandspit, with dunes and salting
jointly owned by the National Trust,
RSPB and KTNC. Great interest to
birdwatchers. Access by footpath.

The Salutation
Knightrider Street, Sandwich
House built by Sir Edward Lutyen,
with garden by Gertrude Jekyll.

Victoriana Museum
Blackburn Hall, Middle Street, Deal
Items from the late eighteenth and
nineteenth centuries on display.

Walmer Castle (EH)
2 miles south of Deal
Similar to that of Deal, but since
1708 has been the official
residence of the Lord Warden of
the Cinque Ports.

White Mill
$1/_2$ mile west of Sandwich on A257
Restored eighteenth-century
smock windmill with machinery still
intact. Open to the public.

four-man teams led by Thomas Elgar of Ramsgate and George Witherden of Bethersden. Witherden's team won by 22 runs to 21.

At a crossroads 2 miles south of Ringwould the B2058 branches off to **St Margaret's at Cliffe**, a growing village with some pleasant weatherboarded houses in the centre and an impressive Norman church. It looks out to sea from its dominant position on the clifftop, some 400ft above the waves. France can be seen on a clear day. In 1696, it is said, a shepherd lost his way and fell over the cliff. Although badly injured he lived long enough to give land to the parish, from which payment was made for the ringing of a bell at 8pm every night from Michaelmas to Lady Day, in order to warn other travellers away from the cliff edge.

The west doorway of the church is impressively carved, while inside there are some fine arches and a recent stained glass window which commemorates three local men who were members of the crew of the *Herald of Free Enterprise* which sank off Zeebrugge in 1987. The window depicts the ship sailing into Christ's outstretched arms, and is a moving memorial to a disaster that rocked all of Britain, including the people of Kent whose losses were so great. Below lies St Margaret's Bay reached by a very steep road that winds down the chalk cliffs that tower over this lovely corner. It is a popular but surprisingly peaceful spot without any 'attractions' other than the beach, the cliffs and the sea. It is a sun-trap, too, from which a number of cross-Channel swimmers set out, and the cliffs in either direction offer interesting walks.

Northwards a $3^1/_2$ mile ($1^1/_4$ hours) walk leads to Walmer Castle, passing Leathercote Point on the way, a 90ft-high memorial obelisk to the Dover Patrol. The path is clearly marked throughout. Three miles of walking in the other direction will lead along the cliffs past a windmill and South Foreland lighthouse where Marconi did research into wireless telegraphy, to reach Dover Castle, one of the many sites of interest in the town.

Dover is an ancient town. As the 'Gateway to England' it has faced armies of invasion, been fortified, settled and developed, and if, for many of the travellers who annually pass through its harbour, it is remembered only for its cliffs of chalk, theirs is the loss. For within these cliffs the town has the history of England spelt out in its buildings.

Standing as they do on the narrowest stretch of the English Channel, it is only natural that these cliffs should have been chosen by man as a settlement, as their strategic importance is obvious. In the Iron Age our ancestors built earthworks for defence. The Romans chose this site for their town, *Dubris*, after having initially been deterred from landing here by a crowd of well-armed locals upon the beach. William the Conqueror saw as one of his priorities the maintenance of sound fortifications here, and Henry II started work on the great castle that is one of the town's marvels.

Crowded together high upon the cliffs dominating the town is a trio of historic buildings that represent the age of the Roman, the Saxon and the Norman. Is the Roman Pharos the oldest building

A ferry on its way past the white cliffs of Dover

within these shores? Certainly this lighthouse has stood here for nearly 2,000 years, erected to a height of 80ft where a beacon was lit to guide the Roman fleet into the safety of the sheltered anchorage below. The tower is well preserved, with a lining of red tiles running all around it. Although it is not much more than 40ft high today, it remains the tallest Roman structure in England. Next to the lighthouse is the Saxon garrison church of St Mary in Castro, itself 1,000 years old and largely built of Roman materials. Around both Roman lighthouse and Saxon church the Normans created their massive castle stronghold, arguably the finest in Britain. The keep stands 465ft above the sea, its walls are 21ft thick at their base, the well goes down 400ft to below the street-level, and the keep is 91ft high. Although it was built as long ago as the twelfth century, it cost the enormous sum of £7,000 to construct and until recently had been continuously garrisoned for 800 years.

At the head of Western Heights there is the **Grand Shaft**, a triple staircase sunk in the cliffs as a connecting route between the town and the barracks which was prepared to repel the threat of invasion by Napoleon. Behind the town is a majestic watermill, Crabble Mill, built in order to provide flour for the troops of the garrison. Elsewhere in the town and on the cliffs are many symbols of other ages, other events that have been historic milestones. There is the Roman Painted House, discovered when a site in New Street was being cleared for a car park. It dates from the second century, with wall paintings and underfloor heating. There is Maison Dieu, founded in 1203 as a travellers' rest house now incorporated into the town hall. On the sea front there is a memorial to Captain Webb, first man to swim the Channel (in 1875), and on the cliffs not far from the castle on North Fall Meadow, there is a granite outline of a plane marking the spot where, in July 1909, Louis Blériot landed his monoplane after the first powered flight across the Channel from France.

To many people Dover is its harbour; an enormously busy place with ships and hovercraft coming and going almost incessantly. In and out of the town, by day and by night, come streams of cars and juggernauts, bound for the busiest port on the busiest stretch of water in the world. This lucrative trade has, of course, dictated much of the direction the town planners have taken. As a result Dover is not a particularly handsome town as a whole, yet taken individually some of its features are of such interest and historic importance that no visitor prepared to spend time exploring its many riches need ever go away disappointed.

The road to Folkestone has little to appeal at first as it leaves Dover, but as Folkestone draws near, so the interest increases. The clifftop path offers a pleasant 8 mile walk (3 hours); for much of the route the Saxon Shore Way combines with the North Downs Way, and the path is joined west of the Western Docks, along Archcliffe Road where the North Downs Way leads over Shakespeare Cliff. It skirts the edge nearly all the way to Folkestone, but makes a short diversion above Abbott's Cliff when the rifle range is in operation. To the people of Kent this no-man's land between Dover and Folkestone has become the most contentious piece of cliff in all of Britain, for beneath it runs the course of the Channel Tunnel. Discussed and argued over *ad nauseum* for nearly 200 years (a candle-lit tunnel was first suggested in 1802), a start was actually made from each coast in the 1880s, and again in the 1960s. Revived once more in the early 1980s the Bill passed through Parliament and received the Royal Assent in 1987, and work began almost straight away with voices raised in protest about the impending loss of national identity, predictions of acts of terrorism, fear of rabies being brought into Britain and, most seriously of all, the adverse effects on the environment. Almost at once environmentalists had something to complain about. Shakespeare Cliff was one of only three designated Heritage Coasts in the south-east of England, yet the government gave the go-ahead for Eurotunnel (the consortium of the Channel Tunnel Group and France Manche S.A. who won the contract to build it) to dump 1.8 million cubic tonnes of spoil at its foot. Yet no matter what one's deep-rooted anxieties and prejudices may be, the 'Chunnel' is a remarkable feat of engineering, often claimed to be 'The greatest engineering project in Europe ever undertaken by the private sector.' Who could deny it?

Remarkably, **Folkestone** has somehow managed to absorb its dual role as both a busy Channel port and a fashionable seaside resort without sacrificing all its charm. Before the coming of the railway in 1842 it was little more than a fishing village, with a sideline of smuggling, but with easier access the town became popular with the Victorians, and it grew into a resort of some importance. Dickens stayed here on several occasions on his way to see his sons at school in Boulogne, and in 1855 spent 3 months in Albion Villas writing the opening chapters of *Little Dorrit*.

The early history of the town shows that a Roman dignitary had a villa on East Cliff with a view over the harbour, and the Normans fortified the hill directly behind the town, confusingly named 'Caesar's Camp', and also established a castle near the harbour not long after the conquest of 1066. This, however, was destined to be demolished by the action of the sea and nothing remains of it today. The church dedicated to St Mary and St Eanswythe contains in a small lead cask, the remains of the daughter of King Eadbald who founded

Folkestone harbour

what many believe to have been England's first nunnery. On such an exposed site the abbey would have been an open temptation to raiding parties of Danes, and it was totally destroyed by them. As a form of protection against invasion during Napoleon's day a line of Martello Towers was positioned along the coast, and the chain begins near Copt Point on the edge of East Wear Bay.

One of the notable features of the town is the cliff-top promenade known as The Leas, where the formal elegance of its layout is enriched with lovely views. From The Leas wind paths among trees and shrubberies and rockeries to the beach 200ft below. There is a good sandy beach below East Cliff and the harbour is a busy place of yachts and fishing vessels. A large amusement centre, splendid sports centre and a very fine indoor swimming pool is found here along with a variety of live theatres and bandstands; gardens, golf and a water-driven cliff lift that has been operating for 100 years.

Sandgate is a suburb of Folkestone, where H.G. Wells came to live at The Spade House overlooking the bay. It was here that he wrote several of his books including *The History of Mr Polly, Tono-*

Places of Interest In and Around Dover and Folkestone

Bleriot Memorial
North Fall Meadow, Dover
An outline of a simple monoplane set in granite marks the
spot where Louis Bleriot landed
in 1909 after the first powered
flight across the Channel.
Behind Dover Castle.

Dover Castle (EH)
Magnificent castle dating from
1180 and perched on the cliffs
overlooking the town. One of the
finest in all England, it occupies
the site of an Iron Age fort.
Within its grounds are the
Roman Pharos (lighthouse) and
the Saxon church of St Mary in
Castro.

Dover Museum
Ladywell, Dover
Founded in 1836, this museum
houses exhibits of local archaeological interest, as well as history
and geology.

Folkestone Arts Centre
New Metropole, The Leas
An arts centre which mounts
various visiting exhibitions.

Folkestone Museum
Public Library, Grace Hill
A museum of local and natural
history with adjoining art gallery
showing various temporary
exhibitions.

Folkestone Racecourse
Westernhanger, 6 miles west of
town on A20

Kent's only racecourse offering
about twenty meetings each
year, usually on Mondays or
Tuesdays.

Folkestone Warren
Extensive chalk cliffs with typical
flowers and butterflies.

Grand Shaft
Dover
Triple staircase sunk through the
cliffs of Western Heights in
Napoleonic times to give access
from the barracks to the town.

Langdon Cliffs
East of Dover, reached from an
unclassified road to St Margaret's
A fine locality for chalkland
flowers and butterflies. Also
superb views.

Maison Dieu
Dover
Situated next door to the
museum, this is one of Dover's
most interesting buildings.
Originally founded in 1221
Maison Dieu was used as a
hostel for travellers and pilgrims
for more than 300 years. Now
incorporated into the town hall
building.

Roman Painted House
New Street, Dover
A well preserved Roman town
house with underfloor heating
system and considerable wall
paintings.

Bungay and *Kipps*. Henry VIII built a castle here using the stones from two abbeys he destroyed. In 1806 this castle was drastically altered to accommodate the building of a Martello Tower, and both the tower and the remains of the castle can be clearly seen from the beach.

Inland a little behind Sandgate, in a narrow wedge of country bordered by the steep wall of the downs, the village of Newington and neighbouring tiny hamlet of Frogholt have become virtually submerged beneath the feeder roads and railway making for the Channel Tunnel. **Newington** once sat among fields, its church tower beckoning in the valley; **Frogholt** slumbered among a bower of leaves in its stream-lined hollow. All that has now changed, transposed by a Euro-dream.

Beyond Sandgate houses appear to grow less crowded and the beginnings of the Royal Military Canal can be seen beside the road. This leads quickly to the pleasant little town of Hythe and the flat open country of Romney Marsh.

5

EDEN VALLEY AND THE GREENSAND RIDGE

The Greensand Ridge enters Kent from Surrey as a line of hills running parallel with those of the chalk downs. They are different to the downs, however, in vegetation, in scale, and in outlook. They are wooded; the river here is the Eden, which in turn feeds the Medway. The land is rich in agriculture, and the views are breathtaking.

From the Ridge it is difficult to believe that man has settled the land below for over 1,000 years. A vast woodland seems to fill the valley, broken here and there by a wheatfield or a meadow. This woodland is small however, compared with the vast forests that once covered half of Kent. Iberian and Celtic tribes settled in the small clearings during the Bronze and Iron Ages, bringing skills with them. Later, in Elizabethan times, the celebrated iron industry of the Weald was developed.

The belvederes along the Greensand Ridge offer some of the very best views in the county. A narrow road leaves Westerham by Squerryes Court at the western end of town, and climbs south towards a wooded rise marking the Greensand Ridge. Less than 2 miles later it emerges from the trees at Kent Hatch, a few short yards from the Surrey border and a small, sheltered indent in the Greensand. As an introduction to the Weald it could scarcely be bettered, for the light floods upward from the meadows, with a pattern of woods and fields stretching off to the distant hills.

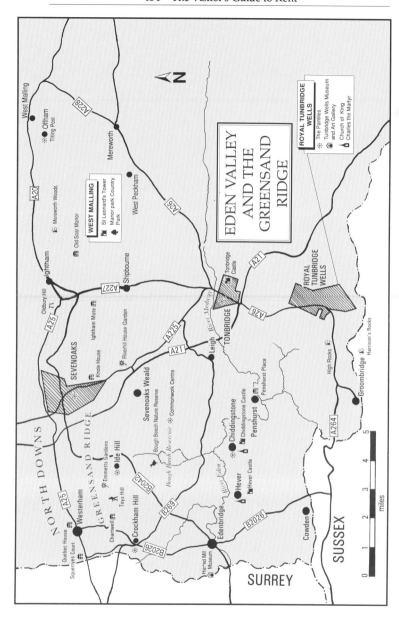

EDEN VALLEY AND THE GREENSAND RIDGE

ROYAL TUNBRIDGE WELLS
🌼 The Pantiles
🏛 Tunbridge Wells Museum and Art Gallery
⛪ Church of King Charles the Martyr

WEST MALLING
🏰 St Leonard's Tower
🍀 Manor park Country Park
🏛 Old Soar Manor

West Malling
Offham
🌼 Tilling Post
A228
Mereworth
🌲 Mereworth Woods
A20
West Peckham
A26
Ightham
Shipbourne
A227
Oldbury Hill
A25
🏰 Tonbridge Castle
A21
River Medway
A26
ROYAL TUNBRIDGE WELLS
Ightham Mote
🌼 Riverhill House Garden
A225
Leigh
TONBRIDGE
A21
SEVENOAKS
Knole House
Sevenoaks Weald
Penshurst Place 🏰
🌼 Bough Beech Nature Reserve
🌼 Commonwork Centre
Chiddingstone Castle 🏰
Penshurst
High Rocks
🌼 Harrison's Rocks
Groombridge
A264
GREENSAND RIDGE
Emmetts Gardens
🌼 Ide Hill
Chiddingstone
🌼 Hever
🏰 Hever Castle
Bough Beech Reservoir
River Eden
NORTH DOWNS
A25
Westerham
🏛 Chartwell
Toys Hill
Crockham Hill
B2042
B269
🏛 Quebec House
🏛 Squerryes Court
🌼 B2026
🏛 Hartield Mill Museum
Edenbridge
B2026
Cowden
SURREY
SUSSEX

miles
0 1 2 3 4 5

Eden Valley from the Greensand Ridge

There is a sixteenth-century house on the right of a road junction, set behind hedges. It was once an inn where Henry VIII is said to have stayed when travelling to Hever to court Anne Boleyn. When he arrived at Kent Hatch trumpeters stationed along the hills would relay a fanfare to announce the king's approach.

Turning left, the road leads along the edge of the hills before a rapid descent into the little village of **Crockham Hill**, a village set on the slopes of the Greensand, with huge panoramas on the run down into the village. The village itself has some good houses mostly hidden from the road; The Royal Oak, which used to display its own well in the public bar, and the cottages forming an adjoining terrace represent the original village that had a toll gate across the road until 1866. There is a Youth Hostel which encourages a closer study of the surrounding area, and in the church, built of local stone in 1842, there lies a memorial to Octavia Hill, one of the three founders of the National Trust. She had spent the last years of her full life in a house built for her and her friend Harriette Yorke on the edge of Crockham Hill Common, and although she was offered a tomb in Westminster

Abbey, it was her choice to be buried in the heart of the countryside she loved.

A footpath leads through a meadow buckled with strange hillocks and hollows, which moves with the pressure of underground water. Greensand, of which these hills are made, is a porous rock, and it easily soaks up rain water. Beneath the surface of rock there lie reservoirs of water on a bed of clay. Some of the water eases itself out by way of a number of springs, but the springs cannot always cope with the demands made on them. The reservoirs fill and the meadow buckles under pressure; or a dry spell reduces the amount held by the hills and the water level drops, and with it the surface of the meadow.

In 1596 a great landslip occurred here, radically altering the shape of the land between the church and Froghole Farm, seen among its oasts across the meadows. In a space of 11 days trees and hedges were taken by the moving hillside and deposited into newly-formed hollows. New hills arose. Pools appeared, 'the cracking of the roots of trees, the breaking of boughs, the noise of its hedgewood breaking, the gaping of the ground, and the riving of the earth asunder; the falling of the torn furrows', could all be heard.

The path (2 miles, 1 hour), across this meadow begins at a gate near the church. It crosses two meadows and a stream before climbing 133 steps through the garden of a lovely little thatched cottage that has stood here for centuries, and then goes left along Froghole Lane. The hillside rises steeply on the right, while off to the left a huge panorama of hills and meadows takes the eye beyond Crockham Hill and out to the distant heights of Leith Hill in Surrey. **Froghole Farm** is a striking piece of architecture with its black timbers and little windows, and double oasts in the yard. At the end of Froghole Lane, more steps climb up to the right, leading to Mariners Hill. At the top of these steps, take the bare imprint of path to the right among trees, for it leads to a seat with a view to remember overlooking the west. Behind it a stile continues the path across the brow of the hill to views of east and south, one of the most magnifi- cent panoramas to be seen anywhere, and it is due to the persistence of Octavia Hill that the National Trust managed to purchase this piece of ground.

Across the tree-shrouded common behind Mariners Hill other paths lead to Chartwell, where Sir Winston Churchill spent 40 years of his life. **Chartwell** was an unpretentious house when Churchill bought it in 1924, but it enjoyed a lovely private view along a narrow valley to the open expanse of the Weald beyond. He enlarged the house, had the grounds landscaped, built his famous wall and found tranquillity among the gardens, where he painted down by the lake. Of his time at Chartwell he once wrote: 'I never had a dull or idle moment from morning to night and with my happy family around me dwelt at peace within my habitation.'

Now the National Trust has preserved much of the house as Churchill had it. It evokes the personality of the man through his library, his studio, his light, bright dining room and in the poolside seat where he fed the fish. There is also a museum, in which countless gifts, awards and uniforms recall the admiration and respect that his long career demanded.

All along the Greensand Ridge there are paths that explore the beechwoods, skirt the edge of the hills with views of the Eden Valley and the Weald below, or turn northwards occasionally into secretive valleys. On the northern edge of Chartwell's car park one such path $(7^1/_2$ miles, $2^1/_2$ hours) sets off towards the woods and a tiny hamlet hidden in one of these valleys, named **French Street**. It is a walk through woodland and French Street is a hamlet which seems not of this time. Follow the lane as it winds to the right into the valley below, and continue along it until a lone house is met standing on the left with more woods immediately behind it. Here another path continues up into the beechwoods of **Toys Hill**, another National Trust property covering more than 200 acres of woodland in which there used to be an impressive house known as Weardale Manor. All this beechwood was a leafy wonderland before 16 October 1987. It was then that hurricane-force winds savaged Kent with unprecedented fury and levelled vast areas of woodland. Toys Hill was one of the worst-hit corners of southern England when nearly 200 acres were lost. Huge beeches weighing countless tons were snapped like twigs. Others were torn from their roots and tossed like so many pieces of litter. The scene was a battleground, with discs of earth and 200-year-old trees laying strewn in disarray, criss-crossed over one another. Spikes of others made crude gesticulations. One giant, at least 60ft tall when standing, now lay horizontal some dozen feet or so above the ground, its monstrous weight supported by the remnants of

A cottage in Crockham Hill

three other victims of the storm.

In the following months the National Trust worked flat-out to make the area safe and to salvage what they could from the devastation. Replanting will be carried out in stages and in due course — not in our lifetime, nor that of our children — the beechwoods of Toys Hill will reflect the glory that was, before October 1987. Until then, visitors to this magical hilltop may at least enjoy views that have not been seen for many generations.

 By crossing the quiet road at Toys Hill another path is found which continues through what was previously Octavia Hill Woods and across two or three fields to reach the high point of Ide Hill, with its fine views and rural atmosphere around the village green. Still heading eastwards, a path goes along the edge of the hills before branching northwards after going through the Everlands estate, and plunges deeply into a coniferous forest, emerging on the outskirts of Sevenoaks. A series of paths lead past a great number of 'stockbroker-belt' houses before reaching the heart of the town.

By road from Crockham Hill to Sevenoaks is a winding route, not

Chartwell, the house and walled garden

without charm, and one which makes it possible to link the various high crowns of the Greensand and so to enjoy the views they offer. Take the B269 leading out of Crockham Hill opposite The Royal Oak and follow it until shortly after Pootings has been passed where a narrow road leads off to the left to Chartwell. Below Chartwell, an even more narrow lane winds to the right, through a collection of cottages named Puddledock, and up to Toys Hill, with Octavia Hill's well-head standing beside a low wall on the right. There are magnificent views down to Bough Beech Reservoir in the valley below. At the nearby junction bear left, driving through the beechwoods until a road to the right signals Ide Hill. This passes **Emmetts** estate, whose gardens are opened by the National Trust to the public on set days during the summer.

Ide Hill is an attractive place with its green and church standing above it, and behind the church a broad panorama over the trees and shrubs to the depths of the Weald.

North of the village the hills fall away into a secretive fold of meadowland which hides a farm or two and a handful of cottages. There is a narrow lane winding through this bowl of greenery between high hedges and sudden open vistas that reveal the blue line of the North Downs beyond the hinted Holmesdale Valley. It is not recommended to motorists, but cyclists may delight in the plunging slopes and sharp bends, while footpaths entice the walker ever deeper into this unknown land where surprise discoveries are to be made, like the remains of a one-time watermill in a tight valley far from highways and a delightful old manor house unguessed by those who restrict their explorations to the A-class roads.

On the edge of Ide Hill near Hanging Bank, with its fine views to Bough Beech Reservoir shining like a natural lake in the broad valley below, the B2042 forks. The left fork passes Whitley Row, a few cottages and a pub, and gains a clear panorama of the Darent Gap in the North Downs before coming down to join the busy A25 at Riverhead. The right branch hugs the very edge of the Greensand Ridge. It is a minor road with lovely views, now that the screen of beeches has been laid flat, and it crosses Goathurst Common and through woods on Bailey's Hill, then by way of a bridge over the deep cut of a bypass and by back streets into that gentle and genteel market town of Sevenoaks.

Sevenoaks, of course, is in the very heart of commuter country, but despite this it retains to a marked degree the atmosphere of a market town. Indeed, weekly livestock and produce markets are held not far from the town station, drawing crowds from the outlying villages with a lively bustle. The town has been in existence since at least 1114 when a record of churches listed it as *Seovenaca*; it was the site of a fifteenth-century battle when Jack Cade and his followers defeated the army of Henry VI before marching on London. There is a plaque recalling this battle on the corner of Solefields Road to the south of the town.

In his classic *Perambulation of Kent*, published in 1570, William Lambarde (who has a memorial in the parish church of St Nicholas) wrote with a certain disdain about Sevenoaks: 'I find not in all historie, any memorable thing concerning it.' It has, however, prospered for centuries and has a notable school, dressed in grey ragstone and endowed in 1432 by the will of Sir William Sennocke who, as an infant in the 1370s was found locally — some say in a hollow tree. He grew to become a very wealthy man and was made Lord Mayor of London.

There are a number of typically Kentish tile-hung cottages along the main street of Sevenoaks, a Regency pub and grand houses that give an air of grace and charm before running to a rather disappointing mixture of bland modern shop-fronts and others that have fought to retain their originality and appear quaint and appealing as a consequence. Not far from the very heart of the town stands the greensward of The Vine cricket ground. When it was given in 1773, the ground was truly in the countryside, but the town has now spread around and below it to the north. The first recorded game of cricket played at The Vine was in 1734 between Kent and Sussex, but its finest hour came in 1782 when the Duke of Dorset (one of the Sackvilles of Knole) led his estate-workers against a team representing All England. The local team won — not only the game, but a wager of a thousand guineas!

Knole Park impresses itself upon the town. The vast deer park, with grassy vales and lofty beeches, occupies at least one third of the town's acreage, while **Knole House** is one of the largest private houses in England, with 365 rooms, and a staircase for every week in the year.

The impressive Knole House with its vast deer park

It was begun in 1456 around an original small manor house bought for the sum of £266 13s 4d by Thomas Bourchier, Archbishop of Canterbury, and used by successive archbishops until Henry VIII decided to take it over in 1532. Elizabeth I granted it as a favour to Thomas Sackville, first Earl of Dorset, who made great improvements and extensions, and it has remained in the Sackville family ever since. Its fame is justified, for among its treasures are rare antiques, exquisite tapestries, an art collection containing notable works by Gainsborough and Reynolds, and an extravagant silver collection housed in a room dismissed as vulgar by the writer Vita Sackville-West, who was born there in 1892. The park itself is a place of quiet contemplation where the great herds of deer wander freely and there are tracks everywhere, so that a whole day could quite easily be spent watching deer, and listening to the birds.

All around the town are villages and hamlets containing gems of interest to the visitor. Not far out of Sevenoaks and protected from the busy hum of town life, **Sevenoaks Weald** shelters among the hills. It was here, at Long Barn, that Harold Nicolson and Vita Sackville West set up home and created a garden before moving on to Sissinghurst where they indulged themselves in the rescue of another garden from the wilderness of neglect, and in so doing performed an act of genius.

It was in Sevenoaks Weald that the restless poet Edward Thomas lived for a while, and where W.H. Davies wrote his classic *Autobiography of a Supertramp*. This is a glorious patch of country with huge panoramas looking south from the slope above the village. Footpaths plunge into a peaceful land. Heading west a series of paths take you alongside the elegant stone-and-tile Wickhurst Manor set in trim lawns, along the ankles of the greensand hills by way of meadows with sheep grazing, and woodland shaws where pheasants cackle, and down to Winkhurst Green on the edge of Bough Beech Reservoir, or round to **Bore Place**. This is a fascinating place. Developed round the Bore Place farm and its Tudor manor by the late Neil Wates, the Commonwork Centre here is an environmental project with special courses on ecology, history and environmental farming methods. Day sessions and residential courses are held, some in conjunction with the University of Kent. Hand-made bricks are fired in a kiln on the farm, there is a nature trail and open days are arranged during the summer to show that successful farming does not have to be dependant upon chemicals and large agri-business ventures.

Below Sevenoaks Weald and to the west of Tonbridge, **Leigh** (pronounced Lie) sits on a twist of road round two sides of its large triangular green. To north and south footpaths tease into gentle landscapes; south to the Medway, or up and over a hilltop to reach Penshurst Place; north to a patchwork of fields that gradually rise to the Greensand Ridge once more. The village of Leigh is expanding, but on one side of the main road are the walls of the Elizabethan red-bricked Hall Place, and on the other a row of charming cottages.

Westwards, the mellow stone of Chiddingstone Causeway's church stands at the head of the slope. The church was built by the architect of Westminster Cathedral and it stands beside a road junction posted to Penshurst.

No matter which of the approaches to **Penshurst** is taken it is down a hill, for the village sits in a bowl of hills just far enough above the river not to be threatened by it. It is a small village, with timbered houses, an inn, a church and a mansion. The gateway to the church is an invitation for the visitor to examine the ancient houses that overhang a courtyard called Leicester Square, whose time-etched beams appear about to collapse. Few churches can have an entrance which creates such an impression as this. The church itself, built of weathered sandstone and dedicated to St John the Baptist, does not disappoint either, without or within. It has stood here for 800 years, but some authorities suggest an earlier place of worship occupied the site as long ago as AD860. It has a font 500 years old and in the Sidney Chapel there is the history of the family who brought the village its fame. They came to Penshurst Place in 1552 when the house was given by Edward VI to his chamberlain and chief steward, Sir William Sidney. It has remained in the family's hands ever since. Sir Philip Sidney described it as 'handsome without curiosity and homely without loathsomeness.'

Like Knole, Penshurst Place is set in a parkland. In its grounds have strolled kings and queens, knights and poets. In its great baronial hall Elizabeth I danced with Dudley, and a poet sang the praises of the walled garden—all 10 acres of it: 'The blushing apricot and wooly peach Hang on thy walls, that every child may reach...' It is one of the finest of stately homes; in its setting, deceptively

Leigh

Penshurst Place

Leicester Square, Penshurst

simple architecture, and countless treasures. All around is a country-side of haunting beauty.

Happily the lanes that wind about these sudden little hills are not made for speed, for this is a countryside to travel slowly. One fine path (2 miles, 1 hour) leads away from Penshurst a little uphill from the village centre on the Leigh road. It heads off to the west, drops down to cross the River Eden, and then wanders among meadow-lands before reaching the timbered farm of Wat Stock. Beyond the farm the way leads to woods and a narrow lane which it crosses, and then strikes off to the north along woods still and climbing fields and beside hedges at the top of the hill ahead where Chiddingstone's church rises above the trees, the Greensand Ridge making a marvel-lous backdrop.

No visit to this corner of the Eden Valley is complete without a visit to the one-street village of **Chiddingstone**, one of the prettiest in Kent, whose fame has spread beyond the confines of the Weald. The National Trust protects the row of half-timbered houses, whose upper storeys overhang the street opposite the church and exude a flavour of Tudor England. The ancient beams and tiny leaded windows are perfect examples of a living past, and they look out at a rural landscape of stretched meadows leading the eye off to the distant wall of the Greensand Ridge.

Opposite these proud buildings there stands a wonderful church which pre-dates the Tudor period. At the end of the street, where the road veers sharply away, stands the popular Castle Inn, and beyond it the spacious grounds and tranquil lake of the manor house known as Chiddingstone Castle. For centuries the home of the Streatfeilds was called High Street House, but the stonework which was used to encase the manor towards the end of the eighteenth century gave it the appearance of a Gothic castle, and from that time onward High Street House became Chiddingstone Castle. The manorial estate included the village within its boundaries, but on the death of Sir Henry Streatfeild in 1936 the castle was sold and the village acquired by the National Trust. Visitors to the village are welcomed also to the castle where the panelling of Tudor times, and some sixteenth-century stained glass, contrasts its essential Englishness with a remarkable collection of oriental objects and Japanese lacquer.

Behind the village houses runs a short footpath to a large block of

The National Trust village of Chiddingstone

much-carved sandstone known to all as the Chiding Stone, one of the alleged origins of the village's name. Among the myths surrounding this stone is that of the wayward villagers being brought here for public example, to be scolded for their sins — a public 'chiding'. But this is only one of a number of similar outcrops to be found in the neighbourhood, others being found in the woods to the south-west.

A couple of miles west of Chiddingstone lies the third of the Eden's chain of delights; **Hever**. Even without its historic past, without the knowledge that it was the home of Anne Boleyn, and that Henry VIII courted her here, Hever would still be impressive. There is no village to speak of; just a castle, a church and an inn, a few scattered farms, one or two houses, and a little school. They occupy an unscarred landscape full of trees, birds and flowers.

The castle dates back 700 years when a small fortified farmhouse was built, with a moat around it and a wooden drawbridge guarding its entrance. The Bullens (as the Boleyn name was originally spelt) added to it, and it was here that the children of Sir Thomas began their fateful lives. Each of the three children added their name to

*Oasts at
Chiddingstone*

Chiddingstone Church

150

Hever Castle and gardens

history, for Mary became Henry VIII's mistress, Anne became his second wife and mother of Elizabeth I, failing to produce a male heir to the throne. She was executed ostensibly for adultery with her brother, George, who was also beheaded on the same charge. Two years later, in 1538, Thomas died at Hever lonely, heart-broken and shunned by his neighbours. On his death Henry gave the castle to Anne of Cleves his fourth wife, from whom he had recently been divorced. She retained it for 17 years.

Hever would have been worth visiting in its original state, but today it is much improved, thanks to the great wealth and indominatable spirit of William Waldorf Astor, first Lord Astor who bought the property in 1903. He then restored the castle, built a collection of Tudor style cottages in harmony with the original building, and with 2,000 workmen laid out a 35-acre lake through which the Eden flows, and created a unique garden that today appears to be the result of hundreds of years of careful tending, instead of a product of our own century.

On the fringe of the castle's parkland stands the church of St Peter with its splendid shingled spire and its much-admired brasses, especially that of Sir Thomas Bullen in his robes of a Knight of the Garter and with his feet resting on a griffin. Another fine brass, 100 years older, is Margaret Cheyne's. With angels at her head and a dog at her feet, she was buried in 1419, but the church was about 200 years old when she was laid to rest.

Behind the church, and leading from the rear of the tended graveyard, a path ($2^1/_2$ miles, 1 hour) goes along the edge of a damp woodland where a stream has carved a deep trench, runs at the back of a row of houses and is led by fences towards Chiddingstone. It is a beautiful path, especially in the spring. Between Park Wood and Tangle Wood, shaded by trees, the path crosses a sunken lane on a wooden bridge. Through Moor Wood near the hamlet of Hill Hoath it plunges between the sandstone walls of a miniature gorge over which ancient beeches claw their roots. The path skirts a farm and finally climbs through the same sloping fields taken on the way from Penshurst, and so reaches its destination in the street at Chiddingstone.

Upstream from Hever flat meadows which are waterlogged after heavy rain mark the outskirts of Edenbridge, a small town

Places to Visit In and Around Sevenoaks and Edenbridge

Bough Beech Nature Reserve
Bough Beech Reservoir, 5 miles
south-west of Sevenoaks
Bird reserve at northern end of
reservoir. Information centre
(manned by Kent Trust for Nature
Conservation) in oast-house
nearby.

Chartwell (NT)
2 miles south of Westerham
Home and gardens of Sir Winston
Churchill for 40 years, now open to
the public. Restaurant in car park.

Chiddingstone
4 miles east of Edenbridge
Delightful Tudor village, protected
by the National Trust.

Chiddingstone Castle
4 miles east of Edenbridge
Castellated manor house containing fine collection of oriental art
treasures, Japanese lacquer, etc.
Extensive grounds, with a lake as
a feature. Fishing by day permit.

Emmetts Garden (NT)
4 miles west of Sevenoaks,
between Ide Hill and Toys Hill
About 5 acres of hillside shrub
garden adjacent to Toys Hill
woodlands. The house is not open.

Haxted Mill Museum
2 miles west of Edenbridge
Working watermill, built around
1680, houses a museum and
picture gallery of mills, with
working models.

Hever Castle
$2^1/_2$ miles east of Edenbridge
Former home of Anne Boleyn.
Beautiful moated castle with Tudor
style houses adjacent. Large,
romantic gardens with lake. Italian
garden with classical sculpture.

Ightham Mote (NT)
5 miles east of Sevenoaks
A superb fourteenth-century
moated manor house, one of the
finest in Britain.

Knole House (NT)
Sevenoaks
One of England's largest houses,
set in the middle of 1,000 acres of
deer park. House contains rare
textiles, antiques, portraits by
Gainsborough and Reynolds, large
collection of silver. Pedestrians
only through park, except visitors
to the house. Park always open.

Old Soar Manor
2 miles south of Borough Green
The solar block of a late thirteenth-
century knights' dwelling.

Penshurst Place
6 miles south-east of Edenbridge
A magnificent manor house, home
for centuries of the Sidney family.

Riverhill House Gardens
Sevenoaks, south of the town, on
A225
Early eighteenth-century house
with Victorian refinements open to
pre-arranged parties only.
Terraced gardens with superb
views open to the public.

Toys Hill
Brasted, 5 miles south-west of
Sevenoaks
200 acres of woodland managed
by the National Trust. Footpath
walks, rhododendrons, fine views.

Doggets Barn, Edenbridge

masquerading as a large village. With two railway stations on separate lines and a light industrial estate creating a busy air, **Edenbridge** has lost its rural atmosphere, but this is easily regained within a mile of its centre. In its centre the High Street ages and grows in character towards the south. Here the Old Crown Hotel spreads its sign over the street; behind it, in a recently renovated square, a lovely old tithe barn houses the town's council chamber. A little beyond there are typical boarded houses turned into shops, and an old disused mill on an all-but-forgotten stream now given a new lease of life as a restaurant. The church stands nearby, up a narrow entrance leading from the square and

The moat at Bloxham Manor

The village green, Groombridge

occupying the site of an earlier Saxon place of worship.

It was the Romans who took the road through Edenbridge. Across the river, that in those times had no name, they built a bridge, but this was replaced in Saxon times by one built by Eadhelm. Thus Edenbridge grew from Eadhelm's Bridge, rather than being the 'bridge over the Eden', the river becoming suitably named as an afterthought. Nowadays the road goes over an attractive stone bridge dated 1836 that replaces both Roman and Saxon originals, and continues to the south in a straight line, towards the Sussex border. Long ago, this corner of the Weald was renowned for its iron-making, and outside the village of Cowden reminders of past industry live on in names like Furnace Farm and Hammerwood.

Cowden's saviour is a road which runs half a mile from it and takes most of the traffic away from its main street. It is a village of great charm with white painted houses, a church with shingles on its tower and spire, with Sussex and Surrey very close. There are several fine old houses scattered about the outlying district, and footpaths and lanes to walk along. By following the lanes eastwards, ignoring the obvious East Grinstead-Tunbridge Wells road, it is possible to

Haxted Mill, near Edenbridge

catch a glimpse of a past era: country hamlets tied still to the land, quiet country pubs half hidden from the outside world.

Groombridge is half in Kent, half in Sussex. Kent has the better portion and it is worth a diversion to visit. An attractive sloping triangular green with tile-hung cottages line two sides and opposite, the moated manor house, Groombridge Place, which occupies the site of a former Norman Castle. At its gates is a lovely church built as the private chapel of John Packer — 'That worthy Patriot' — of Groombridge Place, as a thanksgiving in 1625 for the return of Charles I, then Prince of Wales, from his ill-planned visit to Spain to woo the Infanta.

Beside the church a footpath ($2^1/_2$ miles, 1 hour) leads into the park of Groombridge Place, and this gives an opportunity to gain a view of what is considered by some to be a perfect example of a seventeenth-century moated house. The grounds, which are open to the public via Groombridge Park footpaths, are quite lovely and owe something of their beauty to John Evelyn who was, among many other things, a gifted amateur landscape gardener. The path continues through the park, heading above the stream to the east. After a little over a mile it crosses a lane, passes through the parkland of Holmewood House, and at last crosses the stream — and the county boundary — at High Rocks. This tree-shrouded outcrop is a popular site for family outings, and with rock climbers.

Rock climbers from the south-east also climb the mellow sandstone outcrop of Harrison's Rocks, not far from Groombridge, but accessible without charge, unlike High Rocks. These may be reached by taking the road past Groombridge Station, bearing right at the fork a quarter of a mile beyond the railway bridge, and then turning right shortly afterwards to the car park set on the edge of a forestry plantation. The walk ($^3/_4$ mile, $^1/_2$ hour) through the plantation to the rocks makes a pleasant stroll even for those without the aim of climbing.

And so to **Royal Tunbridge Wells**. The approach from the west is through farmland, which gives way to woodlands that skirt the common. Curious outcrops of sandstone stand in the bracken and grass, and the town comes into view in the hollow below. It was here, on the common, that the wife of Charles I, Queen Henrietta Maria, camped with her retinue in 1630 on her visit to the newly-discovered spa to recuperate after the birth of the future Charles II. The town has grown since then with a plentiful supply of hotels to make the camping-out of royalty unnecessary, but royal patronage continued through the seventeenth, eighteenth and nineteenth centuries until 1909 when Edward VII granted its 'Royal' prefix.

Royal Tunbridge Wells still has the spring that gave rise to its fame. Royalty, the aristocracy, the famous and the curious came here. Its heyday was in the mid-eighteenth century when Beau Nash adopted the role of master of ceremonies and organised society with concerts, balls and other entertainments such as gambling, with the aid of the so-called 'Queen of the Touters', Sarah Porter, whose job was to pester innocent strollers around The Pantiles with the aim of driving them into the gambling halls. The Pantiles remain; a quaint, respectable pedestrian way adjoining the chalybeate spring, with its row of lime trees throwing shade over the clay-tiled paving and its white colonnade retaining an air of harmony, order and tranquillity.

The Pantiles, Royal Tunbridge Wells

Ightham Mote

The common gives the town a sense of space, for it comes down to The Pantiles and the shopping area that is never far away. So resident and visitor alike can be one moment in the country, on gorse-lined footpaths and the next in amongst the shopping crowds. It is a curious mix, but a refreshing one. Elsewhere, Royal Tunbridge Wells recalls its past with several fine Regency houses in the Mount Sion district and the curve of Calverley Park Crescent where white-painted iron pillars support a covered promenade over a terrace originally planned to be a shopping arcade for the houses of Decimus Burton's Calverley estate. Nearby, Calverley Grounds has rose gardens, shrubs, tennis courts, putting greens and a paddling pool for children; it was once the garden of Mount Pleasant House.

The town has survived changing fortunes. It grew from the discovery of its mineral spring. It has courted royalty, became Victoria's 'dear' town and then suffered a brief period out of favour as spas declined in popularity. But it has survived, not least because of its past glories that may still be savoured; and not least because it occupies a position of privilege, sitting as it does on the edge of the High Weald.

Returning to the Greensand Ridge at Sevenoaks it is worth journeying eastwards on a winding of leaf-shaded lanes to continue the exploration of this narrow but scenically delightful range of hills. Immediately below Sevenoaks, on the sunny slope of the ridge, **Riverhill House** crouches beside a sunken track that was once an important highway through the Weald. The house was built in 1714 and gazes over a magnificent sweep of the valley, but it is the garden of lovely specimen trees and shrubs, collected from around the world by an ancestor of the family that now lives here, which make a visit particularly worthwhile. A somewhat wild garden in places, it has an atmosphere difficult to define. But go when the foliage is turning to burnished gold and you will find it a most memorable place.

A lane winds along the crest of the ridge, running at first alongside the boundary of Knole Park, mostly among beechwoods but coming out here and there to open bowls of meadowland, orchards or small hop gardens. An alternative route breaks away to give an opportunity to visit **One Tree Hill** (a beautiful viewpoint) before swooping down the slope to Under River. There are footpaths too, naturally, and one which leads from One Tree Hill that follows the course of an old pack-horse route and takes you directly to Ightham Mote in little over $1^1/_2$ miles (45 minutes). By road the journey is twice as far and you miss the views.

 Of all the medieval manor houses in England, **Ightham Mote** is reckoned to be among the very finest. Small and manageable, set in an idyllic and intimate combe with trees around and a moat washing against the soft ragstone walls, it commands one's immediate affection. The moat is not what gave this fourteenth-century manor its name, but the fact that it occupies the site of an ancient meeting place (mote). It was built round an open courtyard with huge oak beams and two chapels; the older, a medieval one, ranged above the hall, while the other dates from Tudor times with pews, linenfold panelling and a pulpit. It is the timber of Ightham Mote that stands out; the Jacobean staircase, the crown post and rafters of the solar and the

Places to Visit In and Around Royal Tunbridge Wells

Church of King Charles the Martyr
London Road, Royal Tunbridge Wells
Built in 1678, it has a very fine ceiling plastered in part by Wren's chief plasterer at St Paul's. Also an unusual white marble font.

Harrison's Rocks
6 miles south-west of Royal Tunbridge Wells, at Groombridge
A sandstone outcrop lining the edge of a forestry plantation. Rock climbing, forest walks.

High Rocks
2 miles west of Royal Tunbridge Wells
A 70ft-high outcrop of sandstone rocks forming narrow canyons. Scenic walks with rustic bridges over the canyons. Climbing. Occupies the site of a Stone Age camp.

The Pantiles
Royal Tunbridge Wells
Paved area of square clay tiles laid in 1700 beside an attractive row of colonnaded shops. Adjoining is the chalybeate spring where it is possible still to drink the waters.

Tunbridge Wells Museum and Art Gallery
Central Library, Mount Pleasant
Displays of local history, and a fine collection of Tunbridge ware, wooden souvenirs first made in the seventeenth-century.

corbels carved with cheerful peasants at work. The skeleton of a young woman is said to have been found walled-up in the great hall, while another local legend has it that a soldier fell in love with one of the daughters of the house, but while trying to slip through the water gate to see her, fell into the moat and was drowned. The Cromwellian suit of armour he supposedly wore, is now on display. There are two stone bridges across the moat, patterned with lichens and moss.

Ightham Mote was in the hands of the Selby family for nearly 300 years, but its last private owner was an American businessman, Charles Henry Robinson, who saw it as a young man while on a cycling tour. Eventually an opportunity came in 1954 for him to buy it. He subsequently spent a great deal of money on its refurbishment and finally left it to the National Trust in 1985. The Trust discovered dry rot, wet rot and an ugly assortment of other problems, and immediately launched an appeal for £1,000,000 to put it right.

Leaving the house and heading north along the narrow lane, you go through the hamlet of Ivy Hatch and come to **Ightham**, a village of considerable charm with a clutch of half-timbered houses in the centre. In Victorian times the village grocer was one Benjamin Harrison who gained international fame as an archaeologist, mostly due to his discoveries at nearby **Oldbury Hill** on the other side of the A25, a great earthwork covering 151 acres which was used in the Iron Age as a hillfort. This is worth a visit, but in inclement weather you will need wellington boots as the approach can be rather muddy. The best way to it is from Oldbury Lane which cuts away from the A25 by the Cob Tree Inn. Along the lane you pass a fifteenth-century timbered hall house, Old Bury Hall (not open to the public), and soon after take a bridleway rising into woods. This becomes a deeply sunken track, a veritable cleft overhung with trees, and it brings you to the north-eastern corner of the hillfort. Not far from here are low rock shelters used by Palaeolithic hunters and thought to be the oldest 'dwellings' in Kent.

Returning to Ightham Mote the lane continues down into the Weald just west of Shipbourne (pronounced Shibbun) and on to Hildenborough and Tonbridge. But again the visitor who leaves his car and takes to the footpaths has the best of it, for there are two enjoyable cross-country ways to get to Shipbourne, with opportunities to extend the walk farther along the hills to explore more of this delightful countryside. One route takes a track westward from the farmyard across the lane from Ightham Mote. You go as far as Wilmot Cottage then head down into the valley across the fields with Shipbourne Church and neighbouring oast-houses beckoning. The other leaves directly from Ightham Mote heading eastwards, then branches south over meadows and alongside a wood with a huge panorama drawing you down.

Shipbourne is an uncrowded, somewhat straggling village, the best of it lying back from the road. More narrow lanes strike away into the heart of the countryside. Footpaths too, leading to Dunk's Green, past 'orchards' of Kentish cobs. There is a meagre stream, the River Bourne, easing out of the hills here just a short stroll away from the Kentish Volunteer pub. Meagre though it may be, its power has been harnessed to work mills adapted for paper making. One of

Plaxtol Church

Old Soar Manor

these, Roughway Mill, can be seen from the lane which climbs among orchards and hop gardens towards Gover Hill.

Plaxtol occupies a fine viewpoint on the ridge above Shipbourne. On the edge of the village the great mansion of **Fairlawne** overlooks its parkland and the Weald beyond, but the village itself is less pretentious. It is an attractive place draped on a hillslope. The church stands at the head of the slope on a crossroads with a lovely row of weatherboarded cottages nearby, but it is Old Soar Manor which brings most visitors to this corner of the county. To find it involves a study of the map and a twist of narrow lanes among orchards and hop gardens.

Old Soar Manor, owned by the National Trust but in the care of English Heritage, is the solar block of a thirteenth-century manor house built by the Culpepers. There are vaulted undercrofts below, a chapel at one corner and a garderobe (toilet) at another. There are also big windows at either end and a king-post roof. Attached to it is a red brick Georgian farmhouse standing on the site of the medieval hall, and presumably the solar would have been demolished along with the hall had it not made a useful barn for years until its true value was at last recognised.

Rising above the nearby orchards is the great crown of **Mereworth Woods**, nearly 6sq miles of woodland (beech, oak and large areas of coppice) with but one road cutting through. During the reign of the first Elizabeth wild boar were hunted here. Today you are more likely to see its grey squirrels and the occasional deer if you take to one of the many footpaths that make a north-south crossing of this, one of the largest areas of unbroken woodland left in Kent. There is a road which skirts the western edge of Mereworth Woods, joined not far from Old Soar Manor, and it runs along the upper hillside with some glorious views near Gover Hill. Then it swings round to **West Peckham**, a small village with a picturesque green trapped in the midst of orchard country. The road misses the best of the village, but if you take the turning for the church you will find it. The church of St Dunstan overlooks the green. Beyond the hedge on the far side march the serried ranks of apple trees. Go in spring time when the blossoms are out and be deafened by the activity of bees. Along one side of the village green there stands a row of cottages and The Swan Inn, which proudly displays a sign announcing that it recently won a 'Country Pub of the Year' award. The village is old and, like so many of Kent's villages, was mentioned in the *Domesday Book*. Strangely the church was not included in the survey, although it was clearly here when the Normans came for it has Saxon work in the tower. It is an interesting place of worship with an array of carved wooden figures behind the altar, a curious raised chapel with box pews, a seventeenth-century pulpit and a fine screen. Apparently in the late sixteenth century, John Comper (a local resident) had his three children baptised with the strangest and most depressing names imagineable. His son was named Remember Death, and his daughters, Lament and Sorrow. But the church is very much aware of the presence in past centuries of the Culpeper family.

It was Sir John Culpeper who gave the manor to the Knights Hospitallers of St John of Jerusalem in 1408 and it was the same Sir John who built the large house standing some way from the village to the west, called Oxen Hoath. A public footpath allows access through the drive of this mansion, and continues south across fields to Hadlow. But on the way it passes close by a fanciful lake with a neat stone bridge over it, the house standing back admiring broad vistas of the Medway Valley and the Weald beyond.

Continuing along the road out of West Peckham you will cross the B2016 and come to **Mereworth**, a village that is proof enough of the power wielded by aristocrats of the past. In 1720 the Honourable John Fane, later Earl of Westmorland, built a Palladian-style mansion (a direct replica of the Villa Rotunda at Vicenza) deep within the Kentish countryside. But his view was spoilt by the nearby village, so he had a new village built where he could not see it and had the old houses pulled down. He also built the villagers a new church, and this is an incongruous building, a mixture of styles clearly borrowed from St Paul's in Covent Garden and St Martin's in the Fields. Memorials from the old church were also transferred to the new, and this true hybrid of a place has become one of the curiosities of Kent. The other curiosity of Mereworth, the so-called castle, stands mostly hidden by trees today and is not open to the public.

Mereworth stands at a junction of busy roads. The A26 is the main Tonbridge to Maidstone road, while northward the A228 crosses by one of the Battle of Britain airfields and leads to **West Malling**, the heart of which has now been bypassed and made a conservation

Waterfall at St Mary's Abbey, West Malling

The quintain, or tilting post, Offham

area. The unusually wide High Street is lined by mostly Georgian houses; there is an abbey for Anglican Benedictine nuns in Swan Street, and a monastery in Water Lane for Anglican Cistercian monks. Both are places of tranquillity and architectural grace. William the Conqueror's great Bishop Gundulph founded the abbey in the eleventh century (it was destroyed in 1190 and then rebuilt), and he also built St Leonard's Tower nearby. The impressive keep is all that is left of the house in which Gundulph is said to have resided. The tower is situated near the entrance to Manor Park Country Park; 52 acres of parkland with a 3-acre lake overlooked by an eighteenth-century manor house.

A footpath (2^1/$_2$ miles, 1 hour) leads right past St Leonard's Tower, heads through orchard country and around the edges of large open fields with views to the North Downs, and comes to **Offham**, an ancient settlement. The Romans built a road from Smallhythe (see Chapter 7) through the Weald to London, and Offham grew beside it. The village has some fine houses and picturesque corners and is noted far and wide for the quintain on its triangular green. The sport of tilting is thought to have originated with the Romans, and is no doubt more amusing to spectators than participants. The quintain, or tilting post, is an upright post with an arm that revolves when hit. One end of the arm has a flat target, while from the other is suspended either a sandbag or truncheon. Horsemen gallop at the quintain and strike the target with a lance, which in turn spins the sandbag (or other missile). The rider has to dodge quickly out of the way before being struck on the back of the head. The sport was popular throughout the Middle Ages and is sometimes revived on Offham Green during May Day celebrations.

East of Malling the greensand hills are squeezed by the great bow of the River Medway. As you travel farther eastward, so countryside is replaced by housing estates that signal the beginnings of Maidstone. Behind the town rises the long wall of the North Downs, but south of it the Greensand Ridge resumes in an arc towards the Channel coast far off. On its slopes at first fruit farms speckle the hills, while below there spreads a rich agricultural land broken with woods and spinneys, patched with orchards and hop gardens and enlivened by some of the loveliest villages in all of Kent. This is the Weald, that part of the county most deserving of the title, the Garden of England.

6

THE WEALD

Set in its hollow, Tunbridge Wells is very much an urban island in a rural landscape. The Weald is all around. Running roughly eastwards away from the town a series of lush green hills contain within them folding vales, woods and orchards, the quintessential English landscape.

In the Weald are to be found villages of immense charm. Villages whose names give a clue to the country; Biddenden, Benenden, Rolvenden, Horsmonden. Or names that end in 'hurst', Goudhurst, Lamberhurst, Hawkhurst. For the Weald, as has already been noted, was once an almost impenetrable forest — or wood (hurst) — and small communities were established in clearings (dens). Here the Saxons grubbed for existence and their pigs grew fat among the tree roots. In the wilderness of this vast forest there were 'herds of deer and droves of hogs only'. But gradually inroads were made upon the woodland cover. Trees were felled for building, for fuel, to establish areas of cultivation, to fire furnaces and to make charcoal. The cloth trade flourished here and villages prospered. Now, although large stretches of woodland are still a feature of the region, agriculture takes pride of place and in springtime an extravagance of blossom is displayed to fill the air with wonder.

There is much to admire within the Weald, whether in the huge panoramas from the summits of these hills or in individual features. Many of the villages have managed to remain attractive communities justifiably proud of their heritage. There are romantic country seats set in gardens of national fame; vineyards producing wines once more in a region that was first put to the grape by the Romans.

In the heart of the county whole valleys are cultivating hops, and flat lands bearing fruit trees.

To the north and west of Royal Tunbridge Wells a group of hills stub out to fill the square of countryside bounded by the young Medway and one of its tributaries which forms the Kent-Sussex border. The most northerly of these Wealden ridges breaks out from Southborough and has the residential village of **Bidborough** enchantingly set on the crest facing over the Medway's valley to the Greensand Ridge. Hidden from the road is the old village overlooked by its Saxon-based church, a small, crowded place full of silence save for the persistent ticking of the clock whose great pendulum hangs for all to see. But as you emerge from the rather dark interior to a blaze of sunlight, so you gaze over cottage rooftops into a deep green valley. A tight lane drops into that valley and, by 2 miles of twistings, comes to another fine hilltop village, that of Speldhurst.

Speldhurst was first mentioned in a document dated AD768 and stands on the fringe of the Wealden iron country. Opposite the church is the thirteenth-century half-timbered George and Dragon pub. The church is a tasteful Victorian replacement of an original Norman building which was destroyed by lightning in 1791. The stained glass Burne-Jones windows are considered classics of their kind.

Across the meadows from Speldhurst is **Bullingstone Lane** with its string of lovely fifteenth-century cottages caught in a tight valley and with Averys Wood stretching out towards Fordcombe, the first village west of Royal Tunbridge Wells that has a fully rural aspect.

To the south-east of Royal Tunbridge Wells the little River Teise runs along the Sussex border. There is a ridge of hills and a valley; the river forms a pool and a lake. This is the serene setting for the ruins of **Bayham Abbey**. Across the nearby pool, and standing upon a rising hill, is another Bayham Abbey, though this is a gabled mansion of the nineteenth century. The ruins represent an abbey founded nearly 800 years ago by Premonstratensian monks. The mansion stands in Kent, the ruins are just across the border, in Sussex. The river divides the counties.

One of the tributaries of the Teise is the little River Winn that joins the Teise by the abbey ruins. A little over a mile from the ruins

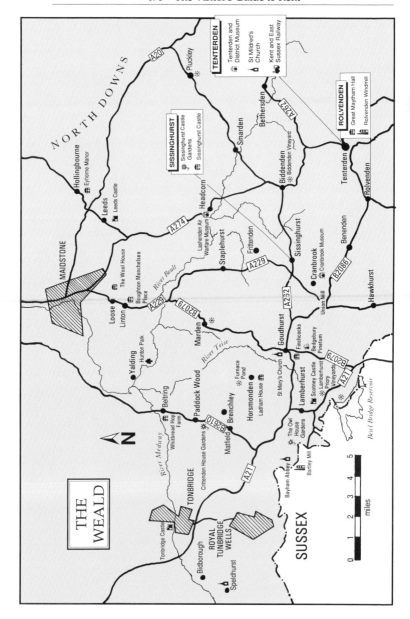

TENTERDEN
- Tenterden and District Museum
- St Mildred's Church
- Kent and East Sussex Railway

ROLVENDEN
- Great Maytham Hall
- Rolvenden Windmill

SISSINGHURST
- Sissinghurst Castle Gardens
- Sissinghurst Castle

NORTH DOWNS

A20

Pluckley

Bethersden

Smarden

Biddenden
- Biddenden Vineyard

Hollingbourne
- Eyhorne Manor

Leeds
- Leeds Castle

Headcorn

Lashenden Air Warfare Museum

Staplehurst

Frittenden

Sissinghurst

Tenterden

Rolvenden

Benenden

A274

A229

Cranbrook
- Cranbrook Museum

Hawkhurst

B2086

The Wool House

Boughton Monchelsea Place

River Beult

MAIDSTONE

Loose
Linton

A229

B2079

Marden

Hunton Park

Yalding

River Teise

Goudhurst

Finchcocks

Union Mill

A262

A232

Bedgebury Pinetum

St Mary's Church

Lamberhurst
- Scotney Castle
- Lamberhurst Priory Vineyards

B2079

A21

Bewl Bridge Reservoir

Paddock Wood

Beltring

Brenchley

Horsmonden
- Furnace Pond
- Ladham House

Whitbread Hop Farm

B2160

Matfield

Crittenden House Gardens

The Owl House Gardens

Bayham Abbey

Bartley Mill

River Medway

N

THE WEALD

TONBRIDGE
- Tonbridge Castle

ROYAL TUNBRIDGE WELLS

Bidborough

Speldhurst

A21

SUSSEX

miles
0 1 2 3 4 5

Bartley Mill

*Cottage with a view,
Bidborough*

(admittedly in Sussex, but near enough to warrant inclusion here) the Winn has been harnassed to power **Bartley Mill**, which was originally owned by the monks of Bayham Abbey. It is an attractive building slumped in a hollow beside a narrow lane that cuts south of the B2169; behind it is the mill pond, and behind that a pair of smaller ponds stocked with trout. The watermill has been restored and is once again operational for the first time since the early part of the century, with flour being milled from corn grown organically on neighbouring land. Contained within the mill building is a bakery, with tea rooms and shop adjacent, so bread bought at Bartley Mill could hardly taste fresher! The mill is open to the public daily throughout the year; the open plan layout of the building making it possible to view every stage of the milling process, and visitors can also fish for trout in the ponds at the rear.

The silence and isolation that surround Bayham Abbey are the more remarkable for the contrast in summer of the thunderous roar of traffic along the A21. If, however, the lanes are followed eastwards around farmhouses and beside ponds the unhurried traveller reaches **The Owl House**. This sixteenth-century smuggler's cottage, all tile and timber, has a delightful garden, while not far away is spread the village of Lamberhurst, with weatherboarded houses and fine rolling country to the east.

Lamberhurst's church stands away from the village with a commanding view of a valley of the Teise. Across the Teise there is a path towards the trees on a hill which hides Scotney Castle. Before visiting the castle and its gardens, it is pleasant to walk along this footpath (5 miles, 3 hours), for it gives a flavour of the countryside.

It begins in the churchyard, beside a large golf course. From the lower gate in the churchyard the path heads down to cross the stream by a footbridge, then up to the grounds of Scotney Castle with its rhododendrons and azaleas. Crossing the castle drive the way continues through a gate and into a slope of parkland with a glorious soft-valley panorama. The route continues towards the south-east, crosses two minor streams and into woodlands to find a track heading left, eventually reaching the hamlet of Kilndown. Left again the path now goes through the woods on its return to Lamberhurst by way of the northern stretch of Scotney's park. It meets the original path above the Teise and concludes an enjoyable loop at the church.

Scotney Castle is full of romance. It stands with a medieval stone bridge, a circular tower and grey ruins. It has occupied this idyllic site for 600 years, for it was begun in 1379 by Roger de Ashburnham. Most of old Scotney dates from the seventeenth century; its picturesque decay was aided by Edward Hussey in the late 1830s. He created the gardens here, too, for in the quarry from which stone was cut to make his Tudor-style house overlooking old Scotney, he planted the great shrubs and fine trees that grip the hills with colour.

Lamberhurst village, which stretches between church and castle, was once a centre for the Wealden iron industry that made the iron railings that went around St Paul's. Today that industry is all but forgotten. Instead there is a growing emphasis on viticulture. In the sixteenth century a Lamberhurst priory housed Augustinian monks who cultivated vines in the Weald. In 1972 that link with the past was brought back to life, and today the village boasts one of the largest vineyards in Britain, producing white wines from grapes of German origin. A vineyard trail is signposted from the main street, and it leads to a specialist farm where viticulture processes from the vine to the bottle are seen.

South of the village lie the outstretched fingers of **Bewl Bridge** **Reservoir**; partly in Kent, but mostly in Sussex. This is the largest inland water in the south-east, formed by the flooding of valleys during the mid-seventies in order to supply a sizable portion of Kent with water. It also provides plenty of scope for boating, fishing and other recreation along its margins, with many footpaths and bridleways leading along its shores and through neighbouring woodlands.

The county boundary winds its way across the reservoir, out to Flimwell and passes to the south of Hawkhurst. On the Kentish side, between Lamberhurst and Hawkhurst, there is a rich heritage of woodland. The hills and their valleys are, in places, parklike with beeches, oak, horse-chestnut and lime; but there is nothing quite as magnificent as the unique collection of conifers — the finest in Europe — of **Bedgebury Pinetum**, part of the Forestry Commission's 2,500-acre Bedgebury Forest.

All who complain — often with good cause — about the insensitive planting of mean rows of single-species conifers swamping parts of Britain, should see how in Bedgebury a beautiful area of

Scotney Castle

The Owl House, Lamberhurst

Lamberhurst, the path that leads to Scotney Castle

Places to Visit In and Around Lamberhurst and Goudhurst

Bayham Abbey (EH)
2 miles west of Lamberhurst, on
B2169
The remains of an early
thirteenth-century abbey
founded by Premonstratensian
monks in a peaceful wooded
valley.

Bedgebury Pinetum
3 miles south of Goudhurst
village, off B2079
Europe's largest collection of
conifers — more than 200
different species — set out in
gentle rolling parkland, as part of
the Forestry Commission's
2,500-acre Bedgebury Forest.
Woodland walks, shrubs, conifer
nursery, visitor centre. Large car
park.

Bewl Bridge Reservoir
South of Lamberhurst, off A21
The largest inland water south of
the Thames. Fishing, water-side
footpaths, large car park and
visitor centre. Canoeing, sailing,
etc, for club members only.

Furnace Pond
Horsmonden, 4 miles north-west
of Goudhurst
A large sheet of water set within
woodlands and hop gardens,
good fishing — day permits
available from house on its bank
— footpath link with fine village
of Brenchley nearby.

Finchcocks
2 miles south-west of Goudhurst,
off A262
An elegant baroque house of
1725. A 'living museum of music'
with historic instruments on
which demonstrations and
recitals are given.

Lamberhurst Priory Vineyards
South of the village, approached
along the B2100 Wadhurst road
One of the largest vineyards in
Britain, open to the public with a
marked trail, wine-tasting and
vineyard shop.

The Owl House Gardens
1 mile north-west of Lamberhurst, off A21
13 acres of gardens in a
woodland setting. The sixteenth-
century cottage is not open to
the public.

Scotney Castle (NT)
$1^{1}/_{2}$ miles south of Lamberhurst,
on A21
Romantic ruins of fourteenth-
century castle set in idyllic
gardens and parkland.

St Mary's Church
Goudhurst
Its setting is perfect, the views
from its doors are far-reaching
and known throughout the
county. Inside, many monuments
to the powerful Culpeper family.

evergreens has been created. This is a scientific collection, an open-air laboratory that started life as a rural Kew after the death of some of Kew Gardens' conifers through pollution. The 200 species of trees, set out on the gentle folding hillsides and valleys, are sufficient to inspire admiration for the combined artistry of nature and the creators of the site. Bedgebury is a place of great beauty, no less lovely for the exotic nature of its trees — cypresses, redwoods, silver spruce, juniper, rhododendrons — in this very English setting.

In order to discover some of the riches of the area, which has so much to offer, it is necessary to take to the byways. On leaving Bedgebury, a pleasant road leads up to **Goudhurst**, set on a steep hill with one of the finest belvederes in all of Kent. It is a pretty village, from the duckpond at the crossroads to the church at the summit of the hill; but cursed by traffic that constantly sweeps round the sharp bends of the main street in a nose-to-tail procession on bright summer days.

Goudhurst's street is a classic composition of tile-hung or weather-boarded houses. At the top of the hill two pubs stand almost side by side; opposite them an old tiled residence overhangs the road, but between pub and house the picture is completed by the squat tower of the fourteenth-century St Mary's Church. From here much of the Weald can be seen to the north in one clear sweep and southwards, it is claimed, one can see as far as Hastings. Inside the church are gathered generations of one of Kent's great families, the Culpepers. They are to be found in a number of the county's churches, but none so numerous as here. There are Culpepers at rest on cushions; she with her hair carefully braided, he protected in his armour. There are Culpepers in brass, stone, and wood. They were a big family with children gathered in quantity. One collection numbers a dozen, another forms a group of eighteen, eleven of them kneeling by their father and mother. Also at rest here is John Bedgebury, a stone's throw from his old estate which passed into Culpeper hands through the marriage of his sister to a Culpeper son.

Outside the church there was once a battle between Kingsmill's gang of Hawkhurst smugglers and a group of local vigilantes led by William Sturt. The smuggling gang terrorised parts of Kent and Sussex during the early eighteenth century, but they met their match in Sturt's vigilantes and the church register records Kingsmill as

Bedgebury Pinetum

Matfield

Brenchley with its oast-house and hop poles, both familiar sights in this part of Kent

being 'killed by the discharge of a lead bullet'.

Down the hill a little to the south-west of the village a side road winds off to a large and elegant Georgian house; **Finchcocks**. It was built in 1725 for Edward Bathurst, and is a charming red brick baroque mansion set in parkland a short distance along the Teise from Scotney Castle. Here, early keyboard instruments form part of an historical musical collection, and recitals are frequently given to the public. As a 'living museum of music' Finchcocks has found a new and interesting lease of life.

Elsewhere, the countryside that surrounds Goudhurst owes

much to the hop. In winter much of the land appears to be laid bare, but come summer and fields everywhere are strung like harps, while September is extremely busy and a glow comes from working oasts at night. Hops have been growing wild in Kent for at least 2,000 years, but they were not cultivated in gardens until Flemish immigrants imported a new strain during the reign of Edward III in the fourteenth century. Yet it was still another 100 years before the hop was universally accepted as a flavouring for beer, thus replacing cloves and cinnamon. Oast-houses followed much later to serve as the kiln, or oven, where the hops are dried, and their distinctive shape with white-painted cowls developed over years of experiment. Square-shaped oasts were a product of the late eighteenth century while rounded oasts appeared in the nineteenth century. But it is not unusual to find both forms side by side in the same farmyard. Nothing is more essentially Kentish than a vignette of oast-houses, hop gardens, orchards and sheep. Goudhurst has them all.

A winding of quiet lanes link Goudhurst with other charming villages and estates caught among the orchards, hop gardens and meadows of the Weald. Among them is **Horsmonden**, around its green, with its church 2 miles (1 hour) away across the meadows and tucked among farm buildings. A footpath to it starts near the village green and goes through some quite delightful country. To the west of the village will be found one of the finest of all Wealden furnace ponds once, although it seems impossible to believe now, at the heart of England's industry. Beyond this pond lies **Brenchley**, a perfect collection of Tudor cottages in an almost perfect street, an avenue of clipped yews leading to the church, and views all around of hills and the Weald. Siegfried Sassoon lived nearby, and he painted it with eloquent prose in *The Weald of Youth*. Various gardens are open at times in the summer, but the landscape around is nature's own garden, and a tour through it reveals some of the best-tended, best-loved country in the south-east.

Matfield stands on its own a couple of miles to the west of Brenchley alongside the B2160; a spacious Wealden village originally grouped around one of the largest village greens in Kent. The green has its duckpond at one end, backed by a charming group of red brick and tile-hung cottages and a Georgian manor, while beside the road another handful of spruce cottages add balance and har-

mony. Just outside the village is Crittenden House Gardens containing two ponds. These are sometimes open to the public.

Not 6 miles north of Goudhurst on the Maidstone road and at the
heart of blossom country is the village of **Marden**, a straggling place
with its ancient stocks set beside the thirteenth-century church.
Orchards lie all around, and in springtime 'blossom routes' are
signposted so that the visitor can follow the byways and see the
glorious colour and tranquillity of the scene. Of course, blossom is
susceptible to the whims of the weather and it is difficult to predict
the precise moment of perfection of this countryside, but as a rough
guide late April or early May is the best time to visit the area. The
Garden of England then lives up to its name.

HEART OF KENT COUNTRY TOUR (50 miles, 2 hours)
This signposted tour leads through the heart of the county's hop and
fruit growing countryside. Parts of the route take you into landscapes described in Chapters 3 and 5 as you cross the Medway and
go onto the Greensand Ridge. Mostly it remains in the Weald. The
route has distinctive brown road signs depicting Kent's 'Invicta'
white horse symbol. As a circular tour it can be joined at any point.
The route is described travelling in an anti-clockwise direction.

From **Brenchley** Church drive downhill among orchards to
Horsmonden, a one-time centre for iron-making, but now very
much an agricultural village with orchards and hop gardens surrounding it. The tour continues eastward to cross the River Teise and
reaches the B2079 where you turn left. Harpers Farm has a trail
among orchards, hop gardens and woodlands and is open to the
public from May to August.

Leave the Marden road to find Curtisden Green on the way to
Staplehurst. On the way you pass Brattle Farm Museum (all sorts of
farming implements and machinery from the past two centuries)
about 1¹/₂ miles from Staplehurst. One of the most notable features
here is the remarkable south door to the church which is decorated
with twelfth-century iron strapwork featuring a Viking ship with
furled sail, sea monsters, fish and dragons.

Follow the A229 northward with views to the greensand hills
rising from the valley of the River Beult. Orchards and fields of soft
fruit intermingle with great velvet-neat parklands draped down

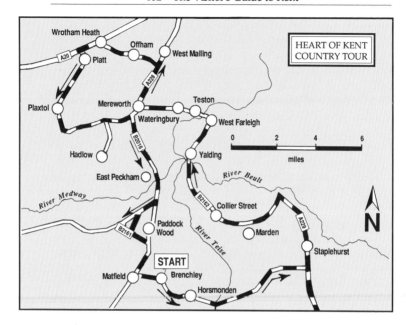

their slopes. Just short of Stile Bridge break away left on the B2079, then head to the right on a minor road to Collier Street and among hop gardens to reach **Yalding**. One of the longest bridges in Kent leads over the Beult into the main part of the village, with its lovely church and wide street lined by a handsome mixture of houses and cottages of various periods. The Medway lies a short distance away to the west with another attractive medieval bridge worth a detour to see. The country tour continues through Yalding and up the hill slope of the Greensand Ridge, cloaked with more orchards and woods, on the way to **West Farleigh**. The route now drops into the Medway's valley and crosses the river by way of Teston Bridge — another superb, if narrow, medieval bridge arching its way across the Medway. On the left bank of the river is Teston Bridge Picnic Site with adequate car parking, toilets and riverside walks.

The main Maidstone-Tonbridge road (A26) is followed through **Wateringbury** and on to **Mereworth**, catching on the way a brief glimpse of the extravagant Mereworth Castle off to the left through the trees. On the edge of the village head north along the A228

towards **West Malling**. Although the tour cuts off to Offham on the ✳
outskirts of West Malling, it is worth continuing into the old market
town, one of the most attractive in this corner of Kent. It has many
good houses, an abbey, a monastery, the Norman keep known as St
Leonard's Tower, and Manor Park Country Park.

Offham is perhaps best known for the quintain (or tilting post) on ✳
the village green, but it also has a pretty assortment of houses,
cottages and pub set in a distinctly agricultural landscape that takes
you to Wrotham Heath. Turning away from the A25 go through **Platt**
(Great Comp gardens nearby), round the edge of Mereworth Woods
and among orchards and hop gardens again, with a short diversion
needed to visit Old Soar Manor, before coming into the hillside
village of **Plaxtol** on the Greensand Ridge.

Continuing to head roughly south, the tour leads through a belt
of farmland with Hadlow Castle seen ahead, joins the A26 once more
going back towards Mereworth but turning away again at a major
roundabout crossed by the B2016. It passes along the edge of **East
Peckham**, crosses the Medway and enters the Weald again at
Beltring, noted for the clustered oasts of the Whitbread Hop Farm.
More hop gardens and orchards accompany the route towards
Matfield, and just before reaching the village signs indicate the way
to Badsell Park Farm Trail (180 acres of fruit and arable farm, with
two nature trails open to the public). From here it is but a short drive
to **Brenchley** where the tour began.

Beyond the River Beult a barrier of orchards arcs from the
Medway Valley. These adorn the hills that are an eastern extension
of the Greensand Ridge. On the river stands **Yalding**. Above and to
the east of the village is a region worth travelling slowly through.
There are lanes that work a route among the orchards and fields of
soft fruit, but better still, a footpath that wanders along the very lip
of the ridge, enjoying magnificent views over the Weald. It takes you
through fields of strawberries and currants, alongside orchards,
across historic parklands too, and as there are other footpaths
skirting the foot of the slope, it is not difficult to work out a circular
tour ($6^1/_2$ miles, 3 hours) that takes in some of the best this countryside has to offer. Below the hills **Hunton Park** occupies about 100
acres of grassland and woods with the thirteenth-century church of
St Mary and the ragstone manor of Hunton Court standing in it. A

footpath allows access, and brings you out to more orchards, oasts and a most attractive fifteenth-century half-timbered house.

Above Hunton Park the hillside is draped with what appears to be one vast market garden. **Linton** stands on the edge of it. A small village alongside the A229, the majority of motorists rushing downhill through it would scarcely notice it. But it is worth finding somewhere to park the car to explore. First go through the car park of The Bull inn (built in 1574) and enjoy the spectacle of orchards plunging down the slope into the huge expanse of the Weald. In springtime when the trees are in blossom this is an unforgettable sight. There is a footpath leading from the pub through these orchards, and if you have the time you could follow it all the way to Yalding and arrange to be met there.

On the other side of the road, nearly opposite The Bull, another footpath takes you through Linton churchyard (the spire of St Nicholas' Church can be seen from far away in the Weald), and into Linton Park, the big white house of which can also be seen from miles away since it stands on the very edge of the hill. Horace Walpole visited Linton Place in 1757 about 20 years after Robert Mann had built it. He was enthusiastic, not just about the house, but its position too. He called it the 'Citadel of Kent, the whole county its garden.' The house is not open to the public, but the footpath through the park is worth following. It leads directly to that other fine deer park, the grounds of Boughton Monchelsea Place.

Although the road which serves it is much more narrow than that of the A229 through Linton, **Boughton Monchelsea** is far better known. It is signposted from the Maidstone road because the house is open to the public — although for views one need only go into the churchyard and gaze out to the south and east. Indeed, from the lychgate it is supposed to be possible on a good day to see beyond the limits of the Weald to the South Downs far off. The village stands to the north of the big house, near the B2163 and not far from Loose (see Chapter 3) on the outskirts of Maidstone. The Romans were here, and a villa from the period of their occupation was excavated in 1841. **Boughton Monchelsea Place** is a large, battlemented, rather dulllooking ragstone mansion which dates from 1567, but manorial rights go back to Norman times when they were granted by William to the Monchensies from whom the village derives its name.

(Boughton, of which there are many in Kent, means 'the clearing in the beech trees'. The Monchensie family died out in 1287.) Robert Rudston who built the present house from locally quarried stone was involved in Sir Thomas Wyatt's rebellion against Queen Mary and had the house confiscated for his troubles. But he was later pardoned and allowed to buy it back again. The deer park below is extensive, and there has been a herd of fallow deer in it since at least 1660. In a sixteenth-century barn near the house there is a display of early farm implements and carriages.

Travelling east along a minor road you come to Chart Sutton, with yet more splendid views, then veer round to the north-east to the road junction at Five Wents and, back on the B2163, come eventually to a village that sits slumped in a fold of hills with the North Downs seen a couple of miles or so away. The village is less known than the castle nearby, and should never be confused with its much larger namesake in Yorkshire. The village is called **Leeds**; it has a squat-towered church, oast-houses and an abbey farm as a reminder that until the Reformation there was an abbey here. The castle provides a vision of Kent that the visitor will never forget. It is one of the finest places England has, a scene of almost unreal magnificence.

It is a shapely construction of mellow stone on two islands in a lake formed by the River Len. In its waters are black swans, ducks and geese, the lake surrounded by greensward and mature woodlands laid out by 'Capability' Brown in the eighteenth century, the oak, beech and horse chestnuts clustered in stately collections to set off the castle itself.

There has been a castle of one form or another in this lake for 1,200 years, ever since Ledian, Chief Minister of the Saxon King Ethelbert of Kent, constructed a wooden fort here in AD857. Some 250 years later, after the Normans arrived, they replaced timber with stone and under the supervision of Robert de Crevecoeur, the basis for the present castle building was established on the smaller of the two islands, known today as the Gloriette. It was in the time of Edward I, however, that the turrets and walls seen today were built, and over several centuries, under one king after another, various adaptations were made and Henry VIII transformed it from a fortification into an extravagant rural palace. Although the main building, joined to the

Leeds Castle and village

Gloriette by a double-storeyed bridge of stone, was only built in 1822, it gives every impression of having been there for many centuries, so well does it fit into the scene.

For over 300 years Leeds Castle was a royal residence, but today it is accessible to the public. There is golf in the park, a walled garden, a woodland garden and footpaths criss-crossing the park. It was Lord Conway of Allington Castle on the Medway, who called Leeds 'the loveliest castle in the world', and there are countless others who would not dispute it.

Returning from Leeds once more into the full sweep of the Weald, you are again among orchards and hop gardens. There are several varieties of hop grown in the Weald for flavouring beer, and it is the female flower that is used. Like the runner bean, the bine climbs its way up strings to reach the top by late June. Six weeks later hops begin to show and by September have matured sufficiently to be harvested. Until comparatively recent years this harvesting was done by hand, and although this was often carried out by local people or gypsies, it is the picture of Londoners in the hop gardens that so easily slips into folk history. In the past, East End families would travel into Kent for a healthy working holiday, and stories and legends abound of those days. Nowadays picking is done by machine, and the atmosphere is quite different from that of old.

On the northern side of the Beult are a number of hilltop villages overlooking the river valley, but south of the river the A229 follows the line of the old Roman road to **Staplehurst**, which has some fine timbered hall-houses. The church has a remarkable oak door, 700 years old, decorated with iron-worked dragons, fishes and snakes. Staplehurst has given three martyrs to history: a pair of Alices burned at Canterbury, and Joan Bainbridge at Maidstone. A stone column bears their names in commemoration.

East of Staplehurst, lanes skirt the lush Beult grasslands to reach **Headcorn**. The village street here only hints at fine things to come, and its lovely church has as its neighbour an ancient oak older than the church itself. Behind the church at the junction of Church Walk and Gooseneck Lane stands Headcorn Manor, an early sixteenth-century hall house with a remarkable two-storey oriel window. Around the square church, gravestones stand at crazy tilted angles, and on the other side a row of cottages of differing styles leads back

to the dog-leg street which in turn signals a quiet lane to **Smarden**,
that pure gem of a Wealden village. It offers a truly wonderful sight,
for the lane traces through a soft green countryside — its Saxon name
meant 'butter valley and pasture' — and suddenly is faced with the
church standing proudly among the trees; to the left a converted
oast-house, to the right a pair of brown and cream timbered houses
squat among the grass. The approach from the east along the road
from Pluckley and Charing offers a view of one of Kent's finest
streets lined with magnificent old houses, the village pump and,
again, the church ahead, this time approached by ducking beneath
an arch formed by the overhanging storey of a charming timbered
building. It is a village with much to commend it.

Only 3 miles or so away, climbing a hill on a ridge, stands
Pluckley, which has the reputation of being the most haunted village
in England. Among its dozen ghosts are said to be a gypsy woman
who burned to death when the pipe she was smoking set fire to her
shawl (another tale suggests it was her straw bedding that caught
fire); a schoolmaster who hanged himself; a highwayman killed by
a sword, and a lady from the family of the local squire who drifts
among the gravestones in search of her lost child.

Returning to Staplehurst, a lane explores the hinterland which is
a delightful corner of the Weald. There are some beautiful old houses
and farms isolated among woods and pastures and streams. **Frittenden** sits on a crossroads, and has a lofty church spire, with
streams and ponds dotted here and there. The Romans were here, so
was Thomas Cromwell, but today it nestles in a sort of back-country
seclusion. It is then but a short run south to **Sissinghurst**, a village
whose name used to be Milkhouse Street, and which has the nearby
estate beautified by Harold Nicolson and his wife Vita Sackville-
West.

When they came to Sissinghurst in 1930 they found '...a castle
running away into sordidness and squalor; a garden crying out for
rescue.' How they performed that rescue is described in Harold
Nicolson's diaries, which show the enthusiastic spirit and romantic
zeal that has resulted in one of Kent's most famous gardens where
individual 'outdoor rooms' express different aspects of their person-
alities. There is a rose garden, a cottage garden, a herb garden, and
a white garden. There is a moat containing it all, and nearby, one of

Sissinghurst

the old Wealden hammer streams; there is the orchard, and beyond it a panorama of the Weald in all its splendour.

The castle is not a castle at all, but the remains of a Tudor manor house built in the sixteenth century by the Baker family of nearby Cranbrook — one of whom, Sir John, was known as 'Bloody Baker' for his persecution of Protestants. In 1752 Walpole described a 'perfect and very beautiful ' court, but he showed contempt for some of its pretension: 'The whole is built for show; for the back of the house is nothing but lath and plaster.' During the Seven Years' War it was used to hold French prisoners — at one time 3,000 were housed there — and Edward Gibbon, the historian, was for a while an officer on guard. Such a role for the manor speeded its decay, and in the first half of the nineteenth century it served as the local workhouse.

What remains is an ancient gateway, a lofty red-brick tower and one side of the quadrangle. There are ageing farm buildings and oast-houses as neighbours, and it is a strange, though not unattractive, sight as one approaches across the meadows, for the unusually high tower rises first out of a sweep of fields and scattered woods long before the rest of the buildings come into view. On the first floor of the tower Vita Sackville-West had her study, in which she wrote her books. Above it, on the second floor, is a room that contains the original hand-printing press used by Virginia Woolf and her husband in the 1920s when they founded the Hogarth Press. The world of letters is as evident in the buildings of Sissinghurst as is the world of colour in the gardens, for in the long, dignified entrance block is an extensive library of some 4,000 books.

The National Trust has taken Sissinghurst Castle into its care, and it has become one of the busiest of all its properties. The normal approach is along the drive leading from the A262, but a more private, peaceful way is to follow the footpaths and tracks across the country. The castle is then seen in a totally rural setting. It announces itself as an integral feature of the landscape.

On the very edge of Sissinghurst village, a few yards east of the church on the A262, a concrete track ($1^{1}/_{2}$ miles, $^{3}/_{4}$ hour), signposted Satins Hill, leads beside a small tennis court. It goes down past a hop garden, then on a true footpath beside orchards to reach the junction of a rough track and a lane. Bear right and follow the track through woods, and out of the woods where the tower is suddenly seen to be rising from the countryside ahead. As one draws near, so the long brick entrance block becomes apparent. It is a worthy approach to such a place.

A small community, Sissinghurst village has a certain air of charm about its street, with typical Kentish houses lining it, a narrow-towered church and orchards to the north. To the east is **Biddenden**, a sprawling village with a broad green, a gabled Old Cloth Hall, some good houses, and the memory of its most notable residents, Eliza and Mary Chulkhurst, 'Maids of Biddenden' who were joined for life at hip and shoulder many centuries ago and whose memory is perpetuated in an Easter charity. A mile or so south of the village, Biddenden Vineyard produces wines from a variety of vines grown on 22 acres of south-facing slopes. When the vineyard was first planted in 1969, a tentative start was made on just half an acre, but the produce was such that expansion was deemed necessary. Today visitors are welcome to stroll among the rows of vines and to buy from the vineyard shop bottles of this Wealden table wine, or the cider that is also made here.

Returning to Sissinghurst, there is an opportunity to walk across fields and through woods to reach Cranbrook, the capital of the Weald. The path (1$\frac{1}{2}$ miles, $\frac{3}{4}$ hour) begins in the Golford road not far from Sissinghurst Church, and cuts south-westwards, crosses a lane above Buckhurst Farm and goes through the woods to reach one of the most attractive small towns in Kent. Alternatively, the motorist has a choice of country routes to take.

Cranbrook owes its prominence and its past prosperity to the cloth trade which flourished here over the course of several centuries. Edward III brought clothmasters from Flanders in the fourteenth century to exploit England's own potential and to break the Flemish monopoly in the trade. As a result Cranbrook's prosperity and population increased, and although the industry that brought riches to this little town has long since departed, it still displays its origins. Its winding streets are lined with weatherboarded shops and houses. There are good houses, fine buildings at every corner. There is the feeling that Cranbrook has been cautiously deserted by the twentieth century and by ugly modern architecture. Even the main road avoids it, so that only the visitor who chooses to go there, does so.

Oast-houses at Sissinghurst

The Union Mill, Cranbrook

One of Cranbrook's more prominent features is Union Mill, a wonderful smock windmill, one of the largest of its kind in England, which stands over the houses of Stone Street. It was built by James Humphrey in 1814 on behalf of Henry Dobell, a worthy piece of craftsmanship with huge sweeps and the original timber frame still intact upon a tarred brick base. When Dobell's business failed, 5 years after taking over the mill, it went into the hands of a partnership of local creditors, thus gaining the name, Union Mill. It is a dominating feature of the town, a touch of England's past for such windmills were once a common feature of the Kentish landscape. When it fell into disrepair in the early 1950s, experts from Holland were called upon to restore it, with funds raised locally. Today the sweeps are again turning and barley is rolled there with electrically driven machinery. At certain times of the year the mill is open to the public; a living museum and a delightful adornment to a delightful town.

The other great building that dominates the town is St Dunstan's Church, which stands behind the High Street shops and houses. On entering there is an immediate impression of space and light, with no sense of confinement, no heavy colouring. It has a collection of strange yet lovely carved oak bosses, thought to be some 600 years old. There is a large immersion tub of stone and a room over the porch known as 'Baker's Jail' where, it is said, 'Bloody Baker' housed the Protestants he had convicted, before their martyrdom. Such grim reminders, however, are rare in this place of sunlight and airy spaces.

South of the town the countryside rolls in many little hills. In the hidden countryside of the Weald lies much of Kent's heritage. The visitor who restricts his travels through the county to a progression from one stately home to another goes away with a limited view of Kent. A better understanding can be gained by an exploration of narrow lanes and village churches; by walking along leafy paths, and to admire the seasonal blossom; in short, to appreciate the countryside as well as its famous houses.

Benenden is country-locked. Noted these days for its girls' public school, a mock-Tudor mansion built in 1859, it is to the traveller passing through a large and lovely green, a broad street and a few good houses. Cricket is played on the green, and there is a story of one such game when the ball went between the stumps without removing the bails! Outside the village, shortly before Rolvenden comes into sight a windmill standing on a knoll above the road catches the sun. **Rolvenden** windmill is a post mill with black timbers and white sweeps, restored in memory of a young man who lived 18 years in its view. It stands beside a huddle of ageing barns on a hillock above a small pond. Behind it the panorama encompasses the Rother Levels. North eastwards Tenterden's tower holds the eye, but nearer is Rolvenden's church, half a mile away.

It is strange to think that this village once had the sea at its doors, for a whale was once found here, and 700 years ago a boat went down nearby. In this boat was found a vase — now housed in Maidstone museum — the skull of a man, and a child's skeleton. Romney Marsh, which lies below the village, once was awash with seas that were driven back. Now, however, there is the Weald on one hand and low, flat marshland on the other. There are some fine unpretentious houses here. The church is an interesting place dating back to the thirteenth century; it contains a private pew which is almost a room in itself; the preserve of the local squire. Frances Hodgson Burnett, author of *Little Lord Fauntleroy* and *The Secret Garden* lived not far away in a large park. Around her former home Sir Edward Lutyens built the neo-Georgian mansion, Great Maytham Hall, in the period just before World War I. Set in spacious grounds to the south of the village, it is at times open to the public.

Rolvenden has a station on the line of the Kent and East Sussex Railway, one of those extraordinarily popular steam railways preserved by a company formed by enthusiasts and which, it is hoped, will eventually run from Tenterden to Bodiam in Sussex. The station lies on the A28 Ashford to Hastings road, at the foot of the hill that climbs up to the town that many consider to be the very finest in all the Weald: Tenterden.

Approaching from Rolvenden, **Tenterden** has a broad main street verged with turf and lined with trees. Along the spacious pavements, eighteenth-century bow-fronted shops, stylish and elegant, bear comparison with the best in England. There is a lively assortment of attractive buildings using a miscellany of materials. There are tile-hung, typically Wealden, houses. There are stucco-fronted shops with wrought iron railings and weather-boarded places, brightly painted. At the back of a rich collection near the

Places to Visit In and Around Cranbrook and Tenterden

Union Mill
Stone Street, Cranbrook
One of the largest working smock windmills in the country.
Accessible daily on the outside.

Cranbrook Museum
Items recalling the town's past reliance on the cloth industry are displayed as well as agricultural and domestic implements.

St Dunstan's Church
Cranbrook
Known as the 'Cathedral of the Weald' on account of its size and light, St Dunstan's has much of interest in it.

Sissinghurst Castle Gardens (NT)
$2^1/_2$ miles north-east of Cranbrook on A262
One of the loveliest gardens in the county, created by the writers Vita Sackville-West and Harold Nicolson.

Bettenham Manor Baby Carriage Collection
3 miles north-east of Cranbrook off A262
A unique collection of Victorian and Edwardian baby carriages, housed in an oast-house beside a fifteenth-century manor house.

Biddenden Vineyard
4 miles east of Cranbrook on Biddenden-Benenden road
About 22 acres of vineyards with harvesting in October. Open to casual visitors and parties.

St Mildred's Church
Tenterden
This has one of Kent's finest towers, and is seen for miles around.
There is much of interest inside.

Tenterden and District Museum
Station Road, Tenterden
Local relics on display recording the area's development over 1,000 years of history. One section is devoted to the Kent and East Sussex Railway whose headquarters are found nearby.

Kent and East Sussex Railway
Station Road, Tenterden
Headquarters of this popular steam railway which will eventually run to Bodiam in Sussex. Along the line Rolvenden Station houses the locomotive workshops, and at Wittersham Road there is a picnic site. A charming rural character is the essence of this railway.

Ellen Terry Memorial Museum (NT)
Smallhythe Place, 2 miles south of Tenterden, in the hamlet of Smallhythe
A sixteenth-century half-timbered yeoman's house and former home of Dame Ellen Terry, the actress.

Tenterden Vineyards
Spots Farm, Smallhythe, 2 miles south of Tenterden
Tours given through 10 acres of vineyards, including winery and tasting room.

Rolvenden Windmill
4 miles west of Tenterden, beside B2086
Restored seventeenth-century post mill standing on a grassy knoll above a small pond. Viewing from the outside only.

Tenterden

crown of the slope, and with its graveyard lined with handsome tilted cottages, there stands the magnificent church of St Mildred, tucked away among neighbouring buildings. At the top of this rise, in the heart of the town, the street narrows and shops, inns and houses crowd for attention. The splendid pinnacled tower of St Mildred's commands the countryside for miles around, yet it seems to shrink upon closer inspection. From its tower a beacon was once hung to warn of the approach of the Spanish Armada; it could be seen from across the Weald and along the line of hills that mark the edge of the marshlands. It is a marvellous tower looking down on a marvellous shingle roof. Inside are slender arches and pillars. The ceiling of the nave is carved and panelled, and there is an intricate stone carving with iron railings protecting it, of an Elizabethan couple, Herbert and Martha Whitfield.

Tenterden is a prosperous little town. It thrived by early association with the enterprising Cinque Ports, and in 1449 became a Corporate Member, a 'limb' of Rye through the shipbuilding industry set up in nearby Smallhythe. It thrived from its activity in the wool trade when Flemish clothmakers settled here as well as in Cranbrook, its rival as 'capital' of the Weald. The town prospered from the development of its market in the fifteenth century, and today its street is thronged with visitors from both home and abroad so that its future seems assuredly prosperous.

It is claimed that Tenterden was the birthplace of William Caxton, that man of Kent who pioneered the art of printing in England. Born and raised among clothmakers, Caxton went to Bruges as a member of the Mercers Company, but there he became fascinated by the processes of printing that were then cautiously being tried. When he returned to England in 1476 he set up his own press at Westminster.

Caxton's name is immortalised on the board of one of the town's many inns, and in the centre of Tenterden is another old inn, the Tudor Rose, a fifteenth-century hall-house opposite the town hall, which was itself built in 1790 and now houses the information centre. The town's museum, situated in a side road which leads to the railway, holds many fascinating items and displays that record the district's development over the past 1,000 years, and there is a section devoted to the railway which now draws many visitors to the town.

The nostalgia that steam locomotives inspire is not always easy to define, but the Kent and East Sussex Railway evokes more than a sentimental wistfulness for the days of yesterday. The journey it offers is an exploration of a peaceful, varied and glorious series of landscapes, from the heights of the Weald to the very edges of the low, crouching land known as Romney Marsh.

There is a walk (6¹/₂ miles, 3 hours) recommended by the Weald of Kent Preservation Society that explores this series of landscapes and combines with a short journey on the railway. The suggestion, published as a route sheet by the society, is to ride on the train from Tenterden to Wittersham Road station, which is reached in about 20 minutes, then to walk back across a stretch of marshland, over fields and through Spots Farm — which has 10 acres of vineyards — to Smallhythe. From this much-visited historic hamlet the route goes through a pleasant little valley to a narrow lake with a heronry nearby. From there through woods and uphill back to Tenterden.

HIGH WEALD COUNTRY TOUR (65 miles, 3 hours)
(See map page 202)

This is the third of the signposted tours recommended to motorists. It explores much fine countryside and links a number of places of interest described elsewhere in this chapter, with a small section contained in Chapter 5 dealing with the Eden Valley. As with the previous two tours, the High Weald Country Tour is circular and described in an anti-clockwise direction. Signposts contain white lettering on a brown background and bear a double oast-house as the symbol.

Beginning at **Tenterden** the tour heads north towards **Biddenden**, passing at Woolpack Corner an opportunity to make a detour to visit Biddenden Vineyard. The main village street is delightful, as is the church, and the village sign showing the Siamese twin sisters who were born here around 1100 is also quite fine. Following the A262 you reach **Sissinghurst**. Sissinghurst Castle, in the care of the National Trust, stands just off the route to the right. Another detour is available from the village, this time to reach **Cranbrook**, a couple of miles away.

Back on the main route continue along the A262 to **Goudhurst** on its hilltop overlooking rich hop gardens and woodland. On the

descent from the hill, almost as soon as you reach the bridge crossing
the River Teise, a signpost directs your attention left to Finchcocks,
a baroque mansion housing a famous collection of musical instruments. From Goudhurst to Tonbridge the route goes through gentle
rolling countryside with surprise views. **Pembury** has been bypassed now, which gives it a new lease of life, as has **Tonbridge** — but
one should go into this town on the Medway to explore the castle
grounds and to wander alongside the river.

Out of Tonbridge head south towards Royal Tunbridge Wells,
but on the outskirts of Southborough turn sharply to the right on the
B2176 and come to **Bidborough** with its superb views overlooking
the north. Make a brief detour here to the left to visit the parish
church which is perched above cottage rooftops. The signposted tour
soon breaks away to drop to the Medway and comes to **Leigh** where
you turn left and continue to Bough Beech. Another diversion will
lead to Bough Beech Reservoir where bird watchers crowd along the
causeway to see a variety of ducks, geese and waders.

The country tour leaves Bough Beech and by way of a twisting
lane brings you within a couple of miles of **Hever Castle**, a magical
small castle set in idyllic landscaped grounds, while the proper route
enters the tiny one-street village of **Chiddingstone**, described in
Chapter 5. The tour continues through a lush green countryside
following sometimes narrow winding lanes to the outskirts of **Penshurst**. This is certainly worth a short detour, for Penshurst Place is
one of the great houses of England, home of the Sidney family for 400
years. There are also vineyards on the edge of the village which can
be visited.

Royal Tunbridge Wells is next. It is reached through more lovely
gentle countryside. The town has much to commend it; its most
famous attraction being The Pantiles, found in the lower part of the
town. A good cross-country route takes you past Bayham Abbey and
on to **Lamberhurst**, with its extensive vineyards. The Owl House
Gardens, its handsome main street and the wonderful Scotney
Castle are reached from the A21. Farther along this road there is an
opportunity to make diversions to both Bewl Water and Bedgebury
Pinetum.

Leaving the A21 at Flimwell the tour bears left and follows the
A268 to **Hawkhurst**. Shortly afterwards signposts direct you north

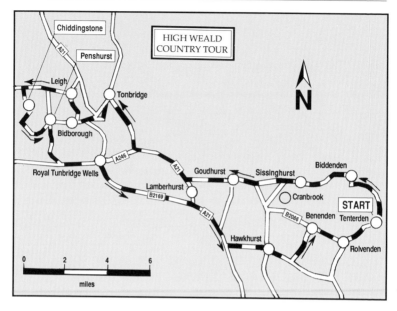

to **Benenden**, famous for its girls' public school. This is on the B2086 which leads to **Rolvenden** (post mill beside the road, and C.M. Booth Collection of Historic Vehicles just beyond the village). Then it is but a short drive along the A28 back to **Tenterden**.

7
THE MARSH COUNTRY

'The world is divided into five parts,' wrote Richard Barham in *The Ingoldsby Legends*, 'namely Europe, Asia, Africa, America and Romney Marsh.' Late on a winter's afternoon, as mists swirl across the great flat expanse of marsh-and grass-land, taking from view all but the spiky reeds and nearby fence posts, one can almost believe it to be true.

Romney Marsh comes as a surprise, so completely does it contrast with the Weald. Here is an area that once was sea; a triangle of levelled meadow and stream; green and flat and smooth as a billiard table, over 16 miles in length by about 10 miles at its broadest. It is the most southerly corner of Kent which grows with the tides as shingle accumulates on the beaches. Backing the marsh are cliffs that once were pounded by the sea, but which now shelter grazing sheep on their slopes.

It is partly due to the Romans that the sea was pushed back and held there, by the construction of sturdy walls. The western marshes, Walland and Denge, and the lesser strip of Guldeford Level beyond the Sussex border — here marked by a stream known as Kent Ditch — are often generally included under Romney's parent name. It was Romney that came first out of the water; Walland and Denge having been reclaimed only since the twelfth century.

It is a triangle of land with obvious borders. To south and east the boundary is the sea with its busy shipping lanes. Running in an arc from Hythe to Rye, backed by the former limits of the land, stretches the Royal Military Canal, dug at a time when Napolean threatened Britain with his Grande Armée at Boulogne. There is an air of solitude and mystery here among the silent, steep-cut dykes. Below the level of the neighbouring sea, the Marsh depends on these ditches to drain the meadows. Solid Norman churches punctuate the sweeping levels, and even their towers seem especially designed not to upset the overall effect of an overpoweringly horizontal landscape.

It is not easy to define the attraction of the Marsh. Part of its appeal may be found among the churches that command a civil audience in a countryside which at times seems anything but civil. Part of it may be the vivid sunsets, the quality of light or the landscape itself. Much of its fascination lies in its history, its constant battle with a sea that retreated, yet threatens beyond the Dymchurch Wall; the knowledge that ships once sailed with valuable cargoes where now people walk. Certainly it is a region estranged from the rest of Kent, and there are those who visit it briefly and depart unmoved by it. For many, however, it holds a unique fascination.

In prehistoric times the Marsh was settled by Belgic tribes who brought with them skills of embanking from the Low Countries. When the Romans arrived work had already begun to tame the shifting coastline, but with their genius for systematic engineering, the Romans pushed a paved way across the eastern marshes. They settled farms, and at Dymchurch evidence was found of a Roman pottery. The Dymchurch Wall is said by some to have first been built during Roman times, as well as the Rhee Wall which runs from Appledore to Romney. Others claim that the Saxons were responsible, at least for the Rhee Wall.

Merscwari — the kingdom of the Marsh — was invaded by Offa, King of Mercia, in the eighth century, and he in turn granted part of it to Archbishop Janibert. Churches and monasteries were established, but the Danes sailed up the Rother, whose fickle course changed the shape of this land, to burn and pillage. The Marsh came back to life; on its very edge Appledore flourished in the Middle Ages, its harbour busy with trading vessels. Now it stands 10 miles from the sea. There was a certain prosperity in towns such as Romney which had 'a good, sure, and commodious harbour, where many vessels used to be at road.' But a series of tremendous gales during the thirteenth century led to great changes in the Rother's estuary, and Romney's prosperity foundered.

Other than the ports the marshes themselves were thinly populated, with ague (malaria) being a common dread, for it was a region notoriously 'bad in winter, worse in summer, and at no time good, only fit for those vast herds of cattle which feed all over it.' Today those vast herds of cattle have been replaced by sheep, the famed Romney Marsh breed that has been transported all over the world; to South Africa, to New Zealand and to Patagonia. The bird population is also numerous and varied

Within easy reach of the Marsh, Tenterden offers three practical approaches. The first runs south towards Rye and crosses the Isle of Oxney. Another goes south-eastwards to Appledore and New Romney along the embankment of the ancient Rhee Wall, while the third follows the line of now-green cliffs that overlook the marshes from the north and links such villages as Ham Street and Ruckinge and Bilsington before reaching historic Lympne and Hythe.

Towards the western end of Tenterden the narrow B2082 turns away from the heights of the Weald beside the William Caxton Inn, heading south for Rye, first reaching the hamlet of **Smallhythe**. There is a strange, red-brick chapel with a splendid early sixteenth-century mellow, half-timbered Priest's House next door and right against the road. Then, a few yards further down, Smallhythe Place stands impressively against a wide view. This large, handsome, typically Kentish yeoman's house dates also from the sixteenth century and was at one time the harbourmaster's house. Standing here it is difficult to believe that in years gone by this quiet, green slope was a port with facilities for ship-building. Ships were built for Hythe and Rye, but the warehouses and quays were burnt down in 1514, never to be rebuilt.

Smallhythe Place then became a farm. In 1899 Dame Ellen Terry, the Shakespearian actress (and for a time Irving's leading lady) came to Smallhythe to live quietly. She spent 30 years here, and when she died in 1928, she bequeathed Smallhythe Place to the National Trust. It is now the Ellen Terry Memorial Museum; the house remains much as she left it, with the presence of its former owner expressed in the possessions that furnish it, while other rooms display a collection of countless theatrical mementoes recalling Henry Irving and Garrick. In the garden can be seen the shape of what is thought to have been a dry dock.

From Smallhythe it is a short step on to the **Isle of Oxney** for one

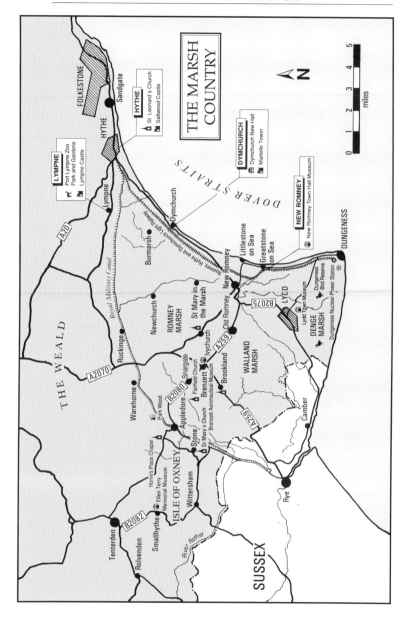

THE MARSH COUNTRY

N

0 1 2 3 4 5 miles

DOVER STRAITS

HYTHE
⌂ St. Leonard's Church
▦ Saltwood Castle

LYMPNE
⚔ Port Lympne Zoo Park and Gardens
▦ Lympne Castle

DYMCHURCH
▦ Dymchurch New Hall
▦ Martello Tower

NEW ROMNEY
▦ New Romney Town Hall Museum

FOLKESTONE

Sandgate

HYTHE

Lympne

Dymchurch

Burmarsh

Littlestone on Sea
Greatstone on Sea

DUNGENESS

A20

Royal Military Canal

Romney, Hythe and Dymchurch Light Railway

New Romney

Dungeness Bird Reserve
Lydd Town Museum
Dungeness Nuclear Power Station

THE WEALD

Newchurch

ROMNEY MARSH

St Mary in the Marsh

Old Romney

LYDD

B2075

DENGE MARSH

Ruckinge

Ivychurch
A259

WALLAND MARSH

A2070

Snargate
Fairfield Church
Brenzett
Brenzett Aeronautical Museum

Brookland

Wareourne

Park Wood

Appledore

B2080

A259

Camber

Stone
St Mary's Church

Home's Place Chapel

Ellen Terry Memorial Museum

ISLE OF OXNEY

Wittersham

Rye

Tenterden

B2082

Smallhythe

Rolvenden

River Rother

SUSSEX

*The Ellen Terry Memorial
Museum, Smallhythe*

Stocks Mill, Wittersham

of its encircling waterways, the unfortunately named Reading Sewer, flows across the southern end of the hamlet. It is all that remains of Smallhythe's once-proud seaway, an insignificant dyke. The road follows it on a winding course and steadily gains height to mount the whale-back ridge that sets Oxney above the spread of the marshes. It is not much of a ridge, but since the surrounding country is so flat it gives the impression of greater height, and the tower of Wittersham Church is a conspicuous landmark. On top there once stood a warning beacon to relay news of coastal raids.

Wittersham is growing. Its church stands back away from development along a lane divorced from the main road. The church dates back to the twelfth century, but its massive sandstone tower is of the fifteenth century; among the windows there is an attractive modern scene depicting a shepherd with his flock in memory of 'a man of Kent' who died in 1945. Life existed here long before the church, long before the Marsh, for it was in Wittersham that the remains of an iguanodon were discovered. It was one of the first animals to take to the land that now is Kent, some 10,000,000 years ago.

Instead of following the Rye road when it breaks to the south at the crossroads a mile east of Wittersham, it is advisable to continue eastwards on the Appledore road. Ahead, the Marsh stretches across a broad horizon. Then the road bears left, with another lane cutting away to the right; both lead to Stone-in-Oxney, but it is wiser to take the minor lane to the right, for it introduces the visitor to a most memorable scene.

This edge of the whale-back of Oxney juts out into the Marsh. The lane prepares to plunge to the levels below and into the waters of the Royal Military Canal. All around is the sky and vast distances unchecked by hills. Then the lane again divides, and by taking the left-hand run it squeezes between high banks and hedges as it dips to the north. A lovely view appears ahead of an old, timber-framed Kentish hall house, half-blocking from view the solid weathered tower of St Mary's Church at **Stone-in-Oxney**. During spring time daffodils line the banks upon which both church and house sit, and the frame of newly-opened buds upon the trees and in the hedges presents a beautiful picture.

The house in the foreground, with its centuries-old timbers frowning under the weight of heavy beams at a wearisome angle, is one of Kent's delightful old dwellings, and has stood witness to a chequered history. The church of St Mary too, has the scars of age; on its site stood another place of worship, but this was destroyed by fire in 1464. Inside, the church is cool, while through the windows comes the damp, watery light of the Marsh beyond. Under the tower there stands a ragstone block, an altar older than the church in which it rests. More than 200 years ago it was discovered when the chancel was being dug up, presumably for the setting of a grave; this stone, when it was first found, bore clearly the carvings of an ox on each side, with signs of fire upon the top. It was an altar to Mithras, the religion brought to Britain by the Romans, and another clue to that period of occupation. It has been defaced by an iron ring that was fixed at the base, presumably for use in tethering the horse of a worshipper during the years when it was discarded from the church itself as unsuitable in a Christian setting.

Set in a windswept landscape a short walk away from Stone is another church that sums up the loneliness of the Marsh country; Fairfield's church, dedicated to St Thomas á Becket. Its solitude — there is no village of Fairfield — makes this one of the most poignant of all the Marsh churches, for it lies away from the road, away from prospective parishioners; away from the world. There is a grass causeway to it, but at times the building has been marooned by floods and worshippers have gone there by boat. To reach it from Stone-in-Oxney, the path (2 miles, 1 hour) directly opposite St Mary's follows south-eastwards round the skirt of Oxney's hill before reaching a narrow road by the driveway to Mackley Farm. Follow the road down to reach the Military Canal and take Stone Bridge across it. Follow the footpath ahead, cross the stream known as Five Watering Sewer to the railway, then turn left along a track to reach the road at Becket's Farm. The church is reached along the road and then by the grassy causeway to its door.

The Saxon Shore Way, one of Kent's long-distance footpaths, comes up the lane from Stone village on the closing stages of its 140-mile journey from Gravesend to Rye. By dropping downhill to the sheltering dwellings of the village, a section of this path ($2^1/_2$ miles, 1 hour) may be taken across the fields to Appledore. A gateway near the post office at the road junction sees the start of this walk which crosses a series of fields, along a hedgerow and off to Luckhurst

Fairfield Church

Farm. Continue across the narrow road that runs beyond the Reading Sewer stream, and then follow this to the right as far as the old Ferry Inn. From here the path goes along the northern bank of the sewer until the stream makes a sudden southwards curve and the way parts company from it, going up towards Appledore village, which it reaches in the road opposite the church.

By road a direct route to Appledore avoids dropping down to the Royal Military Canal by going first north, then east, skirting the edge of the Marsh proper. Halfway along this road the Reading Sewer is crossed once more to leave the Isle of Oxney. The Ferry Inn stands here as a reminder that this bridged stream was once a more substantial waterway, requiring a ferry to convey goods and vehicles. On the wall of the inn a scale of charges is painted.

Appledore; a lovely name, but one that really ought to be applied to a quiet village set deep in the heart of the orchards of the Weald.

The former bulb fields, Appledore

It is a village with wide streets, some picturesque Tudor houses and a church with a squat tower. Here were once the finest bulb fields of southern England — so popular with coach parties during the flowering period when acres of tulips would brighten the land — but now, alas, gone forever. The village sits on the lip of a projection of high ground above the Marsh. There was a Saxon castle defending the area when the Danes landed in AD893 and 250 longships occupied this strip above the tides of the estuary for a year, until King Alfred's smooth diplomacy persuaded them to leave, albeit only temporarily.

Appledore was for a time a port of some prosperity, a part of the thriving Wealden cloth industry, but when the River Rother changed direction during the latter half of the thirteenth century, its importance diminished. Even so, it received the attentions of the French who in 1380 attacked the town and burned the church, where marks of the fire are still to be seen on the tower arch.

Before descending to the Marsh proper, a mile north of the village stands Horne's Place, a farm which occupies the site of William Horne's house that was attacked by Wat Tyler with Appledore men in 1381. Behind it is a domestic chapel. Although it was used as a barn for many years, it has been carefully restored, thus preserving the artistry of the skilled craftsmen of 600 years ago.

Another mile along the Woodchurch road, Park Wood Picnic Site grants access to about 40 acres of oak woodland, with waymarked paths leading to some fine views over the surrounding countryside.

To resume the journey into Romney Marsh it is necessary to return to Appledore, which is then seen in its true light as the gateway to the Marsh. Its dwarfed church overlooks that portion of the Marsh between the village and Warehorne which is below sea-level and known as the Dowels. This stretch of the Royal Military Canal is owned by the National Trust and is a unique property. The $3^1/_2$ miles in Trust's hands were given by Miss D.E. Johnston in 1936, as well as Hallhouse Farm, a fifteenth-century yeoman's farmhouse which is not open to the public.

The canal, which effectively turns Romney Marsh into an island, has never been tested for its original defensive purpose. It was in September 1804 that William Pitt gathered at Newhall near Dymchurch with his generals and the Lords and Bailiffs of the Level of

Romney Marsh 'to consider of the best mode of inundating the Marsh in the case of invasion.' Across the Channel Napoleon waited with gunboats and transport ships, and the Marsh was his closest British soil. A defence was agreed: the building of Martello Towers along the coast, the excavation of a canal — with gun emplacements at strategic points — and the flooding of the marshes. By the time the Royal Military Canal had been constructed in 1807, the invasion scare was over and Pitt was dead.

A walk along the towpath of the canal to the hamlet of **Warehorne**, which sits on the ridge along the borders of the Marsh, gives a lively impression of water and meadow. The path ($3^1/_2$ miles, $1^1/_2$ hours) begins beside Appledore's church before dropping down to the north bank of the canal, which it follows for about 2 miles before crossing a narrow lane at Higham Farm. Half a mile or so after this, the path leads away from the canal — another continues along the towpath — veering to the left to go uphill as far as Warehorne Church and its tiny community.

The rambler in Marsh country, should he leave the quiet lanes, is faced with a bewildering complexity of watercourses. Only the man who has worked the fields all his life may confidently set forth to walk from A to B with the certainty that he will reach his goal without at least doubling the distance of travel. Many of the dykes are too broad to leap, most are too steep-sided to attempt an unconventional crossing. Better by far to enjoy the solitude of the Marsh from the empty lanes, or by sticking to the main waymarked trails that exploit the simple bridges across reed-lined streams. Or travel on a bicycle, for the cyclist surely comes into his own across this flat land.

The B2080 curves in a long sweep to the south-east along the line of the Rhee Wall, effectively cutting the Marsh into two. The country-side is criss-crossed with drainage dykes, a sparse scattering of wind-bent trees in a taut landscape. **Snargate** Church occupies a solitary position, and one wonders where the congregation came from. For 600 years it has withstood the gales and threats of flooding, but it remains sturdy enough. The Reverend R.H. Barham (who wrote *The Ingoldsby Legends*) was rector here during the days when smuggling was still an integral part of Marsh life. His church had clearly been used by local smugglers as a store, for in 1743 (long before Barham's time) a raid by excise men uncovered a cask of gin

Snargate

beneath a table in the vestry and a consignment of tobacco hidden in the belfry. Snargate today is no more than a hamlet and is practically the same size now as it was in Barham's time; a tiny place described by Cobbett as 'a village with five houses, and with a church capable of containing two thousand people!' To the north, towards the rising ground, are one or two shrivelled orchards, but elsewhere sheep or horses graze on little islets trapped between linking ditches. As you approach Snargate from Appledore a narrow, unmarked lane breaks away to the right to stutter its way round to a farm or two for the nearest approach to Fairfield's marooned church. The church is kept locked, but the key to it is available at Becket's Barn Farm nearby.

Brenzett stands at a double crossroads; to the north and east, Romney Marsh; to the south and west, Walland Marsh. By turning right (west) here the traveller comes to Brookland, a sparten hamlet justly famed for its church.

In the marshes, with few real towns or villages and with a regular landscape, it is among the churches that the visitor finds riches. Few are more rewarding than St Augustine's Church at **Brookland**. Seen from the road it is a gem; odd because the timber belfry, shingled from top to bottom and set in three stages, one on top of the other, stands quite separate from the main body of the building like the campanile of an Italian church. Its original timbers date back over 800 years, although the bell frame is thirteenth century with later amendments. Why the belfry should stand separate from the rest of the church is open to conjecture. Probably it always did, built there for fear that the main building could not support the weight of bells; but of all the speculation surrounding it, the most amusing idea is that the tower originally stood upon the church until a local virgin came to be married here — the shock was so great that the belfry fell down! But it is inside that this eccentric place of worship reveals its treasures. There are horsebox pews; a 'graveside shelter' said to keep the preacher dry during foul-weather funerals; a vast chest whose seventy securing nails have engraved heads; a fourteenth-century wall painting that represents the murder of Thomas á Becket. But the most notable feature must surely be the Norman lead font which is small, cylindrical, only 16in high and with forty scenes set out in the ten vertical lead strips; signs of the zodiac and delightful artistic impressions of Saxon life in the countryside: pruning vines, haymaking, slaughtering a pig, threshing and many more.

As in most Marsh villages Brookland has its tales of smugglers and of the local doctor, Ralph Hougham of Pear Tree House, who was regularly called upon to administer to members of a smuggling gang injured either in the course of their illicit trade, or in battle with the excise men. In 1821 such a battle took place on the outskirts of the village between the notorious Aldington gang and the revenue men; an incident that has become part of the folklore of the area.

Beyond Brookland the road continues its curious alignment across Walland Marsh, then over the county boundary at Guldeford Lane Corner by Kent Ditch to skirt the Guldeford Levels and on to the much-acclaimed little town of Rye, in East Sussex, which lies south of the lock where the Royal Military Canal enters the River Rother.

At Brenzett crossroads the B2080 becomes the A259, running straight down to **Old Romney** which is little more than a clump of trees, a few cottages, an inn and a thirteenth-century church containing box pews painted pink for the filming of *Dr Syn*, Russell Thorndyke's imaginative story of the smuggling parson. This is all smuggling country, of course; smuggling and wrecking made the marshland a notorious stretch of fogs, false lights and unquiet movement at night, and the ghosts of their long-dead victims are said to appear now and then as a grim reminder of the past. Daniel Defoe visited the Marsh country and saw dragoons 'in quest of the owlers' riding as though they were huntsmen 'beating up their game'. Owlers and Marsh Pilots, are examples of a variety of colourful names the smugglers were given.

It seems surprising today that Old Romney should at any period in its history have been a busy and productive place. It appears almost deserted, forgotten, as are so many of its neighbourhood hamlets. Yet the Domesday survey records three fisheries here, as well as a mill and the church already mentioned, which used to look onto a wharf. There is no wharf now, nor sea to warrant one — but neither are there fisheries or mill. The village once stood on a small island, but as the Marsh gradually won more land from the sea, so Old Romney (formerly known simply as Romney) lost its island status and became part of it. Its status diminished in other ways too, and New Romney, more a town than village by Marsh standards today, overtook it in importance until Old Romney was left to

Brookland Church with its separate wooden bell tower

Dungeness

ruminate on its past and adapt to a sea-less future.

Leaving the A259 at Old Romney, B2076 runs south to Lydd, and on the way there can be seen the remains of Midley Church, left to crumble among the meadows. **Lydd** rises out of the flattened horizon, with the fencing of Ministry of Defence land to the south, a large army camp, the scrape of neighbouring gravel pits, and the tower of the nuclear power station a few miles away across the shingle wastes. As with several other villages and small towns nearby, Lydd once boasted a thriving port. It was an auxiliary to the Cinque Port of New Romney, taking a share in the heavy medieval trade. The town's character changed dramatically with the shift of the River Rother, that left it a port without the sea, but its great church, often called the 'Cathedral of the Marshes', its guildhall and several fine houses, recall its past and enable it to uphold its dignity.

All Saints Church dominates the town. During World War II it received a direct hit from a German bomb that demolished the chancel while air raid wardens were on lookout duty at the top of the tower. Skilful restoration work has brought the place back to order,

Places to Visit In and Around Appledore and New Romney

Brenzett Aeronautical Museum
Ivychurch Road, New Romney
Contains various aircraft relics
such as a Spitfire, Messerschmitt,
Junkers 88 and Focke-Wulf.

Dungeness Bird Reserve
2 miles south of Lydd, off the
Dungeness road at Boulderswall
Farm
A unique habitat of shingle beach
that attracts a large variety of
birds, including a colony of terns.
RSPB reception centre and
observatory.

**Dungeness Nuclear Power
Station**
On Dungeness Point and approached by road from either Lydd
or New Romney

Modern technology on display in
organised tours of Power Station
'A'.

Horne's Place Chapel (EH)
1 mile north of Appledore
Domestic chapel built in 1366 and
attached to old timber-framed
house.

Lydd Airport
On the north-eastern outskirts of
Lydd, approached along B2075
Pleasure flights all year round from
the Cinque Ports Flying Club.
Also flying lessons.

Martello Tower (EH)
Dymchurch, on A259, south of
Hythe
One of only 43 of the original 103

but it would take more than an architect and a team of masons to create a sense of harmony from the outlying region of mournful desolation. On the outskirts of the town rides the ghost of Sir Robert de Septuans, chain mail and all. Near the army ranges another ghost, that of Katherine Eve who drowned in 1650, is said to appear from time to time in an attempt to lure others to a watery grave. There is a site where horses were buried in the times of the threat of Napoleonic invasion and another where the remains of a customs officer were found, presumably murdered by a smuggler. Out near Lydd Airport, behind Jacques Court Farm, a Spanish galleon is said to lie trapped beneath the shingle.

Between Lydd and the sea lies **Denge Marsh** and the shifting peninsula of Dungeness, a scene of desolation, shingle and scrub and open lagoons that attract birds in great quantities. In spring and autumn numerous migrating birds make this landfall, including such defensive towers built along the coast against the threat of Napoleon's invasion, that survives.

New Romney Town Hall Museum
Town Hall, New Romney
Contains local historic relics, including ancient chests and a loving cup of 1790.

Park Wood Picnic Site
About 1 mile north of Appledore on the Woodchurch road
40 acres of woodland with waymarked paths.

Romney, Hythe and Dymchurch Light Railway
Headquarters in New Romney, but main stations also in Hythe and Dungeness

One of the few genuine miniature steam railways in operation. One third full scale locomotives running a frequent service on 14 miles of narrow gauge track between Hythe and Dungeness.

St Augustine's Church
Brookland, on A259 1$\frac{1}{2}$ miles west of Brenzett crossroads
A remarkable twelfth- or thirteenth-century church with separate timber belfry, and numerous treasures; especially a lead font, one of only thirty-eight in Britain.

St Mary's Church
Stone-in-Oxney, 2 miles south-west of Appledore on Isle of Oxney
Perpendicular church rebuilt after a fire in 1464 containing a Roman altar to Mithras under the tower.

whitethroats, wheatears and willow warblers. Colonies of terns and gulls have exploited the recently excavated pits. Increasing numbers of ducks choose this corner for wintering. Firecrests, merlins and hen harriers make regular visits, and migrant butterflies settle among the flowers. It is a unique area and the Royal Society for the Protection of Birds has a noted reserve on this promontory, with an observatory and reception centre for visitors.

Dungeness is a desolate and austere spot; a melancholy place that has an inexplicable attraction. There is no village, just a line of shacks tethered down on a pebble desert inhabited by fishermen. If there is a Planning Authority here it chooses to use its power with tolerance and discretion, for it is difficult to imagine such a shoddy collection of hutments being allowed to stand more than a month elsewhere. In days gone by those who spent their lives here wore backstays on their feet; pieces of board, a little like snowshoes to

The Romney, Hythe and Dymchurch Light Railway

enable them to move more easily over the endless shingle. Nowadays boards have been laid as pathways from the road to the top of the shingle bank where fishing vessels are drawn up high above the tides; this is a dangerous, deadly place for bathing.

There are lighthouses on the shingle; there was one in 1615, but this was replaced by others as the shingle pushed farther out into the channel. Of those now standing, one was built in 1904, but with the construction of the nuclear power station its light became obscured to vessels south of the promontory, and it had to be replaced. The modern light was begun in 1959. It is tall and slender, with black and white bands and fully automated with a fog warning signal that booms from dozens of speakers. Its predecessor, no longer in use, stands forlornly by in retirement.

The nuclear power station nearby is the most obtrusive construction on this vast shifting promontory. The great complex of concrete and glass, with pipes like outraged bindweed climbing to and fro, offers a scene straight out of Orwell. There are two power stations drawing some 20,000,000 gallons of cooling water per hour from the sea, and a regiment of silver pylons marching inland with their drapery of high voltage cables carrying electricity to places far inland. No matter what one's personal feelings are regarding nuclear power, Dungeness power station has a curiosity appeal, and presumably has been opened to the public as a public relations exercise. Visitors are taken on a selective tour, which includes one of the giant reactors and is open to the public on Wednesday afternoons throughout the summer. But of more popular appeal to the holiday-maker at this end of the Marsh is the Romney, Hythe and Dymchurch miniature railway which terminates nearby. Regular services of this railway ply the 14-mile stretch of narrow gauge track between Hythe and Dungeness and have helped to make this one of Kent's major tourist attractions.

Heading north along the coast, shingle gives way to sand and at both Greatstone and Littlestone on Sea, where the long bay begins to turn towards Folkestone and the distant white cliffs, sea bathing is safe and without the crowds that gather farther along. **New Romney** stands a little way inland, but the flood marks of the great storm of 1287 that robbed the town of its harbour on the Rother, may still be seen round the Norman columns of its church. The tower, 100ft high, has numerous windows and arches and is one of the most magnificent in all the south. There were three churches serving a scattered parish. One, All Saints, lies in ruins a mile or so north of the town beside the B2070; the other is at Old Romney. It was New Romney that gained the distinction of becoming chief of the Cinque Ports, that collection of maritime towns — Hastings, Hythe, Dover, Sandwich and New Romney, with the 'Two Ancient Towns' of Rye and Winchelsea — that together defended Britain's most frequently attacked shoreline. Before England had a navy to protect her, some 700 years ago, the fishing or trading ports of the seven towns were pressed into service as defenders of the realm. Now only Dover is an important harbour, and New Romney, Rye, Winchelsea and Sandwich stand inland.

Inland, north of New Romney, the Marsh spreads itself with an air of peaceful solitude. Scattered parishes are linked by the dyke-lined lanes that in earlier years were white with the flocks of Romney sheep being driven to market. There were sheep fairs at New Romney, at Ham Street on the hills above the Marsh, and at Tenterden.

Places to Visit In and Around Hythe

Folkestone Racecourse
North of Lympne, reached by A20. Regular horserace meetings, about twenty a year.

Lympne Castle
3½ miles west of Hythe
A small castle, built on the site of a Roman watch-tower. It stands on the edge of a former cliff with magnificent views over Romney Marsh and the Channel to France.

Port Lympne Zoo Park and Gardens
Outside Lympne, west of Hythe
A varied collection of exotic animals, set in fine parkland and gardens.

Romney, Hythe and Dymchurch Light Railway
Hythe
Terminus and main station for this major tourist attraction.

Royal Military Canal
Hythe
Runs for 23 miles from Hythe to Rye. Boats may be hired for excursions along it.

St Leonard's Church
Hythe
An imposing Norman church with extremely high chancel and interesting features. One of the curiosities is the crypt which contains over 1,000 skulls and 8,000 thigh bones.

Along the line of the coast the **Dymchurch Wall** shades rows of holiday homes while preventing the sea from flooding the marshes. There has been a sea wall here since Roman times and the various improvements over the years have used assorted materials, including an inner core of blackthorn, before the modern concrete wall was constructed. To one side, there are broad level stretches of firm sand; but on the other side, a sandwich of bungalows and chalets and amusements can be found. A walk along the sea wall displays this contrast well and gives an opportunity to view the strange Martello Towers that once stretched along the south-east coast from Sussex to Suffolk as a means of defence against Napoleon's impending invasion. Of the 103 towers built, 74 were sited between Folkestone and Eastbourne, but only 43 survive; that at Dymchurch has been restored and is open to the public for inspection. Similar in a way to the keep of a medieval castle, the towers were sturdily built of stone and brick with strong, thick walls and roof against attack. Their entrance was by way of a removable ladder, and inside they could accommodate twenty-four men and their officers. The idea came from a similar tower in Corsica; Torre di Mortella. Hence the name, Martello Towers.

Dymchurch is part seaside resort, part residential small town that once fulfilled an important role in the administration of the Marsh, for it was here that the Lords of Romney Marsh held court in the Middle Ages and sent out their orders for the maintenance of the numerous dykes that drain the land. The eighteenth-century New Hall, opposite the church, houses the headquarters of the authority charged with the continued upkeep of the dykes today. At the other end of the small town (which is really only a village) will be found a summer-busy station on the Romney, Hythe and Dymchurch Light Railway, tucked away behind some houses. Dymchurch is also famed as the location for Russell Thorndike's stories about the fictional parson-cum-smuggler, Dr Syn. On alternate summers Dymchurch celebrates with a Dr Syn carnival, when a mock battle is staged on the beach between smugglers and excise men.

Heading north along the wall a narrow side road branches off to the Marsh, with a sign indicating a twelfth-century church. In a matter of only a few minutes holidaymakers on the beaches are left behind, and **Burmarsh** offers a taste of the marshland beyond. The church, with the old rectory on the left and The Shepherd and Crook, a whitewashed village inn on the right, is reached across a narrow ditch. A Norman church, it is typical of so many such churches of the Marsh; **St Mary in the Marsh** is another, with the grave of *The Railway Children* author E. Nesbit by a bush of rosemary; **Newchurch** is another, only its tower boasts a large cross, as does that at Ivychurch — another so-called 'Cathedral of the Marshes'.

Ivychurch takes us momentarily back to the heart of the Marsh, a couple of miles east of Brenzett. Some 300 years ago the Reverend John Streating complained that he lived in an 'unhealthfull place, and among rude and ill-nurtured people for the most part.' Once again there is very little habitation in this secluded hamlet, while the fourteenth-century church is one of the largest around. As it has seating only in the choir and along part of the south wall, the sense of space is made even more profound. During the Civil War, Cromwell's soldiers stabled their horses inside, and in World War II the church was used as a secret food store in case of invasion. But

Ivychurch was also taken by smugglers to store contraband goods, and there is an oft-quoted story of how the rector arrived to take a service one Sunday morning when he was met by his sexton with the warning, 'Bain't be no service, parson. Pulpit be full o' baccy, and vestry be full o' brandy.'

Hythe marks the eastern extremity of Romney Marsh. The coastal bay continues regardless of inland features, to Sandgate and Folkestone, but Hythe has the canal and a colourful history as one of the original Cinque Ports. It has lost its harbour and there is land between the town and the sea, but on a steep hill its large church overlooks what was once an important and flourishing maritime community. In the crypt beneath the spacious chancel lie over 1,000 skulls and some 8,000 thigh bones; a grim collection of Hythe's former citizens. On the outskirts of town lies Saltwood Castle which, for much of its early history, was the property of the Archbishops of Canterbury, but it changed hands and, in December 1170, four knights gathered there to plan the murder of Thomas á Becket.

The Romans left their mark on this corner of the county. Not only did they build the walls to protect the Marsh, and the road called Stone Street, but they also built a fortress called *Portus Lemanis* and a watch-tower high on the cliffs at **Lympne** overlooking the marshes and the sea. The ruins of their fortress remain today, known as Stutfall Castle, and on the site of their watch-tower sits Lympne Castle, a small, Norman structure built around the same time as the church that is its neighbour.

Out of Hythe the road traces the hills that line the Marsh by way of Lympne, but a canal-side walk makes a pleasant outing. A path (3 miles, $1^1/_2$ hours) follows the canal on the north bank, with the miniature railway on the far side for the first mile. It can be very pleasant to walk along this path on a calm, warm summer's day, and there is no difficulty in following the route. Follow the towpath westwards for about 2 miles until the Roman ruins are reached, then bear right as the path climbs uphill. Go left at the top to reach the zoo park, or right into Lympne village with its church and Norman castle.

Westwards the hills lead the traveller into a more varied landscape of trees and hills, with the marshes slipping away below. Villages here are a little more populated than those of the marshlands. **Bonnington** is a gathering of lanes and a church all alone; **Aldington** standing back, but with a steep little road from the church, is a place where Elizabeth Barton lived, the 'Holy Maid of Kent' who was hanged at Tyburn and **Bilsington**, with its remnants of a thirteenth-century priory. Then there is **Ruckinge**, whose church is a sheer delight set in a well-tended graveyard, **Ham Street** whose crossroads tempt a return to the Marsh and **Warehorne**, a community confused among the fields, with a path leading back down to the canal and along to Appledore. A ridge of green caught exposed to the sun and the wind, halfway between the rich diversity of the Weald and the low stretched acres of the Marsh; the land that once was sea.

USEFUL INFORMATION FOR VISITORS

ARCHAEOLOGICAL SITES

Coldrum Stones (NT)
1 mile east of Trottiscliffe
Remains of Neolithic long barrow, about 4,000 years old. Four upright stones with others scattered in rough circle. Free access. Car park nearby.

Kits Coty House
4 miles north-west of Maidstone, off A229
An impressive group of three upright stones with capstone marking the central chamber of Neolithic long barrow. Free access.

Little Kits Coty
3 miles north of Maidstone, off A229
Situated below Kits Coty, Little Kits Coty, or the Countless Stones, mark another prehistoric burial chamber. Free access.

Lullingstone Roman Villa
Eynsford, 8 miles north of Sevenoaks, off A225
Open: April to October, daily 9.30am-5.30pm; November to March, daily (except Christmas and New Year) 9.30am-4.30pm weekdays, Sunday 2-4pm. Fee, car park, toilets.
Excavated remains of Roman nobleman's villa. Fine mosaic floors, remains of early Christian chapel and a pair of portrait busts.

Roman Pavement
Butchery Lane, Canterbury
☎ Canterbury 52747
Open: April to September, Monday to Saturday 10am-1pm; October to March, Monday to Saturday 2-4pm. Fee. Combined ticket for Roman Pavement and West Gate available.
   Underground museum displaying remains of Roman town house, pavement and hypocaust room. Other finds of archaeological interest from elsewhere in Canterbury also on show.

Roman Painted House
New Street, Dover
☎ Dover 203279
Open: April to September, Tuesday to Sunday 10am-5pm;

May to August, 10am-6pm. Fee.
Well preserved Roman town house
with wall paintings and heating
systems. Also displays on Roman
Dover. Organised tours, talks.

BOATING AND SAILING

Bewl Bridge Reservoir
The Manager
Recreation Office
Lamberhurst
Royal Tunbridge Wells
☎ Tunbridge Wells 890661

The following list includes boats
for hire and organised river and
short coastal cruises. It does not
include cross-Channel ferries,
hovercraft or jet-foil crossings to
France or Belgium. For details of
these, consult your local travel
agent. Canoeing and boating are
very popular along the River
Medway between Maidstone and
Tonbridge, and at Hythe boats
may be hired on the Royal Military
Canal.

Achilles
Rilla Mill
Gun Lane, Horsmonden
☎ (0892) 722874
Medway cruises from Castle Walk,
Tonbridge in picturesque narrow-
boat. Trips last $1^1/_2$ hours. Daily,
Easter to October (except Mon-
day); 12noon, 2 and 4pm.

Grove Ferry
The Boat House
Grove Ferry Road
Upstreet
☎ Canterbury 86345
Catamaran *Reneroy VI* gives 50-
minute cruises on River Stour.
May to September daily, 1-5pm.

Kingswear Castle
Historic Dockyard, Strood,

Chatham
☎ Medway 827648
Afternoon cruises from Strood Pier
(or Chatham Historic Dockyard)
along Medway Estuary. May to
September Sunday, Wednesday
and Friday. Some day cruises
along River Medway on Thursday
and occasional Saturday.

Medway Hire Cruisers
Undercliffe Boathouse
Bishops Way, Maidstone
☎ Maidstone 53740
100-seat pleasure boat *Kentish Lady
II* operates cruises from Maidstone
to Allington Castle, daily Easter to
October 1-5pm.
The Medway Regatta in July is an
annual boating jamboree organ-
ised by the Medway Yachting
Association.

M.V. Clyde
Invicta Line Cruises Ltd
46 New Road, Strood, Chatham
☎ Medway 41824
Return trips from Strood Pier to
Southend-on-Sea. Two-hour
voyage, with 6 hours ashore.
Easter to October, assorted days,
check by telephone or in writing
for full details and time-table.

BUILDINGS AND GARDENS OPEN TO THE PUBLIC

Kent has a surprisingly large
number of castles and mansions
and other historic buildings open
to the public. Only the more note-
worthy are detailed below.
    As for gardens, some are
attached to the buildings in the
following list, while others are
smaller, private gardens open on
specific days of the year. The
National Gardens Scheme
publishes a yellow booklet,

Gardens of Kent which annually details almost a hundred gardens that open under this scheme. Write to: National Gardens Scheme, 57 Lower Belgrave Street, London SWIW OLR. *Gardens Open to the Public in England and Wales* has details of some 1,600 gardens operating under the NGS.

Allington Castle
1 mile north-west of Maidstone
☎ Maidstone 54080
Open: daily (except Christmas and Good Friday), 2-4pm.
Home of Carmelite friars since 1951. A fortified castle on the Medway dating from thirteenth century. One-time home of the Wyatt family, with Henry VIII connections.

Archbishops Palace
Mill Street, Maidstone
☎ Maidstone 52642
Open: by appointment only.
Built in 1348 it contains a panelled banqueting hall. Until the dissolution it belonged to the Archbishops of Canterbury.

Bayham Abbey
2 miles west of Lamberhurst
☎ Royal Tunbridge Wells 41835
Open: March to October, weekdays 9.30am-5.30pm, Sunday 2-5.30pm.
Substantial ruins of a thirteenth-century abbey housed by Premonstratensian monks, set in the Teise Valley.

Benenden Walled Garden
In grounds of Benenden School, near Cranbrook
☎ Cranbrook 240749
Open: end March to end April, last week in May, mid-July to mid-September 10am-6pm.
Eighteenth-century walled gardens with medicinal plants, kitchen garden, ladies' garden etc.

Bleak House
Fort Road, Broadstairs
☎ Thanet 62224
Open: daily, March to November, 10am-6pm.
Holiday home of Dickens in which he wrote parts of several of his novels. Set above the harbour with fine views. Rooms on show with Dickens connections, but part of the house is a maritime centre and museum of smuggling.

Boughton Monchelsea Place
Boughton Monchelsea, Maidstone
☎ Maidstone 43120
Open: April to October, weekends and Bank Holidays (also Wednesday, July and August) 2.15-6pm.
Elizabethan manor on the Greensand Ridge, built 1567. Deer park falls beyond the house towards the Weald.

Bradbury House
70 High Street, Milton Regis Sittingbourne
☎ Sittingbourne 23762 (evenings)
Open: by appointment only.
Elizabethan yeoman's house with displays of Victoriana, embroidery, etc.

Chartwell
2 miles south of Westerham, off B2026
☎ Edenbridge 866368
Open: March and November, weekends and Wednesday 11am-4pm; April to October, Tuesday to Thursday 12noon-5pm, weekends and Bank Holiday Monday 11am-5pm. Closed Tuesday after Bank Holiday.
Former home of Sir Winston Churchill from 1924 until his death. With a number of rooms as he knew them, the house is packed with Churchill memorabilia. Extensive gardens, lakes, woodlands, and studio containing many of his paintings. National Trust

owned. Shop, restaurant, large car park.

Chiddingstone Castle
4 miles east of Edenbridge
☎ Penshurst 870347
Open: April to October, Tuesday to Saturday 2-5.30pm, Sunday 11.30am-5.30pm.
Castellated manor house on the edge of delightful National Trust village. Interesting furnishings, paintings, collection of rare Japanese lacquer. Grounds include lakes and caves.

Chilham Castle Garden
Chilham, 5 miles south-west of Canterbury
☎ Canterbury 730319
Open: April to October, daily 11am-5pm.
25 acres of gardens landscaped by 'Capability' Brown. Terraces, lake, trees, rose garden. Medieval jousting and falconry displays featured on Sundays and Bank Holidays.

Cobham Hall
Cobham, 2 miles west of Rochester
☎ Shorne 823371
Open: Easter, late July to early September, 2-6pm.
Extensive house begun in the sixteenth century; a mixture of Gothic and Renaissance architecture standing amid a vast deer park. Now a girls' boarding school, the hall is open during holidays.

David Salomon's House
Southborough, Royal Tunbridge Wells
☎ Tunbridge Wells 38614
Open: Monday, Wednesday, Friday (not Bank Holidays) 2-5pm.
Early nineteenth-century house designed by Decimus Burton containing memorabilia of Sir David Salomon, a Lord Mayor of

London, and his nephew of the same name.

Deal Castle (EH)
☎ (0304) 372762
Open: April to October, weekdays 9.30am-5.30pm, Sunday 2-5.30pm; November to March, weekdays 9.30am-4pm, Sunday 2-4pm.
Built in the shape of a Tudor rose, this is the largest of Henry VIII's coastal fortresses. Exhibition of photographs and prints in the keep. Gatehouse museum with items of Roman and Saxon interest.

Doddington Place Gardens
Doddington, near Sittingbourne
Open: May to September, Sundays and Bank Holiday Mondays 2-6pm.
10 acres of landscaped gardens with extensive lawns, clipped yew hedges, rock gardens, sunken gardens and woodland with azaleas and rhododendrons.

Dover Castle (EH)
Castle Road, Dover
☎ Dover 201628
Open: March to October, weekdays 9.30am-5.30pm, Sunday 2-5.30pm; November to February, weekdays 9.30am-4pm, Sunday 2-4pm.
One of the most impressive, and the most important coastal fortress in the country. Occupies an Iron Age site high on the cliffs above the town. Within its walls the Roman Pharos lighthouse stands near the Saxon church of St Mary in Castro.

Down House
Luxted Road, Downe, Orpington
☎ Farnborough 59119
Open: daily (except Monday and Friday) 1-6pm.
Former home of Charles Darwin

and restored as it was in his day. It is now a Darwin museum which displays and relics from his voyage on the *Beagle*.

Emmetts Garden (NT)
4 miles west of Sevenoaks
☎ Ide Hill 75429
Open: April to October, Tuesday to Friday, Sundays and Bank Holiday Mondays, 2-6pm.
5 acres of gardens on hillside site adjacent to Toys Hill Woods. Fine views; noted for bluebells in spring.

Eyhorne Manor
Hollingbourne, near Maidstone
☎ Hollingbourne 780514
Open: Easter to September, weekends and Bank Holidays, 2-6pm.
Fifteenth-century yeoman's house set in pleasant herb and rose gardens.

Eynsford Castle (EH)
Eynsford, off A225
Open: March to October, weekdays 9.30am-5.30pm, Sunday 2-5.30pm; November to February, weekdays 9.30am-4pm, Sunday 2-4pm.
Remains of twelfth-century Norman castle.

Fordwich Town Hall
Fordwich, near Canterbury
Open: June to September, Monday to Friday 11am-4pm, Sunday 2-4pm.
On the side of the River Stour in an attractive village, this is the smallest town hall in England. A few exhibits, ducking stool, former prison cell.

Fort Amhurst
Dock Road, Chatham
☎ Medway 575840 (evenings)
Open: Easter to September, weekends 11am-4pm.

Defensive fortress built in 1756, now being restored. Tunnels and lower batteries open to the public.

The Friars
Aylesford, near Maidstone
☎ Maidstone 77272
Open: daily 9am-dusk.
First home of the Carmelite friars whose Order was founded in 1242. Restored as Christian retreat. Original fourteenth-century cloisters. Pottery, sculpture and contemporary ceramics. Café.

Godinton House
Godinton Park, Ashford
☎ Ashford 20773
Open: Easter and June to September, Sunday 2-5pm.
Jacobean house containing much fine panelling and carving; furniture, paintings and china. The grounds, laid out in eighteenth century, are formal with good topiary work.

Goodnestone Park Gardens
Goodnestone, near Wingham
Open: mid-April to early July; late August to September, Monday to Thursday 11am-5pm.
Gardens of 7 to 8 acres with roses and assorted trees, woodland and walled gardens, picnic area.

Great Comp Garden
2 miles east of Borough Green
☎ Borough Green 882669
Open: April to October, daily 11am-6pm.
7 acres of formal gardens with wide variety of trees, shrubs and heathers. The house is closed to the public. Teas in old dairy. No dogs.

Great Maytham Hall
Rolvenden, near Cranbrook
☎ Cranbrook 241346
Open: May to September, Wednesday and Thursday 2-5pm.
(No dogs).

Neo-Georgian house built in 1910 by Sir Edward Lutyens around an earlier eighteenth-century house in which novelist Frances Hodgson Burnett once lived. Walled garden on which *The Secret Garden* is supposedly based.

Hever Castle

Hever, $2^1/_2$ miles east of Edenbridge
☎ Edenbridge 865224
Open: April to September, daily (except Thursday and Good Friday) 12noon-6pm.
Moated castle and former home of Anne Boleyn, set in magnificent grounds laid out by the Astors earlier this century. The castle was restored and Tudor style village added by William Waldorf Astor. Gardens with large lake, rhododendron walk, topiary, colonnaded piazza etc.

Iden Croft Herb Garden

Frittenden Road, Staplehurst
☎ Staplehurst 891432
Open: April to October, Monday to Saturday 9am-5pm; Sundays 11am-5pm. November to March, Monday to Saturday 9am-4pm. Closed Sundays. Large herb gardens containing National Origanum Collection.

Ightham Mote (NT)

Ivy Hatch, near Sevenoaks
☎ Sevenoaks 810378
Open: April to October daily, except Tuesday and Saturday 11am-5pm.
One of the finest examples of an ancient moated manor house, set in lovely countryside. Interior has great hall, old chapel and crypt, Tudor chapel etc. Interesting courtyard.

Knole House (NT)

Sevenoaks
☎ Sevenoaks 450608

Open: April to October, Wednesday to Saturday 11am-5pm; Sunday 2-5pm. Park open all year daily.
Dating from 1456, Knole is one of England's largest houses and set in 1,000 acres of deer park. Rich panelling and furnishings, notable collection of portraits etc.

Leeds Castle

4 miles east of Maidstone
☎ Maidstone 65400
Open: all year, April to October daily, 11am-6pm; November to March, weekends only 12noon-5pm.
Glorious castle set upon two small islands in a lake. Dating from the ninth century it was for centuries the favoured home of English queens. Restored and furnished by Lady Baillie in the 1920s. Landscaped parkland with woodland garden, aviary, nine-hole golf course, Culpeper herb garden etc. Licensed restaurant.

Lullingstone Castle (EH)

1 mile south of Eynsford
☎ Farningham 862114
Open: house and gardens, April to September, weekends and Bank Holidays; garden and church only Wednesday to Friday 2-6pm.
Historic family mansion in the Darent Valley. Largely rebuilt in the eighteenth century, it was a manor house mentioned in the *Domesday Book*.

Lympne Castle

Lympne, near Hythe
☎ Hythe 67571
Open: June to September, daily 10.30am-6pm.
Small castle built on the site of Roman watch tower in 1360. Exhibition of toys and dolls, costume display, gardens, remains of the Roman Stutfall Castle below.

Maison Dieu (EH)
Ospringe, near Faversham
Open: March to October, weekdays 9.30am-5.30pm, Sunday 2-
5.30pm; November to February,
weekdays 9.30am-4pm, Sundays 2-
4pm.
Thirteenth-century pilgrims' hostel
where royalty stayed en route for
the Continent. Contains a three-
phase museum.

Marle Place Garden
Marle Place Road, Brenchley
Open: (garden) April to September, Wednesday 10.30am-5pm,
(nursery) 10-acre garden with
shrubs, trees, rockery, Victorian
gazebo, ornamental ponds etc. The
nursery specialises in herbs.

Milton Chantry (EH)
Royal Pier Road, Gravesend
Open: April to September,
weekdays 9.30am-5.30pm,
Sundays 2-5.30pm.
Founded by the Earl of Pembroke
in 1322, Milton Chantry is
Gravesend's oldest surviving
building. Contains a museum.

Minster Abbey
Minster, Thanet, 5 miles south-
west of Margate
☎ Thanet 821254
Open: May to September, Monday
to Friday 11am-12noon and
2-4.30pm, Saturday 3.30-5pm.
Founded in AD670, it was
destroyed less than 200 years later,
but restored in 1027. The Saxon
wing from this time survives, plus
a Norman tower. Now in the care
of Benedictine nuns.

Mount Ephraim Gardens
Hernhill, near Faversham
☎ Herne Bay 751496
Open: May to mid-September,
Sundays and Bank Holiday
Mondays 2-6pm.
7 acres of gardens featuring

rhododendrons, roses, herbaceous
borders, terraces leading to lake,
Japanese rock garden, orchard
walk, vineyard etc.

Old Soar Manor (NT & EH)
2 miles south of Borough Green
Open: April to September, daily
9.30am-6.30pm, Sunday 2-6.30pm.
The solar block of a late thirteenth-
century knight's dwelling.

Owletts (NT)
Cobham, at the north-west end of
village
Open: April to September,
Wednesday and Thursday 2-5pm.
Dating from Charles II's reign, this
red-brick house has a Caroline
staircase and ornate plasterwork.

The Owl House Gardens
1 mile north-west of Lamberhurst
Open: daily (except Christmas,
Boxing Day and New Year) 11am-
6pm.
A noted garden of roses, azaleas,
lake and woodlands. The sixteenth-century half-timbered
smuggler's cottage is not open to
the public.

Penshurst Place
Penshurst, near Tonbridge
☎ Penshurst 870307
Open: April to September, daily
(except Monday) 1-5.30pm.
One of England's great country
houses dating from 1340. Home for
centuries of the Sidney family.
Among the features are the barons'
hall and state rooms. Also toy
museum, Tudor gardens and
venture playground.

Port Lympne Mansion
Lympne, near Hythe
☎ Hythe 60618
Open: daily 10am-5.30pm.
Twentieth-century mansion built
in Dutch Colonial style by architect
Sir Herbert Baker. Terraced

gardens with fine views, and 270 acres of parkland with varied assortment of wildlife. (See also Port Lympne Zoo Park).

Quebec House (NT)
Westerham
☎ Westerham 62206
Open: April to October, daily (except Thursday and Saturday) 2-6pm.
Red-brick gabled house dating from seventeenth century where General Wolfe spent his childhood. Wolfe memorabilia on show. Stable block exhibition on Battle of Quebec.

Richborough Castle (EH)
Richborough, near Sandwich
Open: March to October, weekdays 9.30am-5.30pm, Sunday 2-5.30pm; November to February, weekdays 9.30am-4pm, Sunday 2-4pm.
Ruins of a Roman supply base and Saxon shore fort.

Riverhill House Gardens
Sevenoaks, south of town on A225
☎ Sevenoaks 452557
Open: (garden), April to August, Sunday and Monday, 12noon-6pm; (house) mid-April to August, Bank Holiday Sunday and Monday only 2-5.30pm.
Small country house with terraced shrub and rose gardens, fine collection of trees. Ancient track known as 'Harold's Road' in grounds.

Rochester Castle (EH)
☎ Medway 42852
Open: March to October, weekdays 9.30am-5.30pm, Sunday 2-5.30pm; November to February, weekdays 9.30am-4pm, Sunday 2-4pm. Fine example of a Norman fortress, begun in 1087. Good views of nearby cathedral and river from the tower.

St John's Jerusalem Garden (NT)
Sutton at Hone, 3 miles south of Dartford
Open: garden, April to October, Wednesday 2-6pm. Large garden moated by the Darent.

Scotney Castle (NT)
Lamberhurst
☎ Lamberhurst 890651
Open: April to October, Wednesday to Sunday (closed Good Friday) 2-6pm. Romantic ruins of a small moated castle, set in landscaped gardens. Fine shrubs and trees, lovely views.

Sissinghurst Castle Gardens (NT)
Sissinghurst, near Cranbrook
☎ Cranbrook 712850
Open: April to October, Tuesday to Friday 1-6.30pm; weekends 10am-6.30pm. Well-loved gardens created by V. Sackville-West and Harold Nicolson. A number of small interlocking gardens each with a different theme. Parts of Tudor buildings also open to the public.

Sprivers Garden (NT)
Horsmonden, 3 miles north of Lamberhurst
Open: April to September, Wednesday only 2-5.30pm. Large garden of shrubs, herbaceous borders, old walls and spring and summer bedding.

Squerryes Court
Westerham
☎ Westerham 63118
Open: March, Sundays only 2-6pm; April to September, Wednesday, weekends and Bank Holiday Monday 2-6pm.
William and Mary period manor house with Wolfe connections. Collection of old masters, tapestries, furniture and porcelain. Landscaped gardens include small lake.

Stoneacre (NT)
Otham, 3 miles south-east of
Maidstone
☎ Maidstone 861861
Open: April to September,
Wednesday and Saturday 2-6pm.
Small, half-timbered fifteenth-
century manor house. Exhibition
of embroidery; small but charming
garden. Other fine houses nearby.

Temple Manor (EH)
Strood, near Rochester
☎ Medway 78743
Open: March to October, weekdays 9.30am-5.30pm, Sundays
2-5.30pm; November to February,
weekdays 9.30am-4pm, Sundays 2-
4pm.
Restored flint manor house of the
Knights Templar, dating from the
thirteenth century.

Tonbridge Castle
Castle Street, Tonbridge
☎ Tonbridge 353241
Open: May to September, daily
during school holidays 11.30am-
1pm and 2-5pm, otherwise
Saturday and Sunday.
Remains of Norman castle beside
the Medway. Thirteenth-century
gatehouse contains a small
museum. Nature trail in the
grounds.

Two Sisters Towers (EH)
3 miles east of Herne Bay
Open: March to October, weekdays 9.30am-5.30pm, Sunday 2-
5.30pm; November to February,
weekdays 9.30am-4pm, Sunday 2-
4pm.
Twin towers of a Norman church
demolished in 1809, and the ruined
walls of a Roman shore fort of the
third century.

Upnor Castle (EH)
2 miles north of Rochester
☎ Medway 78742
Open: March to October, week-

days 9.30am-5.30pm, Sunday 2-
5.30pm.
Elizabethan fort built to protect the
Medway dockyards. Ammunition
examples on display and cannons
recovered from ships sunk in the
battle against the Dutch here in
1667.

Walmer Castle (EH)
2 miles south of Deal
☎ Deal 364288
Open: March to October, week-
days (except Monday and when
Lord Warden in residence) 9.30am-
5.30pm, Sunday 2-5.30pm;
November to February, weekdays
9.30am-4pm, Sunday 2-4pm.
Tudor rose shaped castle built by
Henry VIII. Now official residence
of the Lord Warden of the Cinque
Ports. Well preserved, the interior
contains exhibits relating to past
Lord Wardens.
Attractive gardens.

Watts Charity Almshouses
Six Poor Travellers' House, High
Street, Rochester
☎ Medway 45609
Open: March to October, Tuesday
to Saturday 2-5pm.
Elizabethan house founded as a
charity in 1579.

The Wool House (NT)
Loose, 2 miles south of Maidstone
Open: April to September by
written application only.
Fifteenth-century timbered house
believed to have been used for
washing newly-sheared wool.

CATHEDRALS AND NOTABLE CHURCH BUILDINGS

Canterbury Cathedral
Guided tours: April to September,
daily 11.15am and 2.30pm.

Magnificent cathedral, one of the finest church buildings in England.

Church of All Saints
Tudeley
Magnificent stained glass by Marc Chagall commissioned in 1963 in memory of Sarah d'Avigdor Goldsmid. There are twelve windows in all, the last having been installed in 1985.

Church of St Leonard
Hythe
Fine early English building overlooking the town. Acclaimed chancel; charnel house contains huge collection of bones.

Church of St Mary Magdalene
Cobham
The chancel (thirteenth century) contains what many believe to be the finest collection of memorial brasses in the country — perhaps in the world.

Church of St Mary
Goudhurst
Fourteenth-century church on a hilltop. The church contains numerous monuments to the Culpeper family. The tower is open to the public at set times between May and September (Thursday and Saturday) — in addition Tuesdays in July and August (afternoons only).

Church of St Nicholas
Barfreston
Small, but superb Norman church with noted south doorway and east wheel-window.

Church of St Thomas á Becket
Fairfield
A remote, mainly timber church set alone in the wastelands of Romney Marsh. The key is available from Becket's Barn Farm nearby.

Horne's Place Chapel
Appledore
A very small fourteenth-century domestic chapel of manor house attacked by Wat Tyler's men in 1381. Open Wednesdays only 10am-5pm.

Minster Abbey
Isle of Sheppey
Two churches adjoined; one a Saxon abbey, the other dating from thirteenth century.

Rochester Cathedral
After Canterbury, the second oldest cathedral in the land and dating from AD604. Present building begun 1080.

St Augustine's Church
Brookland
Thirteenth-century church with separate wooden belfry tower. Interesting interior features including rare Norman lead font.

Church of St Thomas the Apostle
Harty
Remote and simple church at south-eastern corner of Isle of Sheppey.

COUNTRY PARKS AND PICNIC AREAS

Since there are almost forty separate country parks and picnic areas in Kent, the following lists only the most notable. Leaflets detailing them all are available from information centres. Unless otherwise stated, parks are open daily and are free. In some cases a small charge is made for car parking.

Andrews Wood
Badgers Mount, Shoreham
Off A21 roundabout junction with

A224
185 acres of mixed woodland.
Picnic area, marked forest walk.

Bedgebury Pinetum and Bedgebury Forest
Off B2079, between Goudhurst and Flimwell
100 acres of specimen trees in delightful setting, the pinetum has a visitors centre.
Open: weekends, April to October. Small entrance fee. Car park, toilets.
The forest is adjacent to the pinetum and has some 2,500 acres of mixed trees. Waymarked forest path.

Bewl Bridge Reservoir
1 mile south of Lamberhurst, off A21
☎ Lamberhurst 890661
Open: 9am-dusk
Largest area of inland water between London and the coast. Wide range of activities possible in surrounding countryside; nature reserve (permit only), picnic areas, children's activity area. Entrance fee. Car park, visitors centre, toilets.

Bluebell Hill Picnic Site
Bluebell Hill, 3 miles south of Chatham, off A229
Chalk downland (13 acres) with panoramic views over Medway Valley. North Downs Way runs along northern edge of site.
Footpath walks.
Open: daily (except Christmas), 9am-dusk.

Camer Country Park
North of Meopham, off B2009
Open: daily, 8am-dusk.
46 acres of parkland and woodland. Toilets.

Clowes Wood
2 miles south of Whitstable

580 acres of mixed woodland. Fine views over the Swale. Waymarked footpaths. Toilets.

Eastcourt Meadows Country Park
Gillingham, 1 mile east of the Strand, off B2004
Riverside area of 60 acres. Bird watching, walks, picnic areas.

Folkestone Warren
Folkestone, east of town off A20
350 acres of coastline. Cliffs, walks. Car park fee (summer).

High Rocks
3 miles west of Tunbridge Wells
Open: daily 9am-sunset. Entrance fee, climbers extra.
An area of sandstone outcrops and trees. Walks, rock climbing, gardens.

Knole Park
Sevenoaks, south of town
Historic deer park of 1,000 acres, grounds of Knole House. Pedestrians only (except visitors to house). Dogs must be kept on leads.

Lullingstone Park
South of Eynsford, off A225 (Castle Farm signpost)
300 acres of parkland and woods.

Manor Park Country Park
South of West Malling, off A228
Open: daily (except Christmas) 9am-dusk.
52 acres of mature parkland with 3-acre lake. Walks, picnics, children's play area.

Perry Wood
Selling, 2 miles north-west of Chilham
150 acres of woodland with picnic area. Footpaths, trail for disabled visitors.

Teston Bridge Picnic Site
2 miles west of Maidstone, off A26,
take B2163
Open: daily (except Christmas)
9am-dusk. 24 acres of meadows
beside the Medway. Attractive
bridge, lock and weir. Fishing,
walks. Base for Medway towpath
walk. Car park charge. Toilets.

Toys Hill (NT)
$2^1/_2$ miles south of Brasted
200 acres of woodland on Greensand Ridge. Devastated by the
hurricane winds of October 1987,
but being replanted. Fine walks.
Small car park, fee.

Trosley Country Park
2 miles north-east of Wrotham, off
A227
Open: daily (except Christmas)
9am-dusk.
On North Downs, 160 acres of
woodland and downland. Lovely
views over the Weald, fine walks,
nature trail, picnic areas. Information centre, toilets. Car park
charge.

MILLS

Bartley Mill
Bells Yew Green, near Frant,
Sussex
☎ Lamberhurst 890372
Restored working watermill
originally owned by the monks of
nearby Bayham Abbey.
Open: daily 10am-6pm. Mill and
bakery combined; trout fishing in
pond at rear.

Brattles Mill
Mill Lane, Wateringbury, 4 miles
west of Maidstone
☎ Maidstone 812363
Watermill dating from eighteenth-
century on site of a mill mentioned
in the *Domesday Book*. Can be seen

from the road.
Open: by appointment with
owner.

Chart Gunpowder Mills
Westbrook Walk, Faversham
☎ Faversham 534542
Open: March to November,
Sunday and Bank Holidays, 2-
4.30pm. At other times by
appointment with Faversham
Society. Free admission.
Recently restored mills, once
producing gunpowder for Nelson
and Wellington. The only such
surviving mills in Britain. In care
of the Fleur de Lis Heritage Centre
at Faversham.

Chillenden Windmill
On Wingham to Chillenden road
☎ Dover 840258
Open: any reasonable time. Collect
key from owners.
Restored by Dover Council, this
open trestle mill was built in 1868,
but ceased working in 1949.

Crabble Mill
Lower Road, near Dover
☎ Dover 201066
Open: Easter, Spring Bank
Holiday, September. Mill working
Sunday and Bank Holidays 10am-
1pm, 2-6pm. Wednesday and
Saturday mill open but not
working.
Restored to full working order in
1973. An impressive building with
much of interest. Children under
14 not admitted when machinery
working. At other times only when
accompanied by adults.

Drapers Windmill
St Peters Footpath, College Road,
Margate
☎ Thanet 65841
Open: June to September, Sunday
2.30-5pm, Thursday (July and
August) 6.30-8pm. Guided tours.
Smock mill built around 1850,

restored by the Drapers Mill Trust and now in working order.

Evegate Mill
Smeeth, 5 miles south-east of Ashford, off A20
☎ Aldington 234
Eighteenth-century watermill built on the East Stour. Millhouse dates from about 1650. Now used as antique furniture workshop, but mill enthusiasts may view by appointment.

Haxted Mill Museum
Near Edenbridge
☎ Edenbridge 862914
Open: April to May weekends; June to September daily 12noon-5pm.
Privately owned watermill on the River Eden dating from 1680, restored overshot wheel and machinery, and much of milling history contained within. Exhibitions, picture gallery, working models relating to Kent and Sussex watermills.

Herne Windmill
Herne, near Herne Bay
Not open to the public but viewed from outside.
Recently restored smock mill built in 1789.

Meopham Windmill
Meopham, on A227
☎ Meopham 812110
Open: July to August, Sunday and Bank Holidays 2.30-4.30pm.
Well preserved smock mill and a Grade 1 listed building. Hexagonal shaped mill, built in 1801 and restored to working order. Owned by Kent County Council, but the Meopham Windmill Trust maintains it.

Rolvenden Windmill
On B2086 west of Rolvenden
Recently restored seventeenth-century post mill. Privately owned and not open to the public, but may be viewed from outside.

Stelling Minnis Windmill
Stelling Minnis, 8 miles north of Hythe
☎ Canterbury 720358
Open: April to September, Sunday 2-5pm; Saturday, July to August and Spring and August Bank Holidays.
Smock mill built 1866 and worked until 1970. Mill and auxiliary engine in working order and maintained jointly by East Kent Mills Group and Stelling Minnis Parish Council.

Stocks Mill
1 mile south of Wittersham, beside B2082
Open: June to September, Sunday 2.30-5pm.
Well preserved post mill built in 1781. Privately owned.

Swanton Mill
Lower Mersham, 3 miles south Ashford
☎ Aldington 233
Open: April to October, Saturday and Sunday 3-5pm. At other times by written appointment. Guided tours arranged. Teas available.
Weather-boarded watermill on the East Stour dating from seventeenth century and recently restored to full working order. (In 1975 it won a European Architectural Award.)

Union Mill
Stone Street, Cranbrook
Open: Easter to early September, Saturday 2.30-5pm.
One of the finest windmills in Britain, this smock mill was built in 1816 and restored in the late 1950s. Seen clearly from the outside at all times.

White Mill
On A257 outside Sandwich
Open: Easter to September,
Sunday and Bank Holidays 2.30-
6pm.
A white weather-boarded smock
mill dating from 1760. Recently
restored, with four new sweeps.
Viewing at all times from outside.

Woodchurch Windmill
Woodchurch, 3 miles east of
Tenterden
☎ Ashford 86701
Open: April to September, Sunday
2-4pm.
Smock mill in use until 1926.
Recently renovated. Machinery
and photographic exhibition on
view.

MUSEUMS

Battle of Britain Museum
Aerodrome Road, Hawkinge
☎ Hawkinge 2779
Open: Easter to May, Sundays
only; May to September, daily;
October, Sundays only 11am-5pm.
Displays include remains of British
and German aircraft shot down in
Battle of Britain. Spitfire, Hurri-
cane and ME109e in hangar.
Museum shop.

**Bettenham Manor Baby Carriage
Collection**
1 mile west of Biddenden off A262
☎ Biddenden 291343
Open: by appointment only.

**C.M. Booth Collection of Historic
Vehicles**
Falstaff Antiques, High Street,
Rolvenden
☎ Cranbrook 241234
Open: Monday to Saturday, 10am-
6pm (closed Wednesday after-
noon).

Brattle Farm Museum
Brattle Farm, Five Oak Lane,
Staplehurst
☎ Staplehurst 891222
Open: Easter to end of October,
Sunday and Bank Holiday
Monday, 9.30am-6.30pm.
Various exhibits of historic
farming interest, including
tractors, horse-drawn machinery,
wheelwright's shop; vintage cars
and motor cycles.

Brenzett Aeronautical Museum
Ivychurch Road, Brenzett
☎ (0679) 206061
Open: Easter to September,
Sunday and Bank Holidays 11am-
5pm; July and August, Tuesday to
Thursday 2-5pm.
World War II memorabilia,
engines, Barnes Wallis 'Dambus-
ter' bomb and other armaments.

Buffs Regimental Museum
Royal Museum and Art Gallery
18 High Street, Canterbury
☎ Canterbury 452747
Open: daily (except Sundays)
throughout the year, 10am-5pm.
Large number of exhibits telling
the story of the regiment from 1572
until 1967.

Canterbury Centre
St Alphege Lane, Canterbury
☎ Canterbury 457009
Open: Tuesday to Saturday,
10.30am-5pm.
A permanent centre for exhibitions
relating to the town. Housed in
converted twelfth-century church
of St Alphege.

Charles Dickens Centre
Eastgate House, High Street,
Rochester
☎ Medway 44176
Open: daily (except Christmas,
New Year and Good Friday) 10am-
12.30pm, 2-5.30pm.
Award winning Dickens museum

housed in sixteenth-century house with garden attached in which Dickens' Swiss chalet stands. Tableaux of Dickens characters with audio-visual effects.

Chatham Dockyard
Dock Road, Chatham
☎ Medway 812551
Open: November to March, Wednesday and weekends, 10am-4.30pm; April to October, Wednesday to Sunday and Bank Holiday Monday 10am-6pm.
400 years of history, among the largest collection of scheduled ancient monuments in Britain. Sailmaking, ropery, covered slipways, craft museum, midget submarine etc.

Court Hall Museum
High Street, Milton Regis
☎ Sittingbourne 22162
Open: April to September, Saturday 2.30-5.30pm.
Small museum housed in fifteenth-century timbered building formerly used as court, school and gaol.

Crampton Tower Museum
High Street, Broadstairs
☎ Thanet 62078
Open: May to mid-September, Sunday to Tuesday and Friday 2.30-5pm.
Railway museum dedicated to work of local Victorian engineer Thomas Russell Crampton.

Cranbrook Museum
Carriers Road, Cranbrook
☎ Cranbrook 713497
Open: Wednesday and Saturday, 2-4.30pm (closed January).
Includes items of local historic interest and the Boyd Alexander collection of birds.

Dartford Borough Museum
Market Street, Dartford
☎ Dartford 343555
Open: daily (except Wednesday and Sunday) 12.30-5.30pm, Saturday 9am-1pm and 2-5pm.
Interesting museum which covers the archaeological, geological and natural history of the area. A variety of exhibitions are staged throughout the year. Among the exhibits is the 'Darenth Bowl', a Christian relic dating from Saxon times, discovered in the grounds of a local hospital.

Deal Archaeological Collection
Deal Library, Broad Street, Deal
☎ Deal 374726
Open: daily (except Sunday) 9.30am-5pm, Wednesday 9.30am-1pm.
Local archaeological finds dating from Neolithic times to the Middle Ages.

Deal Costume and Accessories Museum
18 Gladstone Road, Deal
☎ Deal 361471
Open: April to September, Sunday 3-6pm, Monday and Tuesday 2-7pm.
Contains the Salter collection of original costumes and accessories covering the period 1785-1935.

Deal Maritime and Local History Museum
St George's Road, Deal
Open: May to September, daily 2-5pm.
Displays include original boats, figureheads, model ships, photographs and charts.

Deal Timeball Tower
Victoria Parade, Deal
☎ Deal 360897
Open: end May to September, Tuesday to Saturday, 12noon-5pm.
Nineteenth-century semaphore tower containing unusual museum of signalling, satellite and mari-

time communications; working models. Timeball drops at 1pm — originally to enable sea captains to set their clocks accurately.

Deal Town Hall Museum
St George's Road, Deal
Open: by appointment only.
Contains a small archaeological collection, and portraits of, among others, Sir Winston Churchill and Elizabeth Carter.

Dickens House Museum
Seafront, Broadstairs
☎ Thanet 62853
Open: Easter to October, daily 2.30-5.30pm. Also July and August, Tuesday and Wednesday, 7-9pm.

Dolphin Yard Sailing Barge Museum
Crown Quay Lane, Sittingbourne
☎ Maidstone 62531
Sittingbourne 24132 (open days only).
Open: Easter to October, Sunday and Bank Holiday, 11am-5pm.
Housed in original sail loft in old barge yard where repairs are still carried out. Carpenter's shop and forge.

Dover Museum
Ladywell, Dover
☎ Dover 201066
History and natural history of Dover displayed.
Open: daily (except Wednesday and Sunday) 10am-4.45pm.

Dover Old Town Gaol
Town Hall, Biggin Street
☎ Dover 281066
Open: daily 10am-5pm.
A Victorian court and prison with animated figures and audio-visual effects.

Dover Transport Museum
Connaught Road, Dover
☎ Dover 204612
Open: Easter to end of September, Sundays and Bank Holidays 11am-5pm.
History of local transport told with displays and exhibits; vehicles and working models.

Dymchurch New Hall
Near St Peter and St Paul's Church
☎ Dymchurch 872142
Open: during office hours.
Court room of the Lords and Bailiffs of Romney Marsh; exhibits on display.

Ellen Terry Memorial Museum
Smallhythe Place, 2 miles south of Tenterden
☎ Tenterden 2334
Open April to October, Saturday to Wednesday 2-6pm (or dusk if earlier).
Timbered sixteenth-century yeoman's house and former home of actress Dame Ellen Terry.

Finchcocks
2 miles south-west of Goudhurst, off A262
☎ Goudhurst 211702
Open: Easter to September, Sunday and Bank Holidays; August, Wednesday to Sunday 2-6pm.
Set in a Georgian mansion, with a remarkable collection of musical instruments.

Fleur de Lis Heritage Centre
13 Preston Street, Faversham
☎ Faversham 534542
Open: daily (except Sunday) 9.30am-1pm and 2-5pm (closed Thursday afternoons and Bank Holiday mornings).
The history of Faversham, in fifteenth-century former inn.

Folkestone Museum
Public Library, Grace Hill
☎ Folkestone 578583

Open: daily (except Sunday) 10am-1pm and 2.30-5.30pm (Saturday 5pm).

Grand Shaft

Snargate Street, Dover
☎ Dover 201066
Open: end May to September, Wednesday to Sunday 2-5pm.
140ft-triple staircase built in 1809 as a short-cut for soldiers living in the barracks on Western Heights at the time of the Napoleonic wars.

Gravesham Museum

High Street, Gravesend
☎ Gravesend 23159
Open: daily (except Wednesday and Sunday) 2-5pm (Saturday 10am-1pm).
Exhibits and displays recording the history and development of Gravesend's last 200 years.

Guildhall Museum

High Street, Rochester
☎ Medway 48717
Open: daily (except Christmas) 10am-12.30pm and 2-5.30pm.
Local history exhibits, from Stone Age to modern day.

Guildhall Museum

Cattle Market, Sandwich
☎ Sandwich 617197
Open: Monday and Thursday.
Guided tours of the Guildhall at 10.45 and 11.45am, 2.15 and 3.15pm.

Mr Heaver's Noted Model Museum and Craft Village

Forstal Farm, Lamberhurst
☎ Lamberhurst 890711
Open: daily 10am-6pm.
Models and dioramas (animated and lit) of Victorian London, both World Wars etc. Craft shops, puppet workshop, farm shop.

Heritage Museum

Poor Priest's Hospital, Stour Street,

Canterbury
☎ Canterbury 452747
Open: daily (except Sunday) 10.30am-4pm.
Opened in 1987 this offers a journey through 2,000 years of Canterbury's history. Audio-visual show, panoramic time-views, costumed figures, holograms etc. Also includes a display concerning the world's first passenger railway between Canterbury and Whitstable.

Hythe Local History Room

Oaklands, Stade Street
☎ Hythe 66152
Open: daily (except Sunday) 9.30am-1pm, 2-5pm (closes 4pm Saturday, 6pm Monday, 7pm Friday.
Display telling the history of the town (one of the original Cinque Ports).

Intelligence Corps Museum

Templar Barracks, Ashford
☎ Ashford 25251
Open: Monday to Friday 10am-12noon and 2-4pm.
British Military Intelligence history from Queen Elizabeth I to Queen Elizabeth II.

Kenneth Bills Motor Cycle Museum

144 High Street, Rochester
☎ Rochester 814165
Open: daily (except Sunday) 9am-5pm.
An incredible collection of more than 100 motor cycles and motor bike memorabilia.

Kingsnorth Museum

Kingsnorth, Ashford
☎ Ashford 21609
Open: daily 9am-4pm.
Assorted collection of items, including farm tools and domestic implements.

Lashenden Air Warfare Museum
Headcorn Aerodrome, Headcorn
☎ Headcorn 890226
Open: Easter to October, Sunday
and Bank Holidays 10.30am-6pm.

Lydd Town Museum
Town Hall, Queen's Road, Lydd
☎ Lydd 20366
Open: June to September, Wednes-
day and weekends, 2.30-5pm.
Exhibits include manual fire
engine, farm implements and
others connected with smuggling.

**Maidstone Museum
and Art Gallery**
St Faith's Street, Maidstone
☎ Maidstone 54497
Open: Monday to Saturday 10am-
5.30pm.
Local industrial and natural
history displays.

Maison Dieu (Dover)
Town Hall, Biggin Street, Dover
☎ Dover 201200
Open: daily (except Sunday) 9am-
4.30pm (Saturday 9am-11.30am).
Founded 1221 as hostelrie for
'poor and infirm pilgrims'.
Exhibits of armour, flags, portraits.
Fine stained glass.

Manston RAF Museum
Manston Airport, 2 miles west of
Ramsgate
Open: daily 9am-5pm.

Maritime Museum
Pier Yard, Royal Harbour,
Ramsgate
☎ Ramsgate 587765
Open: October to March Tuesday
and Thursday 11am-4pm. April to
September Tuesday to Friday
11am-4pm, weekends 2-5pm.
Items of maritime history.

Medway Heritage Centre
Dock Road, Chatham
☎ Medway 407116

Open: April to October, Wednes-
day to Saturday 10am-4pm,
Sunday 2-5pm; November to
March, Wednesday 10am-4pm,
Sunday 2-4pm.
The story of the Medway Estuary
displayed in redundant church of
St Mary's.

Milne Museum
The Slade, Tonbridge
☎ Tonbridge 364726
Open: Monday and Wednesday
9am-5pm, Tuesday 9am-1pm.
5,000 items of history relating to
electricity, housed in one-time
generating station.

Minster Gatehouse Museum
Minster, Isle of Sheppey
Open: Easter to September, daily
(except Thursday) 2-5pm.

The Model Village
Westcliff, Ramsgate
☎ Ramsgate 592543
Open: Good Friday to October
daily, 9.30am-dusk.
English countryside and buildings
in miniature. Ideal for children.

Motor Museum
11 Cogans Terrace, Canterbury
☎ Canterbury 451718
Open: Monday to Friday, 9am-
5pm.
Veteran and vintage cars and
motor cycles, plus signs etc.

Museum of Kent Rural Life
Lock Lane, Cobtree Manor Park,
Sandling, Maidstone
☎ Maidstone 63936
Open: April to mid-October, daily
(except Wednesday) 10.30am-
4.30pm (weekends 12noon-
4.30pm).
Exhibits in an oast-house; others
displayed outdoors.

Old Town Hall Museum
Market Place, Margate
☎ Thanet 225511
Open: May to September, daily
(except Sunday and Monday)
10am-1pm, 2-4pm.
Displays tracing Margate's growth
from small fishing village to Kent's
premier seaside resort.

Pilgrims' Way
St Margaret's Street, Canterbury
☎ Canterbury 454888
Open: daily (except Christmas
Day) 9.30am-5.30pm.
A time-walk with Chaucer's
pilgrims with the aid of audio-
visual techniques, sights, smells
and sounds of medieval England.

Powell-Cotton Museum
Quex Park, Birchington
☎ Thanet 42168
Open: April to September,
Thursday and Sunday; June to
September also Wednesday, 2.15-
6pm.
Natural history and archaeological
displays.

Precinct Toy Museum
38 Harnet Street, Sandwich
Open: Easter to September daily,
10am-5pm (Sunday 2-5pm).
October weekends only, 2-5pm.
120 years of toys, dolls and dolls'
houses.

Queen's Own Royal West Kent Regiment Museum
St Faith's Street, Maidstone
☎ Maidstone 54497
Open: daily (except Sunday) 10am-
5.30pm.
History of one of the county's
famous regiments with numerous
exhibits.

Ramsgate Motor Museum
Westcliff Hall, Ramsgate
☎ Ramsgate 581948
Open: Easter to November daily

10.30am-6pm.
Collection of veteran cars and
motor cycles.

Ramsgate Museum
Public Library, Guildford Lawn,
Ramsgate
☎ Thanet 53532
Open: Monday to Saturday (except
Tuesday) 9.30am-5pm.

Royal Engineers Museum
Brompton Barracks, Gillingham
☎ Medway 44555
Open: daily (except Saturday)
10am-5pm, Sunday 11.30am-5pm.

Royal Museum and Art Gallery
18 High Street, Canterbury
☎ Canterbury 452747
Open: daily (except Sunday) 10am-
5pm.
Small museum of local interest,
with art gallery offering periodic
exhibitions.

Sevenoaks Museum
Buckhurst Lane, Sevenoaks
☎ Sevenoaks 452384
Open: Monday to Wednesday and
Friday 9.30am-5.30pm, Thursday
9.30am-7pm, Saturday 9am-5pm.
Sevenoaks history outlined by
various exhibits from Roman
artefacts to twentieth-century
domestic items.

Tabor Barns
All Saints Lane, Canterbury
☎ Canterbury 462570
Open: Easter to September
Monday to Friday 11am and 2pm.
The history of Canterbury as told
in audio-visual presentation by a
monk and Tudor housemaid.
Presentation lasts 30 minutes.

Tenterden and District Museum
Station Road, Tenterden
☎ Tenterden 64310
Open: Easter to October, daily 2-
5pm; winter, Wednesday, Satur-

day and Sunday 2-4pm.
Local history displays, and section devoted to Kent and East Sussex Railway.

Tudor House and Museum
King Street, Margate
☎ Thanet 225511
Open: May to September Tuesday to Saturday 10am-1pm, 2-4pm.
The history of Thanet from Neolithic times to seventeenth century, displayed in Margate's oldest domestic building.

Tunbridge Wells Museum and Art Gallery
Central Library, Mount Pleasant, Tunbridge Wells
☎ Tunbridge Wells 26121
Open: Monday to Saturday (except Bank Holidays) 10am-5pm.

Tyrwhitt-Drake Museum of Carriages
Mill Street, Maidstone
☎ Maidstone 54497
Open: Monday to Saturday, 10am-5pm also April to September, Sunday and Bank Holidays 2-5pm.

West Gate Museum
St Peter's Street, Canterbury
☎ Canterbury 52747
Open: April to September, Monday to Saturday 2-5pm; October to March, Monday to Saturday 2-4pm.

Wye College Agricultural Museum
Wye College, Brook, near Ashford
☎ Ashford 812401
Open: May to September, Wednesday 2-5pm; also Saturdays in August.
Fine collection of farming implements displayed in fourteenth-century weather-boarded barn, and nineteenth-century oasthouse.

NATURE RESERVES

The following list is representative only. Others not listed, belonging to either the Kent Trust for Nature Conservation (KTNC) or Royal Society for the Protection of Birds (RSPB) may be visited by permission of the organisations responsible, by permit.

Bough Beech Nature Reserve (KTNC)
5 miles south-west of Sevenoaks
Information centre in nearby oasthouse.
Open: April to October, Wednesday, Saturday and Sunday 11am-4.30pm.
Bird sanctuary at northern end of reservoir with public viewing from road only. Important breeding place for waterfowl, and site for wintering birds.

Church Wood (RSPB)
Blean, 2 miles north of Canterbury
2,000 acre-woodland with footpath access.

Dungeness Bird Reserve (RSPB)
Off the Dungeness-Lydd road
The RSPB has an observatory and reception centre.
Open: Wednesday, Thursday, Saturday and Sunday 10.30am-5pm. Fee payable.
Reserve and a unique shingle habitat. A great variety of birds at all times, and during migration several interesting species make their landfall here.

Elmley Marshes (RSPB)
South Sheppey, bordering the Swale
Open: Wednesday, Saturday and Sunday only, 10am-4pm. Fee payable. Access by footpath only.
Reclaimed marshland and an important wildfowl refuge. Up to

30,000 birds may be seen at a time here. Wintering birds include Brent geese, white fronted geese and hen harriers.

Gazen Salts Nature Reserve (KTNC)
North-west of Sandwich, by A257 Saltings of the River Stour with ponds and rough grassland offering diverse habitats for wildfowl, frogs, toads, newts and butterflies. Unrestricted access, but parties of ten and more must first contact the chief warden.

Ham Street National Nature Reserve (NCC)
Off B2067 between Hamstreet and Ruckinge
Good example of Weald Oakwood with butterflies and typical plants. Access by public footpaths only.

Hothfield Common (KTNC)
3 miles north-west of Ashford, off A20
140 acres of bog, heath and woodlands. Acid bog plants, fine trees and good bird life.

Northward Hill Bird Reserve (RSPB and NCC)
1 mile north of High Halstow
Mixed woodland on the edge of High Halstow marshes noted for its many breeding birds and Britain's largest heronry. The reserve has partial access via the Saxon Shore Way. Access by permit.

Queendown Warren (KTNC)
2 miles south of Rainham, off M2 near Farthing Corner
Chalk grassland with scrub and woodland, with a varied flora and insect population.
Open: all year.

Sandwich Bay Nature Reserve (KTNC and RSPB)
2 miles north of Sandwich via toll road
About 700 acres of foreshore, salt marshes and dunes ideal for observing migrating marsh and seabirds.
Open: all year.

Stodmarsh (NCC)
5 miles north-east of Canterbury
Extensive reedbeds, open water and wet meadows in the Stour Valley with bitterns, godwall, marsh harriers etc breeding. Numerous warblers, and large numbers of wintering ducks. A National Nature Reserve. Partial access on footpaths.

Shell Ness National Nature Reserve (NCC)
Isle of Harty, south-east Sheppey
Mudflats on the Swale ideal for birdwatching. Access along public footpaths and sea wall. Information boards show various habitats.

South Swale Nature Reserve
North of Faversham
Much of the coastal strip bordering the Swale to west and east of Faversham Creek is nature reserve. Nagden and Graveney Marshes in particular favour the bird watcher. Access along footpaths and sea wall.

Wye Downs Nature Reserve (NCC)
On road from Wye to Hastingleigh
Chalk downland with typical flowers and butterflies. Nature trail leaflets available at information centre.
Open: summer only.

Yockletts Bank (KTNC)
Bossingham, 5 miles south of Canterbury
60 acres of woodland coppice.

Spring wild flowers, butterflies in summer. Assorted woodland birds, including nightingales.

STEAM RAILWAYS

Kent and East Sussex Railway
Tenterden Town Station, Tenterden
☎ Tenterden 2943
Trains run: April to October, weekends, June to July, mid-week August, daily. Specials at Christmas and New Year. Contact railway for full details of services.

Standard gauge steam railway running from Tenterden to Hexden Bridge with work in progress to extend the line.

Romney, Hythe and Dymchurch Light Railway
New Romney
☎ New Romney 2353
Trains run: Easter to September, daily, March and October weekends only. Contact railway for full details.

The only main line railway service in the country on narrow gauge track. Almost 14 miles of 15in gauge running from Hythe to Dungeness across Romney Marsh.

Sittingbourne and Kemsley Light Railway
Milton Road, Sittingbourne
☎ Medway 32320 (weekdays)
Trains run: Bank Holidays, some Saturdays and Sundays, Tuesday, Wednesday, Thursday; Saturday and Sunday in August. Contact railway for full details of services.

Narrow gauge (2ft 6in) line running for 2 miles between Sittingbourne and Kemsley Down. Seven narrow gauge steam locomotives, two diesels and three standard gauge steam locomotives on show.

Stone Lodge Railway
Cotton Lane, Stone, near Dartford
☎ Dartford 28260
New standard-gauge steam and diesel railway being developed on 'green field site' by the Thames. Railway heritage centre and museum. Contact railway for full details.

TOURIST INFORMATION CENTRES

Ashford
Lower High Street
☎ Ashford 37311 ext 316

Broadstairs
Pierremont Hall
☎ Thanet 68399

Canterbury
34 St Margaret's Street
☎ Canterbury 766567

Cranbrook
Vestry Hall
Stone Street
☎ Cranbrook 712538
(summer only)

Deal
Town Hall
High Street
☎ Deal 369576

Dover
South-East England Tourist Board
Townwall Street
☎ Dover 205108
Town Hall (summer only)
☎ Dover 206941/211056

Faversham
Fleur de Lis Heritage Centre
Preston Street
☎ Faversham 534542

Folkestone
South-East England Tourist Board
Harbour Street
☎ Folkestone 58594

Gillingham
Farthing Corner
(M2 motorway services)
☎ Medway 360323

Gravesend
10 Parrock Street
☎ Gravesend 337600

Herne Bay
The Bandstand
Central Parade
☎ Herne Bay 361911

Hythe
Prospect Road car park
☎ Hythe 67799

Maidstone
The Gatehouse
Old Palace Gardens
☎ Maidstone 602169

Margate
Marine Terrace
☎ Thanet 20241/2

New Romney
Light Railway Station Forecourt
2 Littlestone Road
☎ New Romney 64044

Ramsgate
The Argyle Centre
Queen Street
☎ Thanet 591086

Rochester
Eastgate Cottage
High Street
☎ Medway 43666

Royal Tunbridge Wells
Town Hall
Mount Pleasant Road
☎ Tunbridge Wells 26121 ext 3163

Sandwich
St Peter's Church
Market Street
☎ Deal 369576 (summer only)

Sevenoaks
Buckhurst Lane
☎ Sevenoaks 450305

Sheerness
South-East England Tourist Board
Bridge Road Car Park
☎ Sheerness 665324

Tenterden
Town Hall
High Street
☎ Tenterden 3572 (summer only)

Tonbridge
Castle Offices
Castle Street
☎ Tonbridge 844522

West Malling
Millyard Craft Centre
Swan Street
☎ West Malling 843484

Whitstable
Horsebridge
☎ Whitstable 275482

Information is also available from
the tourist department of the Kent
County Council who publish a
number of leaflets.
Write to: Tourism Section,
Economic Development Depart-
ment, Kent County Council,
Springfield, Maidstone NE14 2LL,
☎ Maidstone 671411.

VINEYARDS, HOP FARMS AND BREWERIES

A visit to one of the county's
vineyards makes an interesting
outing, and wine tasting features

as part of the visit. Each year the number and acreage of Kentish vineyards seems to increase, but the following list covers those known at the time of going to press.

Biddenden Vineyard
Little Whatmans, Biddenden
☎ Biddenden 291726
Open: May to October, daily 11am-5pm, Sunday 12noon-5pm; November to April, Monday to Friday 9am-5pm and Saturday 11am-2pm.

Elham Valley Vineyards
Breach, Barham near Canterbury
☎ Canterbury 831266
Open: June to September, daily (except Monday) 10am-6pm.

Lamberhurst Priory Vineyards
Ridge Farm, Lamberhurst Down
☎ Lamberhurst 890286
Open: during daylight hours. Tours by appointment May to October.

Penshurst Vineyards
The Grove, Grove Road, Penshurst
☎ Penshurst 870255
Open: April to 24 December, daily 10am-6pm.

Staple Vineyard
Church Farm, Staple, near Canterbury
☎ Ash 812571
Open: May to September, Monday to Saturday 11am-5pm. Sunday 12noon-4pm. Tours available.

St Nicholas of Ash Vineyard
Moat Farm, Ash, near Canterbury
☎ Ash 812670
Open: daily 9am-6pm (guided tours 11.30am, 2 and 3.30pm).

Syndale Valley Vineyards
Newnham St Peter, Faversham
☎ Sittingbourne 89693
Open: May to 24 December daily 10am-5pm (guided tours by appointment.

Tenterden Vineyards
Spots Farm, Smallhythe, near Tenterden
☎ Tenterden 63033
Open: May to October, daily 10am-6pm. Tours by appointment.

A visit to a hop farm unravels some of the mystery of this typically Kentish industry, and a tour of one of the county's oldest family breweries helps complete the picture.

Harper's Farm Trail
Harper's Farm, Goudhurst
☎ Goudhurst 211853
Open: May to August, daily during daylight hours.

Shepherd Neame Brewery
17 Court Street, Faversham
☎ Faversham 532206
Open: all year by appointment, Monday 2.30pm, Tuesday to Thursday 10.30am and 2.30pm.

Whitbread Hop Farm
Beltring, Paddock Wood
☎ East Peckham 872068
Open: April to September, daily (except Monday) 10am-5.30pm and Bank Holidays.

YOUTH HOSTELS

Canterbury
54 New Dover Road
☎ Canterbury 462911

Crockham Hill
Crockham Hill House
Edenbridge
☎ Edenbridge 866322

Dover
Charlton House
306 London Road
☎ Dover 201314

Kemsing
Cleves
Pilgrims Way
☎ Sevenoaks 61341

USEFUL ADDRESSES

British Tourist Authority
   Information Centre
64 St James Street
London SW1

Camping Club of Great Britain
11 Grosvenor Place
London SW1W 0EY

Cyclists' Touring Club
Cotterell House
69 Meadrow
Godalming
Surrey GU7 3HS

Department of the Environment
(Ancient Monuments Commission)
22 Savile Row
London W1X 2BT

Countryside Commission
John Dower House
Cheltenham
Gloucestershire GL50 3RA

English Heritage
PO Box 1BB
London W1A 1BB
☎ (071 973) 3000

Kent Trust
   for Nature Conservation
PO Box 29
Maidstone

Ramblers' Association
1-5 Wandsworth Road
London SW8 2LJ

Royal Society for the Protection of
   Birds
The Lodge
Sandy
Bedfordshire SG19 2DL

The National Trust
(Kent and East Sussex Regional
Office)
Scotney Castle
Lamberhurst
Tunbridge Wells TN3 8JN

Youth Hostels Association
Trevelyan House
St Albans
Herts AL1 2DY

INDEX